STUD[illegible] THE
ROMANIZATION OF ITALY

STUDIES IN THE ROMANIZATION OF ITALY

Mario Torelli

EDITED AND TRANSLATED BY

HELENA FRACCHIA AND MAURIZIO GUALTIERI

The University of Alberta Press

First published by
The University of Alberta Press
Athabasca Hall
Edmonton, Alberta
Canada T6G 2E8

ISBN 0-88864-241-5

CANADIAN CATALOGUING IN PUBLICATION DATA
Torelli, Mario
Studies in the Romanization of Italy

Translated from Italian.
Includes bibliographical references and index.
ISBN 0-88864-241-5
1. Rome-History-Republic, 510-30 B.C.
2. Rome-Antiquities. 3. Etruria-Antiquities. I. Title.
DG78.T67 1995 937'.02 C93-091300-0

Typesetting by The Typeworks, Vancouver, British Columbia, Canada

Printed and bound by Best Book Manufacturers, Louiseville, Quebec, Canada.

Printed on acid-free paper.

The Alberta Foundation for the Arts

COMMITTED TO THE DEVELOPMENT OF CULTURE AND THE ARTS

CONTENTS

ABBREVIATIONS

AA	*Archäologischer Anzeiger*
AArch	*Acta Archaeologica*
AASO	*The Annual of the American Schools of Oriental Research*
AC	*L'Antiquité Classique*. Louvain-la Neuve, Institut d'Archéologie
Acta Antiqua	*Acta Antiqua*. Magyar Tudomanyas Akademia
Acta Inst. Rom. Fin.	*Acta Instituti Romani Finlandiae*
AE	*L'Année Epigraphique*
AJA	*American Journal of Archaeology*
Acta 6	*Akten des VI Internationalen Kongresses für Griechische und Lateinische Epigraphik*
AJPh	*American Journal of Philology*
ANRW	*Aufstieg und Niedergang der römischen Welt.*
AnnScAt	*Annuario della Scuola Archeologica Italiana di Atene*
Archeologìa Laziale	*Archeologìa Laziale*
Arctos	*Arctos. Acta philologica Fennica*
ASMG	*Atti e Memorie della Società Magna Grecia*
Athenaeum	*Athenaeum. Studi periodici di Letteratura e storia dell'Antichità*
Atti Soc. Tosc. Scienze Naturali	*Atti della Società Toscana di Scienze Naturali*
Atti Taranto	*Atti Convegno di Studi sulla Magna Grecia*

BCAR	*Bollettino della Commissione Archeologica Comunale in Roma*
BdA	*Bollettino d'Arte*
Capitolium	*Capitolium*
Chiron	*Chiron. Mitteilungen der Kommission für alte Geschichte und Epigraphik des Deutschen Archäologischen Instituts*
CIE	*Corpus Inscriptionum Etruscarum*
CIL	*Corpus Inscriptionum Latinarum*
Coll. Latomus	*Collection Latomus*
CRAI	*Comptes rendus de l'Académie des Inscriptions et Belles-Lettres*
DdA	*Dialoghi di Archeologìa*
EAA	*Enciclopedia dell'Arte Antica*
EAA Suppl.	*Enciclopedia dell'Arte Antica Supplemento*
EE	*Ephemeris Epigraphiké*
Epigraphica	*Epigraphica. Rivista italiana di Epigrafia*
Etphilarchbelg	*Etudes de Philologie et Archéologie belges*
FA	*Fasti Archeologici*
Gallia	*Gallia. Fouilles et Monuments archéologiques*
Glotta	*Glotta. Zeitschrift für griechische und lateinische Sprache*
Hermes	*Hermes. Zeitschrift für klassische Philogie*
Historia	*Historia Zeitschrift für alte Geschichte*
II^2	*Inscriptiones Italiae*^{2}
ILLRP	*Incriptiones Latinae Liberae Rei Publicae*
ILS	*Incriptiones Latinae Selectae*
JHS	*Journal of Hellenic Studies*
JRGZ	*Jahrbuch des Römisch-Germanischen Zentralmuseums*
JRS	*Journal of Roman Studies*
Klio	*Klio. Beitrage zur alten Geschichte*
Latomus	*Latomus. Revue d'études latines*
MA	*Accademia Nazionale dei Lincei: Monumenti Antichi*
MAAR	*Memoirs of the American Academy in Rome*
MAL	*Monumenti Antichi dei Lincei*
MEFR	*Mélanges de l'Ecole française de Rome*
MEFRA	*Mélanges de l'Ecole française de Rome, Antiquité*

MemAccLinc	*Memorie dell'Accademia Nazionale dei Lincei*
MemPontAcc	*Atti della Pontificia Accademia Romana di Archeologia, Memorie*
MGR	*Miscellanea greca e romana. Studi pubblicati dall'Istituto italiano per la storia antica*
MonPiot	*Monuments et Mémoires publiés par l'Académie des Inscriptions et Belles-Lettres Monuments Piot*
NSc	*Notizie degli Scavi di Antichità: Accademia dei Lincei*
NSc Suppl.	*Supplement to Notizie degli Scavi di Antichità*
PBSR	*Papers of the British School at Rome*
Philologus	*Philologus: Zeitschrift für klassische Philologie*
PIR[2]	*Prosopographia Imperii Romani*[2]
PP	*La Parola del Passato. Rivista di Studi Antichi*
RA	*Revue Archéologique*
RAL	*Rendiconti della Classe di Scienze morali, storiche e filologiche dell'Accademia dei Lincei*
RAAN	*Rendiconti dell'Accademia di Archeologia, Lettere e Belle Arti di Napoli*
RE	*Paulys Real-Encyclopädie der Klassischen Altertumswissenschaft*
RevEtGr	*Revue des Etudes Grècques*
RendLinc	*Rendiconti dell'Accademia Nazionale dei Lincei*
RendPontAcc	*Rendiconti della Pontificia Accademia di Archeologia*
RhMus	*Rheinisches Museum für Philologie*
RFIC	*Rivista di Filologia e di Istruzione Classica*
RIASA	*Rivista dell'Istituto Nazionale di Archeologia e Storia dell'Arte*
RivFil	*Rivista di Filologia*
RömMitt	*Mitteilungen des Deutschen Archäologischen Instituts,* Römischen Abteilung
SCO	*Studi Classici e Orientali*
StEtr	*Studi Etruschi*
StMatStRel	*Studi e materiali di storia delle religioni*
St. Misc	*Studi Miscellanei. Seminario di archeologia e storia dell'arte greca e romana dell'Università di Roma*
StSardi	*Studi Sardi*

StStor	*Studi Storici*
Suppl. Libya Ant.	*Supplement to Libya Antiqua*
TLE	*Testimonia Linguae Etruscae*
WienSt	*Wiener Studien. Zeitschrift für klassische Philologie*
ZPE	*Zeitschrift für Papyrologie und Epigraphik*

EDITORS' NOTE

THE ORIGINAL PAPERS in this collection included extensive references in the notes. In order to make this vast body of detailed bibiliographical references on the Romanization more helpful and more readily accessible to the reader, we have compiled the individual items in a comprehensive bibiliography chapter by chapter. Numerous overlaps have been eliminated and the references have been updated. A concordance for articles in *Notizie degli Scavi* is also included in the Bibliography at the end of the relevant chapter sections.

Substantial changes were made in sentence structure and word order to avoid a phraseology that would be quaint, exotic, or merely awkward in English but we have tried to retain the very vivid personality and presentation of Professor Torelli. Professor Torelli has gone over the English translations to smooth out any ambiguities or changes in meaning. Site names or references to art works, museums, et cetera, have been left in the original Italian; although this may be awkward for the reader it is, in our view, more accurate.

In transcriptions of inscriptions, Italic type has been used where the text is intelligible. Letters enclosed in parentheses constitute the abbreviations found on the stone. Letters in brackets indicate supplements made to the extant text, while a series of three dashes in brackets indicates a lacuna of indeterminate length. Letters printed in capitals indicate text which is meaningless as it stands or fragmentary and uninterpretable.

The original sources for the chapters are as follows:

1. "The Creation of Roman Italy: The Contribution of Archaeology," Public Presentation (revised), University of Alberta, Edmonton, Alberta, Canada, April 1986.

2. "La situazione in Etruria," in *Hellenismus in Mittelitalien*, P. Zanker, ed., pp. 97–109 (Göttingen 1976).

3. "Ascesa al senato e rapporti con i territori d'origine: Italia: regio VII (Etruria)," Epigrafia e Ordine Senatorio, *Tituli* V (1982): 275–99.

4. "Per la storia dell'Etruria in età imperiale," *Rivista di filologia e di istruzione classica* XCIX (1971): 489–501.

5. "Un *Templum Augurale* d'età repubblicana a *Bantia*," *Rendiconti dell'Accademia dei Lincei*, new series 8, XXI (1966): 293–315.

6. "Una nuova epigrafe da *Bantia* e la cronologia dello statuto municipale Bantino," *Athenaeum* LXI (1983): 252–57.

7. "Aspetti Storico-archeologici della romanizzazione della Daunia," from Atti del XIII Convegno di Studi Etruschi e Italici Manfredonia, 1980, in *La Civiltà dei dauni nel quadro del mondo italico,* Leo S. Olschki, ed., pp. 325–36 (Firenze 1984).

8. "Monumenti funerari romani con fregio dorico," *Dialoghi di Archeologìa* II (1968): 32–54.

9. "Edilizia pubblica in Italia centrale tra guerra sociale ed età augustea: ideologia e classi sociali," *Les "Bourgeoisies" Municipales Italiennes aux IIe et I^e siècles av. J.-C.* (1983): 241–50.

10. "Innovazioni nelle tecniche edilizie romane tra il I sec. A.C. e il I sec. D.C.," *Tecnologia, economia e società nel mondo romano,* Atti del convegno di Como, September 1979, pp. 139–61 (Como, 1980).

PREFACE

Professor Mario Torelli, of the University of Perugia (Italy), was invited to the University of Alberta in April 1986 as a Distinguished Visiting Professor in the Department of Classics. The impetus for this collection of essays was Professor Torelli's public lecture and departmental seminars presented in Edmonton, as well as conference papers presented in Italy on various aspects of the Romanization of Italy.

Owing to the interest expressed by various colleagues and the collaboration of Mrs. N. Gutteridge, director of the University of Alberta Press, who applied for a translation grant to the University Community Projects Committee, we have been able to publish the text of the public lecture and translate some of his previously published papers on related subjects in order to provide an English-speaking general audience with a *summa* of recent work on a topic of major interest and relevance to all students and scholars of ancient Italy.

E.T. Salmon in *The Making of Roman Italy* dealt with general aspects of the Romanization of Italy in his historical outline of the third to first centuries B.C. (Ithaca, 1984) while W.G. Harris dealt more specifically with central Italy in his study *Rome in Etruria and Umbria* (Oxford, 1971).

The papers collected in this volume, with the exception of Chapter 1, address case studies dealing more specifically with the archaeological and epigraphical evidence for various aspects of the Romanization process in central and southern Italy, areas in which several University of Alberta excavations have been conducted in the last decade. These papers shed considerable light on the multiple situations and the related responses set in motion by Roman intervention into those specific areas and by the creation of a unified political and administrative system which eventually made Rome and Italy the center of a Mediterranean empire.

In the first chapter, a revised version of the public lecture, Torelli outlines the background for the case studies presented in this collection. In this introductory essay he emphasizes a fact fundamental to the understanding of the phenomenon of the Romanization of Italy: the unequal levels of cultural development in ancient Italy at the time of the expansion of the Roman hegemony over the rest of the peninsula. Torelli effectively delineates the cultural geography of ancient Italy during the important and little understood third century B.C. Torelli also provides a synthetic picture of the material culture and artistic production of the various cultural areas within the Italic territories between the third and first centuries B.C. A clear distinction emerges between the world of cities, such as Etruria, Latium, and Campania, as well as the coastal areas of Magna Graecia, and the world of the "noncities," the Apennine hinterland of Samnium, Lucania, and that part of the Adriatic region between Picenum and Apulia. Torelli demonstrates that such a distinction should not be seen as a clear-cut division between two worlds: clear stimuli towards the urbanization process can be detected in the archaeological record in those regions which he defines as "peri-urban." Conversely, the picture which emerges from his analysis is one of great variety of socioeconomic situations which Rome had to incorporate within a unified political and administrative structure. Thus, despite the early military conquests of the fourth and third centuries B.C., by which Rome managed to extend her supremacy over the whole of the Italian peninsula, it was only in the crucial half century between the Social War and the beginning of the Principate that one can actually detect the results of the Romanization process in large parts of Italy. Indeed, it is only under Augustus that the diversity of structures and cultural and economic levels become assimilated into a unified system.

The thorough archaeological picture provided by this overview of mid- and late-Republican Italy constitutes a basic reference point for more detailed discussions of the regional situations. The topic was discussed in November 1988 at an international conference on *La romanisation du Samnium aux IIe et Ier s.av. J.-C* held at the Centre Jean Bérard (Naples, Italy). The Romanization of Basilicata (ancient Lucania) was the subject of another conference held in April 1987 at Venosa (Italy). In

1989, G. Volpe analyzed the evidence for the Daunian area (*La Daunia nell'eta' della Romanizzazione*, Bari, 1990).

Etruria, the focus of Chapters 2 to 4, has been a favorite field of study for scholars working on the problem of the Romanization of Italy. Studies in recent years dealing with the Romanization of Etruria range in scope from the analysis of the historical developments between the fourth and the first centuries B.C. (Harris 1971) to the analysis of changes in the rural landscape of sample areas (A. Carandini, ed., *La Romanizzazione dell'Etruria: il territorio di Vulci*, Milan, 1985). In Chapter 2 an overview of the artistic production of the region during the late Hellenistic period is presented and examined in conjunction with the economic and social situation of second and first century B.C. Etruria. In Chapters 3 and 4 the epigraphical evidence for two important factors, that is, the participation of members of the Etruscan aristocracy in Roman political offices and the introduction of local Roman magistracies, in determining the role of Etruria within the Roman world is presented. In Chapter 3 Torelli updates a paper he wrote in 1969 to incorporate new evidence and recent discussions on the prosopography of Roman senators of Etruscan origin. Chapter 4 reviews B. Liou's book on *Praetores Etruriae* (Bruxelles, 1969) which Torelli uses as a springboard to discuss a number of local magistracies in Roman Etruria. This chapter extends the chronological range of the analysis of Etruria into the second century A.D.

Ancient Lucania also receives particular attention in this collection of essays in light of the important epigraphical evidence from the Latin colony of Bantia and the equally important discovery at that site of a *templum augurale* of the Late Republican period which Torelli himself explored. Chapter 5 contains a physical reconstruction of the *templum* together with a stimulating discussion of its significance in Roman Lucania, based on fragmentary archaeological evidence and a thorough scrutiny of the little known written sources. The analysis includes the question of the role of augury in both the Etruscan and Italic worlds and its continued importance in Roman society and religion. In Chapter 6, Torelli adds considerable detail to the picture of Republican Bantia in his discussion of an inscription from the excavations at the site which shed new light on the chronology of the *Tabula Bantina Osca* and on the *templum augurale* itself.

Daunia, the northernmost section of Apulia, is the focus of Chapter 7. This essay studies the earliest stages of Rome's intervention into the South of the Italian peninsula (between the second half of the fourth and the early third centuries B.C.), against the background of Daunian culture and settlement organization. This chapter discusses in detail the historical circumstances of the foundation of the earliest Latin colonies in the southeast of the peninsula and especially the early stages of the settlement at Venusia (the border region between Daunia and Lucania), for which a comprehensive study is still missing in spite of much field work done in recent years in that area.

The last three chapters bring the discussion back to a wider geographical area, analyzing cross-regionally selected aspects of the Romanization as it is reflected in the development of funerary architecture, public building, and construction techniques. Chapter 8 is dedicated to a class of funerary monuments which emphasize the importance of the local cultural context to the phenomena of Romanization and, at the same time, illustrate the mechanisms by which the Romanization affected artistic form and production. A class of funerary monuments with Doric friezes has long been linked with the spread of Roman colonization (for example, the chronology of their appearance in southern France) although lacking a study of their development and distribution. The analysis included in this volume, however, underlines the importance of the local cultural substratum and the social and economic conditions of the tombs' proprietors in order to clarify certain aspects of their structure and geographical distribution. Thus, although focusing more specifically on a single class of monuments, the paper is of major methodological significance for the scrutiny of the effects of Romanization on the local artistic expression. At the same time, the discussion brings up a lucid example of the key role of patronage in the development of Roman art.

Torelli also looks at public building in central Italy during the late Republican period (Chapter 9) and at the spread of new Hellenistic architectural types which take place concurrently with the great building renewal of the early second century B.C. in the city of Rome. After an apparent Italic *koiné* in architectural typologies which lasts until the late third century B.C., the gap between the center (Rome) and the periphery of the least developed regions of Italy becomes particularly evident, in spite of the impulses toward urbanization brought about by the Roman presence in the Italian peninsula. Torelli emphasizes the role of *euergetism* of the local elite families, on the one hand, and donations on the part of the senatorial aristocracy, on the other, as important factors in the diffusion of new architectural types. Some of Torelli's remarks are critical to the study of the development of Late Republican architecture in general. His discussion about the early basilica and its functional and ideological links with the *atria publica* provides a useful interpretative paradigm for the development of Roman Republican architecture.

Chapter 10 analyzes the spread of Roman construction techniques and offers considerations of programmatic importance for the organization of Roman Italy and for the Roman world in the wider view. In discussing the development and diffusion of *opus reticulatum* Torelli underlines how this particular construction technique was considered the indication of *urbanitas* in the impressive urban development of Italy between the late first century B.C. and the first century A.D. The subsequent analysis of its diffusion within Romanized Italy provides the groundwork for the discussion of the organization of the technique itself and its direct links with the economic conditions of the time, thus presenting a very illustrative picture of new building developments within Romanized Italy and, more generally, in the early Roman empire.

In sum, the papers collected in this volume encompass a detailed analysis of the socioeconomic and cultural background to the Romanization of Italy and at the same time provide a full picture of the material evidence from a number of Italian regions and a variety of local situations in the period between the Late Republic and the Early Empire.

Helena Fracchia
Maurizio Gualtieri

ACKNOWLEDGEMENTS

OUR COLLEAGUE AND FRIEND, Professor R.J. Buck, and the staff at the University of Alberta Press have been extremely helpful and kind in reading over the text: it is a pleasure to thank them.

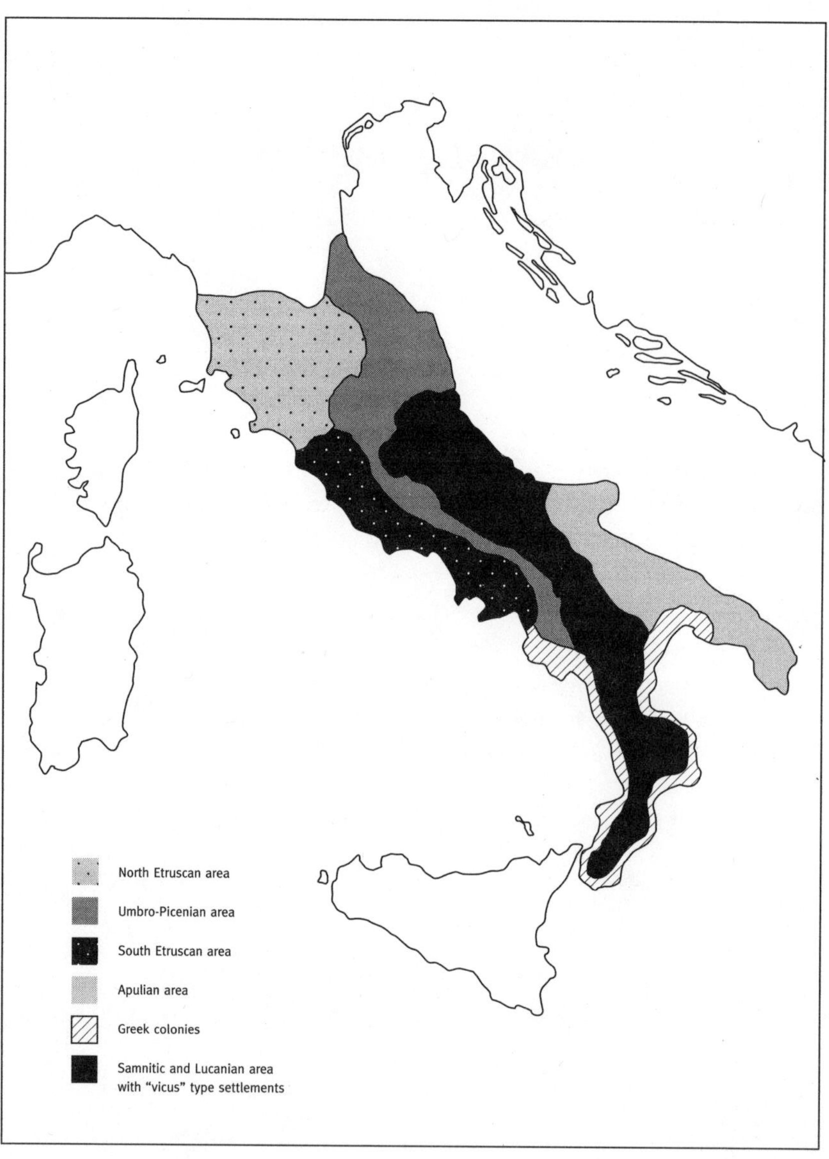

North Etruscan area
Umbro-Picenian area
South Etruscan area
Apulian area
Greek colonies
Samnitic and Lucanian area
with “vicus” type settlements

1

THE CREATION OF ROMAN ITALY: THE CONTRIBUTION OF ARCHAEOLOGY

IN THE STUDY OF "ACCULTURATION," archaeological evidence is a faithful reflection of the historical reality in its articulation of both structures and ideological forms. Indeed, the study of material culture—or archaeology in the widest sense—provides a detailed picture of the main transformations which occurred in the production process. Changes in the typology of urban and rural settlements reveal the different ways in which the productive forces are distributed in a territory. Thus, the alterations which occur in the previously established equilibrium in a given economic and social structure can be significant. The circulation of archaeologically detectable goods gives us an indication not only of the level and quality of commercial exchange but also of the degree of social organization and of differences in the levels of accumulated wealth. The types of goods produced in specific areas can provide some indication about the degree of craftsmanship development and the scale of workshops. Precise statistical data on the finds from settlement areas and cemeteries may enable us to determine figures for social mobility and to understand the interconnections between the latter and the stratification of society. No less indicative are the data which can be extracted from archaeological finds pertaining to the sphere of "ideal" forms such as cults, funerary customs, changes in taste and the very structure of artistic forms. Provided that we take into account the necessary differences between the finds themselves and ideology and between the latter and structure, all these data are very useful in understanding structural developments. In addition, these data provide an overall view of the cultural trends of the ruling classes, both in connection with the heritage of the preceding traditions and the relationships of hegemony or marginality to external cultures.

Such statements about the potential value of archaeological evidence must be set against the background of very fragmentary evidence. As well, the tradition of studies on the Italic culture is in a deplorable state, as is our comprehension of the structural heterogeneity of the areas occupied by populations of Italic language. Until very recently, scholarly research has laid exclusive emphasis on data pertaining to ideological forms and thus on those elements that are closest to the cultural manifestations of Hellenistic and Roman derivation. As a result, we ignore almost totally the aspect of material culture. And in consequence we are much better informed about the higher manifestations of Hellenization or Romanization and of the ideological aspects than we are about the so-called "indigenous" aspect. Often these "indigenous" aspects have been the object of distorting speculation, in search of the phantom "Italic *genius*" or the like. Luckily for us, however, the more serious historical and archaeological research of recent years has created the background for modern historical considerations. For example, we can note the fundamental, numerous contributions of M.W. Frederiksen and W. Johannowsky for Campania, and of A. La Regina for the Samnitic areas, in addition to the papers presented at the Colloquium in Göttingen on "Hellenismus in Mittelitalien." My paper is based very much on this work and aims at providing a general view of the problem.

Another fact of fundamental importance in the understanding of such a complex phenomenon as the Romanization of Italy is the very unequal level of development found in the territories inhabited by peoples speaking Italic languages. This is especially the case for the period preceding the establishment of Roman hegemony on the peninsula in the third century B.C. and during the phase of Romanization in the second and first centuries B.C. These territories included areas where there was a very high degree of economic, social, and cultural development, areas from which Rome derived important technological and cultural stimuli, such as Campania. Both the part of Campania Romanized at an earlier stage by way of colonial settlements (such as Cales) and the part that remained formally independent until the Social War, such as the area of Nuceria, Cumae, or Teanum, are examples of this phenomenon.

Within the "Italic" area, a definition which essentially corresponds to a linguistic rather than socioeconomic and cultural concept, we may distinguish a plurality of regions. This plurality of regions reflects fairly well the diverse articulation of the structures of ancient Italy at the moment of the various movements in the archaic period of the Umbro-Sabellian tribes, as well as the effects deriving from the economic and political presence of Rome, active in the area for two centuries before the *bellum sociale.* The destructuring action fostered by Rome by means of her colonies, or as a consequence of the wars of conquest or of the Hannibalic war, is extremely important. Entire regions of southern Italy, such as the plains of Apulia, Lucania, and a large part of Bruttium, are hit by violent destructions in the second half of the third century B.C., particularly in the final decades of the century: this fact radically changed the local habitat. From Daunia to the Salentine region, from the valleys of the Bradano, Basento, and Sinni rivers to the Brettian plains of the Crati River, the Roman conquest left behind a scorched earth. Older and more recent excavations of Apulian, Lucanian, and Brettian settlements and precious surveys of Lucanian and Apulian areas have consistently revealed destruction and heavy depopulation, with a few meaningful exceptions represented by some Greek colonies and by a few major indigenous centers (the example of Canosa is outstanding). The shrinking urban areas and the rapid decay documented by a drastic reduction of public and private building and in craft production reveal visible and long-lasting consequences even in those major settlements which had survived, and which had been favored, to some extent, by the Roman conquest, such as Canusium and Herdoniae in the Daunian area.

We can distinguish three regions in the Italic territories. A first region is represented by Oscan Campania: here, in spite of the Samnitic conquest of the fifth century B.C. and the wars of the fourth and third century B.C., a very marked development of ancient date had never been completely stopped. The well-known case of post-Hannibalic Capua, first dismembered and then soon resurrected as a city, is representative of the depth and strength of the roots of the urban model in the region. The archaeological evidence clearly shows that between the end of the third century B.C. and the beginning of the first century B.C. the local aristocracies are among the richest in the Italian peninsula. Public and private building are undertaken on a large scale. The amount of wealth which accrues to the region as a consequence both of the booty from the Hellenistic East in the wake of Roman conquests and the development of a specialized local agriculture testify to this continuity. Although the origin of the "Graeco-Italic" amphorae is still controversial and one would like to know more about it in order to understand the earliest phases of the agricultural development in the peninsula, the distribution all over the Mediterranean area of Dressel I amphorae, exported as containers of Italic produce (mostly from Latium and Campania) is the best evidence of the high level of the second century B.C. development of agricultural production in the region.

The Campanian area, between the Apennine slopes and the sea, is closely tied to southern Latium and presupposes two major centers of development, the port and Roman colony of Puteoli and the agricultural and commercial center of Capua, again inside the *ager publicus populi romani*. Around Capua the Oscan cities of Nuceria, Pompeii, Nola, Teanum, Trebula, Caiatia, Telesia, Caudium, Abellinum and Aeclanum, the Latin colonies of Suessa, Cales, Saticula, Beneventum, and the colonies of Sinuessa and Liternum, with extensive tracts of *ager publicus* are distributed. The Samnitic cities took substantial advantage of the great prosperity of this coastal region between Latium and Campania and their culture cannot be distinguished from that of the other Latin and Roman cities in the region. This is the consequence of a profound social, economic and political interaction which constitutes the foundation of the *koiné* Romano-Italic culture of the third and second centuries B.C.

We have tangible evidence of such prosperity, which characterizes mainly the last three decades of the second century B.C., in the well-known monuments and archaeological complexes. A large part of the public buildings in Pompeii, the area of the forum with the temples of Jupiter and Apollo, the Basilica, the Stabian baths, the massive restructuring of the Triangular Forum, together with the Samnitic palaestra, the Temple of Isis, the Temple of Zeus Meilichios, and the rebuilding of the large theater pertain to this period. Above all, we find important developments in private building, represented not only by the earliest examples of suburban villas of *otium*, such as the first phase of the Villa of the Mysteries, but also by immense urban dwellings, such as the Houses of Pansa and of the Faun. The latter, with its 3,000 square meter extension, is much larger than the only known residence of the Hellenistic East, the almost contemporary palace of Attalus II at Pergamum. Luxury spreads in an astonishing manner: the aristocratic houses of Samnitic Pompeii not only show elements of design inspired by the *luxuria*

Asiatica, such as *oeci Cyzyceni* and *Aegyptii*, but are also richly decorated with stuccoes, first-style paintings and mosaics, which surpass in quality and size the most refined houses of the Hellenistic East. Even the other cities of Oscan Campania reveal a level of luxury not inferior to the one which by chance has been preserved at Pompeii. For example, note the forum and the baths of Cumae (the latter building, datable to around 180 B.C., includes an Oscan inscription on a marble *labrum*, and a rare instance of an extensive use of vaults, which is contemporary to the earliest example in Rome, that in the *porticus Aemilia*). The theaters of Allifae and Sarno and at Teanum, of exceptional size, the sanctuaries of Diana Tifatina, Teanum, Aeclanum, close in conception and construction type to the contemporary scenographic sanctuaries of Latium, such as Praeneste, Tivoli, and Terracina, are equally significant. Indeed, the list could be much longer.

The data so far summarized confirm the high degree of cultural homogeneity existing between the Samnitic cities and Roman cities of the Campanian area. A slightly different picture is provided, however, by the rural settlements. Large rural villas like the one excavated at San Rocco, in the territory of Capua, are, at the very least, little known and poorly documented in the areas of the Campanian *socii*. All the examples of villas so far known in some way, namely those of the countryside of Pompeii and Stabiae, show a particular development of the *pars fructuaria* only after the Social War, and particularly from the Augustan period onwards. The very size of the *ager* of these cities, quite modest indeed, does not lead to the development of satellite settlements of the country-village type, while the latter type of settlement is well documented in the very large territories of Capua and Beneventum. There are some rare exceptions, such as the *pagus Felix Suburbanus* of Pompeii dating to the colonial foundation, but it probably was developed already in the Samnitic period and this is the exception that seems to confirm the rule.

The craft production of these cities is still poorly known. If the red fabric of the great production of black glaze pottery of the second century B.C. is indeed the clay of Pithecusa, the so-called Campana A—as shown by J.-P. Morel—then we can consider Neapolis as the production center of this ware. On the other hand, nothing yet can be said about the presence in the Samnitic cities of workshops producing the well-known Campanian bronzes, a parallel development of the workshops certainly existing in the territory of Capua. The art works of the time are considered to derive from workshops of late Hellenistic tradition, which existed in the main cities of the East or at Rome or was even passed on by itinerant craftsmen. These workshops are responsible for the high quality marble works such as the cult statue of Jupiter from Pompeii and the many trapezophoroi, also from Pompeii (as well as the best mosaic works such as the well known mosaic of Alexander). Instead, the products of indisputable Campanian origin, such as figured capitals or decorative sculpture in tufa or limestone, probably derive from workshops situated in Capua. Overall, one gets the impression of total dependency on the main Roman centers of Campania and Latium or on the Hellenistic cities of the East for luxury crafts, while only the minor crafts are partly developed in the Samnitic cities. Cases such as the one of the terracotta trapezophoroi from Pompeii and Capua, made in Neapolis or Puteoli (as seems likely, on account of the characteristic red-clay of Pithecusan type), or the black glaze pottery at Teanum imported from the nearby Latin colony of Suessa, make one think that even the minor local craft production was restrained in its development by the massive production of the Roman or Latin cities of Campania. According to W. Johannowsky, the *torcularia* in lava-stone from the extinct volcano of Roccamonfina were also made in the Roman or Latin cities of Campania. This example provides evidence of the possible derivation not only of craft traditions but also of technological developments.

The archaeological data from Campania seems to indicate that the Oscan cities were certainly integrated into the Roman economic system and into the most advanced cultural manifestations of the Italian peninsula; however, the basic condition was one of relative dependency on the nearby territories under Roman domination, where the extraordinary development of slave-based production and the more favorable political situation fostered a greater development of the productive forces. In the areas of the Campanian *socii*, which were the only beneficiaries (together with the *cives romani*) of the great growth of wealth in the Italian peninsula, there were some limited strata of the urban population which appear to have been open to the influences of Hellenistic culture and of its way of life, as is documented in public and private buildings and in the introduction of oriental cults and exotic fashions (such as the early development of *ephebia*), but which were, nonetheless, clearly conservative. The almost complete absence of portraits before the Social War and the persistence of strongly rooted ideological traditions, such as the use of hypogean family tombs, seems meaningful, in spite of the fact that by the late second century B.C. there are found in Rome and other developed areas of the peninsula portraits of Hellenistic origin, individual *naiskoi*, and *epitymbia* or funerary monuments deriving from the eastern tradition. The sepulchral monument of Galba in Rome dated to circa 105 B.C. and the so-called *heroa* from the Licinella area in the Latin colony of Paestum are examples of this development.

The second Italic region is the one immediately bordering the most developed areas in the Italian peninsula. Far from being geographically and economically uniform, it extends along the borders of Etruria, Latium, Campania, and Apulia, along the valleys of the tributaries on the left bank of the Tiber and on the Apennine foothills overlooking the Tavoliere. It includes Picenum and a small stretch of Umbrian territory to the north, Samnitic and Lucanian territory to the south, and was close to the most developed areas of Etruria in the archaic and classical periods, of Greek and Etruscan Campania and of the Greek colonies in southern Italy. In this region, as far as we know (which is not much, unfortunately), urban civilization had appeared in a discontinuous manner and often very late, seldom before the fourth century B.C; however, in the period immediately preceding the Social War, urbanization of the area was completed. In spite of centers of very ancient origin, such as the Samnitic settlements on the borders of Campania or the Umbrian settlements of the Tiber valley, we must include in this category centers which acquired a form of urban organization in a relatively recent period, such as the centers of Bruttium and Lucania, more directly in contact with the world of the Greek colonies. The Lucanian town of Laos suffices to illustrate the phenomenon. The urban civilization of these areas, however, merely reflects the bordering regions, just as the culture of these areas is largely conditioned by the nearby Etruscans, Latins, Campanians, and Greeks (in addition to the Latin and Roman colonial settlements). Often the cities occupy a very small area, sometimes various public buildings and public works are missing, but not infrequently one finds significant works comparable to those of the most important cities, as happens in many cities of Samnium bordering Campania or Umbria. Heterogeneous and sporadic evidence of an archaeological or epigraphical nature indicates a marked interest in city planning and in monumental works, such as roads, porticoes, fountains, construction or reconstruction of city walls and city gates, in the course of the last decades of the second century B.C.

The models of Hellenistic culture are introduced in this area in a haphazard manner and in a way which is controversial and archaeologically difficult to interpret. The introduction of genuinely Greek models (or more accurately, models from Magna Graecia) is documented at a fairly early stage for the whole region. Archaic examples are relatively isolated and certainly mediated through the Etruscans, such as the princely burials from Monteleone near Spoleto in Umbria, or of Fabriano or of Pitino near San Severino in Picenum, or are transmitted through Greek colonial settlements, such as the wealthy tomb from Armento in Lucania. Recall the presence of strigils in Samnitic and Umbrian tombs of the fourth century B.C. and, at a later stage, the presence of beds of the Delian type in tombs from Arna in Umbria. This type of luxurious symposium and the funerary bed derived from it are closely paralleled in remote and diverse areas such as Corfinium among the Paelignans and Amiternum in the Sabine land. Everything, indeed, appears to be mediated through the more developed cities of bordering areas, as is confirmed by the analysis of the scarce local craft production, such as the late Hellenistic cinerary urns from Umbria, totally dependent on prototypes from Perugia, or the finds from the Ansanto votive deposit, which imitate Campanian or Apulian terracottas, as do the ones in many other votive deposits from Hirpinia and Lucania. In this context, the Greek colonies and the cities of inner Etruria are particularly meaningful as propulsive centers for the earlier period. Increasingly, from the third century B.C. onwards, the Latin colonies from Ariminum to Luceria, from Venusia to Spoletium and Paestum serve as points of transfer. Models of urban life and types of craft production often derive from Paestum, and only at a late stage and in an occasional manner do these urban models and crafts production spread into non-Roman areas. Black glaze pottery, for example, is first imported and only later, in the course of the second century B.C., locally imitated after Etruscan, Roman, and Campanian forms. The well-known Popilius bowls of Megarian type, produced at Mevania in Umbria in the second century B.C., are emblematic of this situation, as these bowls bear the Latin signature of the owner-potter and reveal the creation of branches at Ocriculum. They confirm that the scarce craft production in the area is either derivative from earlier production (such is the case of the small so-called Italic bronzes) or from the movement of craftsmen.

The characteristics of this group of territories, which I define as "peri-urban," are those of a peripheral and dependent area vis-à-vis the major leading centers, which exist at the periphery or, in the case of the Latin colonies, inside the areas discussed. In this region we find a not very homogeneous type of Hellenistic-Roman culture, which has been received in both a direct and disorganic manner. This culture spreads in direct proportion to the level of economic development and, therefore, is tied to the more favorable conditions for agricultural production in the lowlands and in the lower foothills. The spread of urban models, sometimes very late, derives mostly from the Roman world and shows that before the Social War the relationship between city and countryside concurrently with the integration of developed agriculture and sheep-grazing is far from being clear cut. The pagano-vicanic forms of organization are relatively rare in the northern region and more frequent in the southern region because there is a different ratio in these areas between inhabitants and arable land. Furthermore, the rural villas of standard type (but not the farm) are completely absent.

The third Italic region is represented by the Apennine area, between the Adriatic Sea and the central mountain chain that extends from the Umbrian hinterland to the mountainous areas of Lucania, namely the area inhabited by the great tribes of Sabellian stock, the Praetuttii, the Vestini, the Marsi, the Paeligni, the Marrucini, the Frentani, the Samnites (Pentri and Carecini), the Hirpini, and the Lucani. In the period immediately preceding the Social War, in those areas where the Roman conquest did not leave a waste land as it did in many parts of Apulia, Bruttium, and Lucania, the typical habitat is represented by pseudo-urban structures, fortified circuits on hilltops, often enclosing few houses or farms (well documented especially in the south at Roccagloriosa or Serra di Vaglio) and rare public buildings (such as the rather mysterious one at Aufidena), but more often just traces of frequentation are found. What we would call "services," namely cults, fairs, markets, festivals, assembly areas, are included in sanctuaries of various sizes set in the open countryside, near raw materials or mountain passes, sanctuaries-enclosures which vary from small terraced areas with a small or medium-sized temple and sometimes a modest portico to monumental complexes with many temples, porticoes, and theaters. The latter complexes sometimes assume the character of a political tribal center: this is the case at Pietrabbondante for the territory of the Pentri. Within that territory we know of at least five more sanctuaries on a smaller scale (Schiavi, Vastogirardi, San Giovanni in Galdo, Quadri, Agnone) which have a similar function within a paganic organization, for a territory which includes at least twenty-six *oppida*. Another fairly well known example, in the territory of the Paeligni, is the great sanctuary of Heracles Curinus. There, at least twelve more minor sanctuaries (San Michele Arcangelo at Vittorito, Prezza, Popoli, Civita di Raiano, Pacentro, Corfinio, Scanno, Casale di Cocullo, Castelvecchio Subequo, Bugnara, Molina, Seciano), and a total of twenty-eight *oppida* are documented. Another case is that of inner Lucania with a major cult center at Rossano di Vaglio and minor sanctuaries at Ruoti, Armento, Serra di Vaglio, Grumento, Lavello, and Rota. Indeed, the list could be extended further. It is important to underline the radical change which occurred, with total prevalence in the countryside and an almost complete absence in the city between the third and first centuries B.C. in this territory. The hilltop fortified enclosures, the small family farms scattered in the countryside (the survey in the Biferno Valley by G. Barker has identified a number of them), and the series of country sanctuaries perform the functions otherwise and elsewhere performed by the city. As a consequence, the rural villas for agricultural production are completely absent, as indeed is noted by the ancient sources "Vici . . . appellari incipiunt ex agris, qui villas non habent, ut Marsi aut Peligni." "We start calling *vici* the settlements in those areas which have no villas, such as among the Marsi or Peligni."

This world of "noncities," under the stimulus of increased agricultural production in the fertile and more developed lowlands, began a nucleation process in the last decades of the second century B.C. This nucleation process is especially clear among populations inhabiting strategic points in the local economic system, near transit points in valley floors, transhumance trails, or near important crossroads. In looking at this phenomenon, we cannot ignore the existence of a well-defined stimulus, even if episodic and not clearly organized, towards urbanization. Elements of this process derive from more than a single site in the area. Corfinium, which becomes the capital of the *socii Italici*, the Italian allies, at the time of the revolt, has yielded a great concentration of tombs of the late second/early first centuries B.C., which makes one think of a process of urbanization already under way before the Social War. Over twenty-five years ago, at Saepinum, an impluvium house with a Samnitic inscription was found in the east corner of the Forum. Recent excavations at the west side of the Forum have provided evidence for the major remains of an aristocratic house with a polychrome mosaic decorated with a hunting scene. On the north side of the Forum there are a series of storerooms: all are datable to the late second century B.C. and destroyed by fire, probably to be connected with the Social War. From such examples (certainly the most meaningful and the best documented so far) one gathers that socioeconomic and cultural motives induced the aristocracies of the area to adapt themselves to patterns of urban life. Other types of cultural and formal choices such as the plan of the theater at Pietrabbondante, imitating the one at Sarno, and the moldings of the podium of Temple B in the same sanctuary, faithfully copied from those of the Patturelli temple at Capua emphasize this fact. For architectural and decorative works, for their private luxury, the local ruling classes depend almost exclusively on the importation of both objects and craftsmen. The imports of bronzes and fine wares in the native cemeteries of the Paeligni and Vestini come from the nearby areas to the northwest, namely Ancona, Volterra and Todi. Similarly the architecture of the territory of the Pentri and Carecini derives from the works of Campanian workshops. The locally produced finds and common wares, deriving from the pre-Roman layers at Saepinum and from the burials at Corfinium, show, in general, a strikingly low level of technology (such as a coarsely refined impasto), very few forms, mostly of archaic tradition, and a rather primitive type of decoration. Even the local fine wares (such as the black glaze pottery) reveal a very mediocre quality and limited productivity, confirmed by the recovery, so far unfortunately isolated, of a kiln dump near the circuit wall of an *oppidum* in the territory of Boiano.

A similar picture is found in those territories under Roman domination with land redistribution. In the territory of the Sabini, episodic pressures toward urbanization in areas still settled *vicatim* are felt, for example, by comparing Trebula Mutuesca, still a *vicus* around 140 B.C. and transformed into a municipium under Augustus, with Amiternum, where the burials of the late second century have yielded rich finds, documenting the beginnings of an urban form of organization which, at least formally, remained a *praefectura* until the Augustan period. Thus, where there was no planned political intervention for the urbanization of the site (as is the case of the Latin colonies), the general conditions created by the local economic reality fostered a uniform development of the society virtually independent of the political status of the inhabitants.

Such is the picture, in summary, of the Italic territories at the eve of the Social War. In it, we find a varied reality, even within the major socioeconomic divisions analyzed here. On one side, a world dominated by cities, as in Oscan Campania, and on the other side, a world dominated by the countryside, as in the Samnitic and Lucanian Apennine region, with a series of intermediate situations characterized by a process of discontinous and still not prevalent urbanization. But it was a complex reality, where, toward the end of the period of independence from Rome, the trend toward urbanization manifests itself in a spontaneous manner, under a two-fold pressure: one pressure was economic, represented by the development of agricultural practices, and the other was cultural, fostered by the local aristocracies craving *luxuria*. As a consequence, the prevailing cultural models and the artistic production are those presented by the Roman world, sometimes directly by Rome and sometimes indirectly through the Latin and Roman colonies. The reception of these models varied according to the level of local development, although "indigenous" traditions strongly persisted if the ideological forms were of a religious nature. The culture of the "peripheral" groups, where it is possible to detect it, generally reflects strong ties to traditions of the early Hellenistic or even Classical period, in the form of contemporary bronze and terracotta votives.

The picture of the Augustan period is noticeably different. The great diversity of structures and of cultural levels which manifested itself during the period preceding the Social War turns into an evident uniformity. Everywhere, the urban model is the prevalent one: the *oppida* and the sanctuaries of the Apennine areas are abandoned or lie fallow, *municipia* and colonies with their own well defined territories occupy the areas which were once Italic and a substantial uniformity of culture spreads into an enormous area, which includes Latium, Campania, Sabine territory, Samnium, Umbria, the Picenum area, and the hilly areas of Lucania. It is the late Hellenistic culture, with its peculiar, well known developments, as it spreads out of its characteristic areas, which expresses, in a more modest fashion than the original models, the political and social solidarity of the Augustan *tota Italia*, of large middle classes made up of colonists of Sulla, Caesar, the Triumvirate and Augustus and by the remaining local aristocracies, now ruling established municipal towns. The substantial unity of this culture, which excludes Etruria, Bruttium, and a large part of Apulia—manifests itself in the adoption of common models which reach as far as Cisalpine Gaul, the Narbonensis, and the more Romanized part of Spain: I refer to an examination of the diffusion of a type of funerary monument with a Doric frieze belonging to this period (see Chapter 8). The cities have regular plans, *fora* surrounded by public buildings and full of honorary monuments, walls with towers and city gates, often richly decorated. The proto-urban settlements of the Apennine territory, in Samnium, Sabina, and Lucania become fully urban almost suddenly. The case of Saepinum, better explored in recent years, shows that the forum area had been built following a unitary plan, in a few decades in the first half of the Augustan period, a unitary plan to which the city walls of the period 2 B.C./A.D. 4 and the theater are also to be linked. But Saepinum, as many other cities in the region, is in large part an artificial creation: the extent of the inhabited area is hardly larger than that reserved for "service" areas, and the rural landscape, as far as we know, does not appear to be substantially different from the one of the previous century. These "artificial" cities, in most cases, had a short life span and, as E. Gabba has observed, the vitality of rural areas was in this zone far greater than that of the cities, whose very origin and existence were tied to the convergence of the need for an agricultural economic development and the cultural choices of the elites.

The development and diffusion of the villas for agricultural production in the Italic milieu is of great interest. The archaeological data, still far from systematic, would seem to show that the rural villas do not exist at all in the central Apennine areas (the case of Lucania, at least in the eastern sector, is quite different). In the other areas of the Italian peninsula rural villas appear or grow in number and size until the end of the first century B.C. After that date, this type of settlement slowly declines and by the end of the second century A.D. practically disappears, at least as a major productive structure crucial to the economy of Italy.

Craft production at the beginning of the first century A.D. confirms the indications provided by population analysis. The dependency of the former Italic territories on some traditional production centers appears complete as far as the fine wares are concerned, which in fact are not even locally imitated any longer. The great oil and wine production (and therefore the manufacture of amphoras) is progressively shifted to northern Italy and to Spain. The great uniformity of local sculptural production shows the existence of a few workshops producing on a large regional scale, while the importation of marble products from the capital satisfies the need for luxury by the municipal *clientelae*. Results of a recent study on a class of minor products are relevant here, for example, the *impluvia* of the houses in Pompeii. The gap between the "center" and the "periphery" becomes progressively more evident for the current production of decorative art by comparing the paintings from Rome and the paintings from Campania. The late Hellenistic local figurative tradition, which was still fashionable with the municipal ruling classes between the end of the republic and the beginning of the empire, gradually diminishes in the marginal areas and in the social level of its patrons. Rather, the late Hellenistic figurative tradition manifests itself more and more as a "Gesunkenes Kulturgut" a "debased" culture, or according to a fortuitous definition by R. Bianchi Bandinelli, "plebeian art," becoming an expression of groups in a position of cultural and economic dependency or enterprising and volatile freedmen of the Julio-Claudian period. Symptomatic, finally, is the complete disappearance of what had been the figurative culture of the local "middle" and "lower" classes of the second century B.C. The last votive deposits are dated in the first quarter of the first century B.C. when those products (terracottas, small bronzes) and those religious customs typical of the "poor" culture of the late Hellenistic period also disappear.

The Romanization of the Italic territories appears therefore as a phenomenon which took place in the crucial half century between the Social War and the beginning of the empire, in a collateral and dependent manner with respect to the immense social and economic take-off of the most advanced areas in the Italian peninsula which were already under the direct control of Rome and characterized by the slave-based mode of production. The precedents of this mode of production are largely represented by the social and economic events of the second century B.C., in which, however, characteristics of marginality of economic and ideal forms are implicit. This marginality, occurring at the moment of the so-called "political unification" of Italy, in the midst of the reign of Augustus, brings forth the signs of a not-too-distant collapse, which happened between the end of the first and the beginning of the second centuries A.D.

2

THE SITUATION IN ETRURIA

A COMPREHENSIVE HISTORICAL PICTURE of Etruria between the middle of the second century B.C. and the Augustan age has recently been delineated by W.V. Harris.[1] In order to do the same for the field of art history, it is necessary to remember, however, that our archaeological evidence is still incomplete and imprecise,[2] with the result that many of my statements here are provisional and should be treated as working hypotheses, both in general terms and in specific details. This needs to be said at the outset, as the problems are of considerable complexity, and the solutions which are put forward are to be considered in light of both the character and quality of our information.

There are at least three problems to examine. The existing documentation needs to be considered not only as classes of material but also in terms of production centers and in relation to the known chronological fixed points. Hence it is necessary to establish the degree of continuity in the individual classes of material and, generally, to establish the measure of continuity between the characteristics of the early and middle Hellenistic styles and those of the late Hellenistic phase, which is our main focus. Both of these problems are tied, however, to the understanding of various historical phenomena and above all to the understanding of the social situation of the period. Both of these aspects are, in turn, critical to the correct interpretation of art historical facts which, in antiquity as today, are connected to the culture and interests of the patronage.

The situation of southern Etruria is well known in general and only a few points are controversial. At Caere, there are no large aristocratic hypogea which can be dated to the period after the floruit of the fourth cen-

Fig. 2.1

tury to the end of the first quarter of the third century B.C. The tombs of the Alcove, of the Reliefs, of the Inscriptions, of the Triclinium and Torlonia, can be dated to this period.[3] The great ceramic industry, however, is by this time already firmly established in Rome,[4] and there is no other artistic activity documented in this area. In the third and second centuries B.C., Caere produces only votive material[5] and a few examples of terracotta temple decoration. The most noteworthy piece, now in the Vatican, is the classicizing fragment of a relief with tendrils and a human head.[6] The evident abandonment of the great Pyrgi's sanctuary between the first and second quarters of the third century B.C. is also programmatic,[7] as is the fact that in the Late Hellenistic period only a somewhat modest decorative addition is made to the small sanctuary at Punta della

Vipera,[8] by that time already associated with the Roman colony of Castrum Novum.

The decline of Late Republican Veii is no less obvious. We can scarcely attribute to Veii more than a few votive pieces,[9] while the appearance of several villas in the area of the old city is symptomatic. The earliest of these villas, that at "Fosso della Mola," is datable to the first half of the first century B.C.[10]

The situation at Tarquinia is particularly interesting in that only three painted tombs are securely datable to the late Hellenistic period. The Tomb of the Typhon (ca. 150 B.C.)[11] is permeated by a baroque pathos. In the Tomb of the Cardinal (ca. 120 B.C.), a long frieze with underworld scenes is characterized by large summary outlines, and an austere paratactic composition alternates with impressionistic polychrome friezes of gladiators: both friezes are contemporary. Lastly, the flat and lifeless frieze from the Bruschi tomb (ca. 120 B.C.) clearly represents a style which is midway between the styles of the other two tombs.[12] Elsewhere, I have considered the question of the other less monumental hypogea and I shall refrain from summarizing what has already been stated about the sociological aspects.[13] Rather, it is worthwhile to note that the Tarquinian production of nenfro sarcophagi,[14] which exhibit a clear typological and stylistic evolution for the entire fourth and early third century B.C. becomes standardized into the so-called "Fassadentypus." The "Fassadentypus" is characterized first by a plain but still graceful style with an animated and vibrant composition (third century B.C.). Later a series with very little decoration becomes commonplace. This last series includes sarcophagi with plain chests or chests decorated with sea monsters and patera (or the like) and are probably datable to the first half of the second century B.C. as is illustrated by neighboring Tuscania where (for example, a tomb in "Pian di Mola") the sarcophagi in nenfro are replaced from circa 150 B.C. until the middle of the first century B.C. by the characteristic terracotta sarcophagi.[15] The Tomb of the Salvii at Ferento[16] which contains sarcophagi in the later and lifeless Tarquinian tradition (e.g., some reclining figures on the door have only vague anatomical details) is another example of the same development. Bear in mind that these very poor sarcophagi belong to the family of minor local nobles (120–50 B.C.) into which the future emperor Otho would be born.

The architectural evidence from Tarquinia is interesting in several aspects. The "Ionic-Italic" type of capital is already in use in the third century B.C., as is clearly demonstrated by its close association with the late classical and proto-Hellenistic antefix type from the Ara della Regina temple and from the suburban sanctuary at "Ortaccio."[17] Evidence also exists for the redecoration of the "Ara della Regina" temple. The new adornment consists of interesting if crude Doric- and Ionic-type friezes, datable to the late second century B.C.[18] A later refurbishing in the full first century B.C. uses "Campana" plaques.

Instead, the situation at Vulci is problematic. A strong transformation is evident in the necropolis at Vulci in the course of the first half of the second century B.C. In that period, between 250 and 150 B.C., the tombs, for the most part, are of the classical "François" type with a T-shaped plan. That they then lose the facade decoration is proven by a series of small nenfro pediments and by a unique terracotta *naiskos* in the Florence Archaeological Museum, while curious *hypogea* "a corridoio" remain the dominant tomb form for the entire first century B.C.[19] Other artistic production in the area of Vulci is practically nonexistent: at the end of the third century B.C. the characteristic production of incised mirrors, the pride of the fourth century B.C. city, disappears and here, as elsewhere, is replaced by a series of relief mirrorcases which may have been imported from Campania. Additionally, the exceptional painted tombs of the fourth century (the "Francois" tomb) and the third century B.C. (the Campanari tomb), with large nenfro sculpture in the round, are no longer found.[20] The production of architectural terracottas is episodic and in any event badly documented, but a grandiose and unpublished *domus* (the so-called "terme") from the beginning of the first century B.C. infers the existence of an unsuspected private architecture on a par with that of nearby Cosa. Cosa itself is an exception in the entire south Etruscan area. The suspicion that this exception may be due, more than anything else, to our own ignorance of the Etrurian urban situation has largely been dispelled by the excavations of nearby Rusellae,[21] where the public and private building activity is comparable generally to that of other central southern Etruscan cities. Unfortunately, little attention has been paid to the results from the Rusellae excavations. Cosa, with its exceptional civil architecture in *opus incertum* of the second half of the second century B.C. is an example of the northwards expansion of the great architecture of Latium and Campania.[22] This development may be explained by Cosa's particular status as a Latin colony. Either its diverse socioeconomic arrangement or its pledge of *civitas optimo iure* by the local magistrates after the Fregellan war (124 B.C.) would present equally good motives for undertaking a large scale building program. Nevertheless, the evidence of the architectural terracottas from Cosa, well known thanks to their excellent publication,[23] provides us with several points to consider. Three aspects particularly lend themselves to comparison: first, the repertoire of the original decoration of the so-called Temple of Jupiter which, in my view, still belongs to the first years of the colony,[24] second, the vaguely classicistic vein in the decoration of the *Capitolium* of circa 150 B.C., and third, the final arrangement of the Capitolium with "Campana" plaques of the full first century B.C.

Turning to the internal portion of Etruria, the area from Falerii to Volsinii, the panorama changes only superficially. The continuity of tradition between the two Falerii, especially in the tomb typology of the characteristic loculi deposition, is of great importance. The final date of Faleri Veteres (241 B.C.) provides only in part a terminus for the temple architecture and decoration. Only in two extraurban sanctuaries, Celle and Sassi Caduti, do we find further embellishments which are securely datable to the period after the fall of the city, whereas the great urban temples of Scasato and Vignale have provided only homogeneous terracottas datable to before 241 B.C. This fact has implications for the votive deposits. It seems possible that the famous portrait from the Vignale votive deposit, on the basis of its relief, may be dated prior to 241 B.C. Among the decorations in the later epoch, the phase of the Sassi Caduti temple in which the "Campana" plaques were used is noteworthy.[25] From Falerii Novi we have principally the famous altar with a triumphal scene,[26] which dates to the mid-first century B.C. and thus is contemporary to a series of funerary monuments with reliefs of arms and other late Republican motifs. These funerary monuments, to judge from the ancient sources and epigraphic evidence, are linked to the settlements of Roman veterans in the area.[27]

The area of the so-called rock-cut necropoleis, now scientifically investigated (beginning with the Castel d'Asso necropolis) by E. and G. Colonna,[28] share a common evolution in their splendid development in the fourth and third century B.C. and again in the extreme modesty of the later tomb remains which are, in fact, reused between the second and mid-first century B.C. These conclusions, deduced from both excavations and detailed architectural analyses, are of fundamental importance for the chronological placement of the more northerly rock-cut necropolis at Sovana, which is of a high architectural level and contains such monumental examples as the Lattanzi and Hildebranda tombs.[29] Both tombs are most certainly to be assigned to the third century B.C. in accord with the less well known but parallel situation at Vulci.

At Bolsena-Volsinii there are also the remains of rock-cut architecture, similarly florid in its sculptural style but not without some elements of pathos.[30] The French investigations in the ancient city have revealed portions of the complex urban stratigraphy:[31] the more significant architectural remains are dated to the end of the late Hellenistic period under scrutiny here. The picture of Volsinii seems to develop in a surprising manner, especially after the mid-first century B.C. There is a remarkable deployment of energies in public construction with more modest but evident activity in the private sector, such as houses and tombs. Among the latter group a recently restored tomb in the form of a house reflects the typological and stylistic developments of Rome itself.[32] The character of this activity perhaps owes more to the preceding period than to the specific favorable circumstances of the moment, as certain aspects of the ceramic mass production would seem to indicate.[33]

The situation in central Etruria is different in many ways. Undoubtedly the coastal area suffers a decline not unlike that which afflicted the maritime region to the south of Argentario. Rusellae took on a monumental appearance only in the imperial period, Vetulonia seems to have been a center of very modest appearance, at least to judge from the portions excavated, and Populonia, even in light of the most recent soundings, does not provide any evidence datable to the late Hellenistic period, a situation consistent with the rather grim picture painted by Strabo.[34] For none of the above named cities can we find noteworthy artistic activity, with the exception of Vetulonia with its morsels of architectural sculpture and the handsome, unique pediment of Talamone (150 B.C.) which, however, is tied to the figurative tradition of the hinterland, from Volterra to Chiusi.[35] In the great cities of the interior—Chiusi, Perugia, Cortona, Volterra, Arezzo and Fiesole—one can instead recognize a culturally and artistically homogeneous region characterized by remarkable but discontinuous traces of a formal and high cultural level between 400 and 200 B.C. Considerable achievements in sculpture and vase-painting place Chiusi and Volterra in the forefront of the cities in the region. At the beginning of the second century B.C. there is a sudden and vast diffusion of generally uniform quality goods which satisfied the needs of a not particularly exacting but certainly extensive clientele. Hand in hand with this artistic phenomenon go certain other more lofty achievements, both in the context of public and private use of art.

At Chiusi, some ateliers producing sarcophagi had continued along the same lines of development as their more southern counterparts in the third century B.C. From the early second century until the first decades of the first century B.C., workshops instead produced small stone and terracotta urns which were iconographically and stylistically inspired by middle and late Hellenistic models.[36] Whereas in general the stone urns were much more refined and fulfilled the needs of a cultured and sophisticated urban clientele, the terracotta urns had a wider diffusion, especially in the countryside. Stamps reproduced the elements found in the local late Hellenistic repertoire (the duel of Eteocles and Polyneices was a favorite motif) to which certain popular overtones were added by the use of a vivacious polychromy. There were also terracotta pieces of considerable importance, such as the two sarcophagi of *Thanunia* and *Larthia Seianti*, probably from the mid-second century B.C.[37] The decoration of the two sarcophagi demonstrates the debasement of the orginal Doric frieze, now contaminated with pilasters used as decorative division, a widely recognized motif in the urns of Chiusi, Volterra, and Perugia.

But the center of great Hellenistic exuberance is Volterra with its famous production of alabaster urns: the Pergamene and Asiatic inspiration of the urns is well known.[38] Numerous workshops were active from the end of the third century B.C. until the first quarter of the first century B.C. (although the later production demonstrates a clear degeneration on the formal level).[39] The Volterran workshops exerted considerable influence on the Perugian ones and to a lesser degree on the artists at Chiusi: in fact, already from the fourth century B.C. Perugia appears to be culturally subordinate to Volterra.[40] The celebrated urn of the "two old people"[41] illustrates the talents of the Volterran artists in the use of clay. Their mastery in the production of architectural terracottas has now also been confirmed by one of the temples on the acropolis which is as outstanding in its Asiatic Hellenism as are the urns.[42] The buildings on the acropolis clearly attest to the prosperity of Volterra in the second century B.C.

Perugia developed in a subordinate role, mass-producing urns in travertine, for the most part on a not very high level: nevertheless, examples like the Tomb of the Volumni illustrate the elevated level of the local aristocracy by the inclusion of a group of stone and plaster urns within the general conservatism evident in the plan of the tomb.[43] Preeminent among the urns is that of *Arnth*, the founder of the sepulchre: his urn is exceptional for its stylistic balance of baroque pathos and classicistic tendencies.

The portrait of *Aule Meteli*, the so-called "Arringatore," is no less interesting. This bronze life-size statue made at Perugia depicts the man from Cortona in the new style of portraiture imported directly from Rome.[44] Perugian architectural experiments, in particular the Porta Martia, with its lovely Hellenistic *caenaculum* illusionistically peopled by divine figures and horse-heads.[45] The flattened form of the pilaster capitals (widely repeated on contemporary urns) documents the apparent evolution of the capitals and of architectural decoration in general from the swollen baroque formulae of third century B.C.

Arezzo offers us, in addition to a mediocre production of cinerary urns, an extraordinary series of terracotta fragments (often cited but not exhaustively published) of figured pediments and friezes belonging to one or more temples. The figures have dramatic expressions that, on the one hand, echo several specific classicistic pieces, but, on the other hand, are reminiscent of the urns of the Volumni and perhaps less forcefully recall the slightly earlier pediments from the Roman colony at Luni.[46] To go beyond the cultural history in the context of economic history, around the middle of the first century B.C. the beginning of the coral-red ceramic production stands out as an important moment: Arezzo certainly had already held a prominent position in the previous black-glaze production.

Fiesole, also, had been for a long time rather less important than other southern cities. The reconstruction of the small temple at Fiesole, given by G. Maetzke,[47] is of interest. Although the building has a very provincial outlook, Hellenistic forms appear in the porticoes attached to the temple facade, an architectural solution which is found in other Etruscan sacred architecture.[48]

At the end of this analysis we must ask ourselves: What are the traditional elements in the local early and middle Hellenism that reappear in the late Hellenistic Etruscan culture?

The principal factors of continuity which have come out of this analysis are those imposed by religious traditionalism: specifically, the production of architectural terracottas and votive material in both bronze and terracotta. In this case, however, as in all other manifestations of Etruscan culture, the data in our possession shows that the decorative tradition of architecture in the third century B.C. appears to be surpassed by the innovations of the second half of the second century B.C. A particularly important example of such innovations are the "closed" pediments which are decorated in very high relief (Talamone, Arezzo) and which, perhaps, follow a fashion begun in Rome and then repeated elsewhere in Italy. Furthermore, from the mid-second century B.C., the purely architectural decoration, well-illustrated by the Cosa sequence but also attested to elsewhere in Etruria, shows a predilection for new forms. The new forms include the elaboration of the decorative elements in the Doric and Ionic traditions, or other plant motifs, taken from preceding formulae but executed with different intricacies and spirit, with little turgidity and less insistence on flowery details. In turn this phase was superseded by the middle of the first century B.C. by the revetment tradition of the Campana plaques, neoattic in taste and of urban origins. We have no evidence of temple decoration of a traditional type—even if modified in the late Hellenistic mode—after the beginning of the first century B.C. The local production of the terracottas ought not, then, continue beyond these two centuries. The votive deposits, for which the chronological *terminus* is around 50–40 B.C.,[49] contain a large number of minor bronze and clay objects. The deposits certainly dated to after the beginning of the third century B.C. contain the most mediocre bronzes—in no way comparable to the handsome bronze votives or candelabra finials of the fourth century B.C. which come from small workshops mostly dedicated to production for a sacred use. In the second century B.C., the quality of the bronzes sank even further with elongated forms and a very summary execution of details. The great bronze production of the fourth century/first half of the third century is by now only a memory. The mirrors and cists are no longer produced by the end of the third century B.C.[50] and are replaced by an ever growing influx of imported products, most likely from Rome and Campania. For the terracotta votive material the situation is not dissimilar. In the fourth and third centuries B.C. the large "ideal" type heads of classical, late classical, and proto-Hellenistic inspiration are widely appreciated but already in the second half of the third century B.C. the forms flatten out. Veiled busts are not modelled in back, and inconsistent details are not only found but will dominate the production, with few and marginal exceptions, for the entire second century B.C.[51] At the end of the second century and for nearly fifty years of the first, one can add handsome physiognomic portraits in the round to this mass production; however, this is a phenomenon restricted to Caere and owed to influences emanating out of nearby Rome. A break in continuity is sharp and unequivocal between the "mid-Italic" tradition which is tied by objective data with an absolute chronology, by comparanda and by historical probability to the first half of the third century B.C.[52] and these very different and late manifestations of portraiture to which the "Arringatore" justifiably belongs on the basis of its style and destination. At the most one could speak rather dubiously of "revival" even if in my view the "mid-Italic" tradition has been largely ignored—and not only stylistically—by late republican portraiture.

In all other sectors, from funerary architecture to painting, there are no real signs of continuity but only imitations of old fashions for reasons of prestige as, for example, in the "archaic" plan of the Tomb of the Volumni and in the very few late Tarquinian tombs. Beyond a generic religious conservatism found throughout Etruria (but also in Rome) which is expressed in more outwardly apparent forms (preservation of customs and of rites) than in elements of a true formal repertoire, the break between the two traditions, that of the fourth to third centuries B.C. with that of the second and part of the first centuries B.C., could not be greater and more evident.

From the foregoing summary examination of the material and of the cultural traditions, several conclusions of particular interest in the contexts of art history and cultural history have emerged.

The Etruscan area in this period can easily be divided into two large sectors: a southern area which includes a coastal annex extending as far as Populonia, with a northern limit at the territory of Vulci and Volsinii, and a northern area, centered on Chiusi, Perugia, Volterra, and Arezzo. The southern area is characterized by a fairly sudden halt in high quality artistic production between the first and second quarters of the third century B.C., almost perfectly concomitant to the definitive takeover of the area by Rome which was accompanied by a relevant and drastic abandonment of the territory: the takeover was spread over the years 281 (Tarquinia), 280 (Vulci), 273 (Caere), 265 (Volsinii) and 241 B.C. (Falerii). After the middle of the third century B.C., the various artisan activities slowly disappeared with only the occasional barbarized survivals, for example, Tarquinian sarchophagi. In the emerging relatively important areas of the periphery (Tuscania, Ferento) a modest local production of objects which in the past had been imported from the nearby greater cities begins to develop. Around the mid-second century B.C. and for a few decades thereafter, rare and discontinuous signs of an artisan revival occur in architectural decoration (Cerveteri, Tarquinia, Vulci, Volsinii, Cosa, Talamone, Vetulonia), in painting (Tarquinia) and in funerary sculpture (Tuscania). The models for these activities are, in general, those of Asiatic late Hellenism with its emphasis on pathos, but sometimes with classicistic overtones. Nonetheless, the phenomenon has an obviously episodic character with extremely rare cases of continuity of workshops (Tuscania) which seem to die out in the first quarter of the first century B.C. This movement was brought about on the cultural level by imitation of forms which were widely diffused in Etruria and elsewhere, especially in Rome and on the social level by Roman colonization, particularly in the old territories of Tarquinia and Vulci.[53] The same Asiatic flavor with rare classicistic accents pervaded the northern artistic production but the phenomenon has altogether different structural characteristics. Unlike that which happens in the south, we find a vast "middle-class" patronage with peaks of greater sophistication in both the public and private spheres (Çhiusi, Perugia, Volterra). The diffusion and persistence of small workshops is owed to this "middle-class" patronage, while the impetus for more sensitive formal experimentation is owed to the needs of the local aristocracies. The interdependence of the two levels of patronage is evident.

The two situations then, that of the south and that of the north, clearly indicate the existence of two different realities for which a reason must be sought within the socioeconomic structure as purely political explanations will not suffice.[54]

Elsewhere I have attempted to analyze the process of the assimilation of the Etruscan aristocracy into the Roman ruling class.[55] The conclusions of that study are generally applicable here, given the precocious interest of the south in a rapid absorption into the Roman political class, whereas in the north the local aristocracy seems more reluctant to be absorbed, if not actually jealous of their own autonomy. This explains rather well the decline of the patronage in southern Etruria and the existence of culturally advanced "peaks" in the north, but it does not suffice to explain the presence of a vast "middle-class" patronage in the north which was a strongly felt presence from the second quarter of the second century until the first quarter of the first century B.C. Furthermore, a purely sociological explanation which is limited to the higher strata of society does not suffice. One must analyze the social structure in its entirety and pay particular attention to the profound interrelations of the social structure and the economic structure.

A brief analysis of the economic and social situation in Etruria of the second century B.C. turns up interesting evidence. The south, as much as survived of the socio-economic structure after the Roman conquest, quickly adapted to the rapid spread of "slave labor" as a mode of production (thanks also to a similarity to the economic, political, and social situation of fourth and third century B.C. Rome). Thus, acceptance of slave labor in the second century B.C. lead to the first *latifundia*. In the north, however, the archaic Etruscan mode of production based on *servitus* was preserved throughout the entire third century under the security of Roman protection. Only after the rebellion of the *servi* in Etruria in 196 B.C., and especially after the events of the Bacchanalia, the Etruscan cities of the north, perhaps after Roman pressure, granted civil status to the *etera/servi* in the city and countryside. The blossoming forth of the *Vornamengentilen* at Perugia, Chiusi, Volterra, and Arezzo (studied by Rix) testifies to this development. The "reform" did not totally abolish the old servile status, as the famous fragment of *Ninfa Vegoia* illustrates. It did, however, cancel substantially the fundamental discrimination which in early centuries the Roman patricians had tried unsuccessfully to impose on the *plebs* who were politically disenfranchised because they had no *gens*. The ancient Etruscan *servi* gradually acquired an ancestry and political rights and thus evolved into a type of intermediate group between the aristocracy, the true and proper slaves, and however many were still in the rank of *etera*.[56]

The chronological coincidence between this reform and the flowering of the "middle-class" patronage, to which the *Vornamengentilen* belong, to judge from their cinerary urns of mediocre quality and their rather degenerated artisan products, is illuminating. It should be no surprise that Etruria was fiercely opposed to the reforms of Drusus or that she may have shown a far-reaching sympathy for Marius since it is clear that the Roman repression, from the Sullan violence to the Octavian massacres at Perugia, served physically to eliminate or silence this "middle-class," and thus imposed on the surviving aristocracy the virtual necessity to conform to the economic and political laws of Rome.

This economic and political scheme was followed by a clear cut cultural plan. After the first decade of the first century B.C., the influence emanating from the capital city now became dominant. Until this time, the peripheral areas had struggled to imitate the formal artistic expression either in their own fashion or by importing ideas. One by one the local workshops ceased, although they had tried to resist with a repertoire of barbarized Hellenistic motifs. The imitation of the classicism flowing out from the capital, both ideologically and formally, in the last decade of the first century B.C. became the ordering artistic principle of the day, both for the vestiges of the local aristocracy and for the new upper classes composed of the Sullan and Augustan centurions. Was this imposition accomplished easily? One would say yes, to judge from the overview of the first imperial period, the flood of dynastic honors flowing from every corner of Etruria which, if it does not hold the record in all of Italy for homages to the imperial house certainly comes close. Some interesting curiosities, such as the copy of the *elogia* from the Forum of Augustus, displayed together with the Lupercal on an altar in the city of Arezzo, or the loose copy of the Capitoline she-wolf at Fiesole allow us to understand that it may have been necessary for the Sullan colonists to underline publicly their being "Romans," just as at Tarquinia the last survivors of the old Etruscan nobility similarily emphasized their ancient stock and small local triumphs.[57]

The confrontation between the Etruscan *veteres*, humiliated and scattered, and the Etruscan *novi*, proud of the better lands but insecure of their own possession of them, was not an easy one as we are taught by the revolts at Fiesole and Perugia. The imposition of a new mode and new relationships of production—and thus of a new culture—has never been an easy task, but the result was positive, if by the first century A.D., the sources can speak with satisfaction of the "*Tusca ergastula*."

NOTES

1. Harris 1971.
2. Torelli 1970–71: 431, but also the convincing and broad synthesis by Bianchi Bandinelli, *Etruschi e Italici*, Roma, 1973.

3. On the tomb of the Inscriptions, Cristofani 1965: 221 ff and on the tomb of the Reliefs. Cristofani 1965, used in conjunction with the Cerveteri fasicule of the *CIE* (also by Cristofani), comments on other tombs and their relative chronology incorporating archaeological, epigraphic, and historical sources.
4. *Roma* 1973: 43 ff.
5. On the material from Caere in the Museo Gregoriano Etrusco del Vaticano (Helbig 1963: 14, *passim*), Hafner 1965–66: 41 ff. and 1966–67: 29 ff. has added extensive comments, often with many new and interesting ideas. Still important even if outdated, Kaschnitz von Weinberg 1925: 325 ff.
6. Bianchi Bandinelli 1973: 300 and fig. 346.
7. *NSc Suppl. 1970: passim.*
8. Torelli and Pallottino 1967: 331.
9. On the new votive deposit from the small sanctuary at Porta Caere, *NSc* 1973: 227 ff.
10. On the villa, Ward Perkins 1961: 69, nr. 839558.
11. Cristofani 1971.
12. Basically unpublished. For the Tomb of the Cardinal, see the work of Van Essen 1928: 83 and Blazquez 1965: 3.
13. Torelli 1970–71: 436.
14. Herbig 1952 has collected the information according to the museum collections (*n.b.:* the chronologies are low).
15. On the recent discoveries (tombs of the *Curunas* and the tombs in the "Pian di Mola" area) see *EAA Suppl.* 1970: "Tuscania." These tombs are important for the chronological information they provide about the terracotta sarcophagus production: see also Turr 1963: 68.
16. Degrassi 1961–62: 59.
17. Unpublished, although discovered in 1968.
18. The Tarquinian architectural terracottas are not well known (although M. Cataldi is now working on them) because they were discovered after the comprehensive work by Andren 1939–40. There is a brief presentation as well in *NSc* 1948a: 193 ff.
19. Messerschmidt and von Gerkan 1930: for a summary of the situation at Vulci, *EAA* VII: "Vulci."
20. Dohrn 1965: 377 and with chronologies rather low, Hus 1966: 665.
21. Laviosa 1969: 577.
22. Brown 1951: 7 and 1960: 9; Boethius and Ward Perkins 1970: 122.
23. Brown, Richardson and Richardson 1960: 151. On "Campanian" revetments in general, see Borbein 1968.
24. Torelli and Pallottino 1967: 343.
25. Andren 1939–40: 120.

26. Weinstock 1971: 86, 129, pl. 14.
27. Amply documented (*CIL* XI, 3109: early centurion; 7496: similar; 7499: standard bearer; above all 7495: *trib. mil. leg. Gemellae*) for the presence of veterans in the second half of the first century B.C. This may be because of the viritane assignations or perhaps because of an actual colonial deduction (cfr. the *colonia Falisca* of Pliny *N.H.* 3, 51. had been rather quickly abandoned, together with the triumviral colony *Inunoia quae appellatur Faliscorum* of the *Lib.Col.* 217L, in contrast with *CIL* XI, 3083 where *municipes* are noted. See *infra* note 53.
28. Colonna and Colonna 1970. On the rock-cut necropoleis, Koch, von Mercklin, Weickert 1915: 161 ff. (Blera); *NSc* 1963: 1 (San Giuliano); Boethius et al. 1962 (San Giovenale); Gargana 1931: 297 (San Giuliano); Rosi 1925: 1 and 1927: 59 for general comments.
29. Bianchi Bandinelli 1929.
30. Cfr. the head at Museo Barracco in Rome, Pietrangeli 1949: 54, nr. 204.
31. Bloch 1947: 9; 1950: 53; 1963: 339 with regular reports from 1963 onwards in *MEFRA*. See also Gros 1970: 186; Balland and Tchernia 1966: 52; Goudineau 1968: 375.
32. Colonna 1965: 106, figs. 14, 16.
33. "Ruvfies" and "Numnal group" *askoi*, cfr. Colonna 1967: 560 and Cristofani 1968: 258.
34. Rusellae, Laviosa 1969: 577; Vetulonia, Renzetti 1950–51: 29 (archaeological map of the area) and Talocchini 1963: 435 as well as frequent notices yearly in *StEtr.* Populonia, in addition to the old work by Minto 1943, cfr. De Agostino 1955–56: 255; 1962: 275; *NSc* 1957: 1; *NSc* 1961a: 63.
35. Vetulonia, Andren: 1939–40; 239 figs. 294–7; Talamone, *NSc* 1951: 251; *NSc* 1962: 285; *NSc* 1965a: 30 and 81.
36. Important comments by Thimme 1954–55: 25; 1957: 87; 1959: 147.
37. On these sarcophagi, the excavation data have been collected by Bianchi Bandinelli 1925: c. 305. On the tomb of the Calini Sepus at Monteriggioni, Bianchi Bandinelli 1928: 133. On the tomb of the Pellegrina at Chiusi, Levi 1931: 475. On the tombs at Papena, Phillips 1965: 5; 1967: 23 and at Malignano, Phillips 1967–68: 617. These last tombs are important for the urns with the coins issued between 205 and 155 B.C. which are associated with them: Crawford 1968: 281 on the coins from late north Etruscan tombs. On other late tombs, *infra* note 57.
38. Hanfmann 1945: 45; von Vacano 1960: 48; Dohrn 1961: 48; Laviosa 1964; Pairault 1972.
39. Pairault (1972a: 11) has recently studied some of these workshops.
40. As is the case for the pottery from Volterra, exported to Perugia and the

territory (the masterpiece of the main red-figure Volterran artist, the Esione Painter, comes from Perugia): Beazley 1947: 124 and Montagna Pasquinucci 1968.

41. This class has not been studied, even if the famous piece from Volterra is frequently illustrated (cfr. Santangelo 1960: 75).
42. *NSc Suppl.* 1973. I thank my colleague M. Cristofani for allowing me to see the material and for having discussed with me such interesting material. Excavation notices are found in *FA* 1958: 170, nr. 2632.
43. Von Gerkan and Messerschmidt 1942: 122 (with rather low dates).
44. On the statue, Dohrn 1968: on the origins of the family (inferred from *CIL* XI, 1905) see Torelli 1971: 495. The statue certainly comes from a sanctuary: on the exact provenience, Susini 1965: 141.
45. Riis 1934: 65 and Boethius and Ward Perkins 1970: 76.
46. Andren 1939–40: 283, figs. 337–40.
47. Maetzke 1955–56: 227; Bocci 1961: 411; *NSc* 1961a: 52. Cfr. also Caputo and Maetzke 1959: 41 (relief). The other temple at Fiesole of Santa Maria Primerana is also important: *NSc* 1948: 58.
48. Cfr. the building at the side of the small temple at Punta della Vipera which is very like a stoa of the third century B.C., Torelli and Pallottino 1967: 332, fig. 1, area E.
49. This last date, from a secure context, comes from the deposit at Veii near Porta Caere (see note 9). The deposit was sealed by a very modest building of 40 B.C. circa. We find the same situation at Gabii (Balil 1970: 173, nr. 2441) while the imprecise stratigraphic interpretation (*NSc* 1959: 102) led the author to date the closing of the votive deposit from the Porta Nord at Vulci to 90 B.C. In my opinion, the deposit is datable to the period before 80 B.C. as is demonstrated by some of the heads (Paglieri 1960: 74) in a Rhodian-Pergamene emotional style. This is a parallel phenomenon to the appearance of votive heads in the "veristic" style about which I will speak later. I have not seen the study of Terrosi Zanco 1966: 268 which dates the closing of some of the votive deposits with Etrusco-Italic ex-votos to the first century A.D.
50. *Roma* 1973: 258.
51. *Roma* 1973: 138, and on the elongated type of ex-voto see Terrosi Zanco 1961: 423.
52. The relationship of "middle-Italic" portraits with pieces such as the head oinochoe Tiskiewitz and the one at London (Haynes 1965: 523 and 1959: 110) and the Perugine cinerary urn in Leningrad (Vostchinina 1965: 317) is symptomatic since these pieces represent the evolution from the late classical tradition of the Mars from Todi to the Chiusine type of sculpture illustrated

by the cinerary urn of Chianciano and the Berlin E32 statue. This in turn gives rise to the squared aspect of the "middle-Italic" heads and thus is an important chronological element as is the head from the votive deposit of Falerii, Vignale (*Roma* 1973: 32) which is associated with pieces not seemingly later than 241 B.C.

53. On the colonization of southern Etruria in the second century B.C., Harris 1971: 147. Obvious name changes occur in Tarquinia of the first century B.C. and I think that a Gracchan colony may have been placed there, as is noted by the *Liber Coloniarum:* Torelli 1975. In the area of Tarquinia there was in any event the maritime colony of Gravisca and the Latin colony of Cosa was in the area of Vulci as well as the *praefecturae* of Heba, Saturnia, and Statonia.
54. As is known, between Tarquinia, Vulci, Volsinii, Falerii for the South and the other large northern cities, there was no substantial difference in the juridical condition until the Social War as all were indistinctly *sociae.* Formally the position of all the Etruscan cities was the same for Rome.
55. Torelli 1969: 285 ff.
56. See Torelli 1974–75: 3.
57. On the problem, see the remarks and bibliography in note 53. The use of Hellenistic chamber tombs is documented up to the end of the Augustan-Tiberian age (*supra* note 37 and Torelli 1968: 47). See also the documentation on recent discoveries, unfortunately rather summarily published, if at all: Fiesole: *NSc* 1957: 267; Arezzo: Maetzke 1954: 353; *FA* 1960: 267, nr. 4088; Volterra: Fiumi 1946–47: 349 and 1957: 367, and 1959: 251; *FA* 1963: 186, nr. 2706; 1964: 206, nr. 2920; San Gimignano: *FA* 1962: 169, nr. 2573; Montepulciano: Tarugi 1960: 339; Montalcino: *FA* 1962: 164, nr. 2518; Asciano: *FA* 1959: 174, nr. 2739; 1963: 162, nr. 2409; Chiusi: *FA* 1965: 193, nr. 2677; Vetulonia: *FA* 1963: 184, nr. 2694. The dating and interpretation given by Minto 1951: 60 for the Angori and Pythagoras "tanelle" at Cortona (where the general typology is still obscure: cfr. Maetzke 1954: 345 ff.) is incorrect. The Hellenistic influence of these second century B.C. monuments is evident, as is the Hellenistic origin and the typology of the barrel vaulted tombs at Perugia and Chiusi, once again rightly emphasized by Richardson 1964: 211.

BIBLIOGRAPHY

Andren, A.

1939–40 *Architectural Terracottas from Etrusco-Italic Temples.* Lund.

Balland, A., and Tchernia, A.

1966 "Bolsena: Scavi della Scuola Francese di Roma: Pavimenti tardo repubblicani o protoaugustei," *NSc:* 52–78.

Beazley, J.D.

1947 *Etruscan Vase Painting*. Oxford.

Bianchi Bandinelli, R.

1925 "Clusium. Ricerche archeologiche e topografiche su Chiusi e il suo territorio in età Etrusca," *MA* XXX: 211–578.

1928 "La tomba dei Calini Sepus presso Monteriggioni," *StEtr* II: 132–76.

1929 *Sovana*. Firenze.

1973 *Etruschi e Italici*. Roma.

Blazquez, J.M.

1965 "La Tomba del Cardinale y la influencia orfico-pitagórica en las creencias etruscas de ultratumba," *Latomus* XXIV: 3 pp.

Bloch, R.

1947 "Volsinies Etrusque-Essai Historique et Topographique," *MEFR* LIX: 9–39.

1950 "Volsinines Etrusque et Romaine Nouvelles découvertes archéologiques et épigraphiques," *MEFR* LII: 53–120.

1963 "Gli Scavi della Scuola Francese a Bolsena," *StEtr* XXXI: 399–424.

Bocci, P.

1961 "Nuovi Scavi del tempio di Fiesole," *StEtr* XXIXA: 411–15.

1961a "Fiesole: Campagne di scavo negli anni 1961–62 nella zona adiacente al tempio etrusco," *NSc:* 52–62.

Boethius, A. et al.

1962 *Etruscan Culture, Land and People*. New York.

Boethius, A. and Ward Perkins, J.B.

1970 *Etruscan and Roman Architecture*. New York.

Borbein, A.H.

1968 *Campanareliefs. Typologische und stilkritische Untersuchungen RömMitt. Erg. Heft. XIV.* Heidelberg.

Brown, F.
1951 *Cosa I: History and Topography MAAR* XX.

Brown, F.E., Richardson, E.H. and Richardson, L.
1960 *Cosa II: The temples of the arx MAAR* XXVI.

Caputo, G. and Maetzke, G.
1959 "Presentazione del relievo di Fiesole antica," *StEtr* XXVII: 44–63.

Colonna, E. and Colonna, G.
1970 *Castel d'Asso.* Roma.

Colonna, G.
1965 "Bolsena (Viterbo). Area dell'antica Volsinii," *BdA* L: 106.
1967 "Rivista di epigrafia etrusca," *StEtr* XXXV: 560–61.

Colonna, G. et al.
1970 "Pyrgi-Scavi del Santuario Etrusco" *NSc Suppl.*

Crawford, M.H.
1968 "Coins from a Cemetery at Malignano," *AJA* LXXII: 281–83.

Cristofani, M.
1965 *La tomba delle Iscrizioni a Cerveteri.* Milano.
1966 "Le iscrizioni della tomba dei Relievi di Cerveteri," *StEtr* XXXIV: 221–38.
1968 "Rivista di epigrafia," *StEtr* XXXVI: 258–62.
1971 "Tarquinia" *Monumenti della pittura Antica,* fasc. V. Roma.

Cristofani, M. et al.
1973 "Volterra: Scavi 1969–71" *NSc Suppl.*

De Agostino, A.
1955–56 "Nuovi contributi all'archeologìa di Populonia," *StEtr* XXIV: 255–68.
1957 "Populonia (Livorno). Scoperte archeologiche nella necropoli negli anni 1954–56," *NSc:* 1–52.
1961 "Populonia (Livorno). Scoperte archeologiche nella necropoli negli anni 1957–60," *NSc:* 62–102.
1962 "La cinta fortificata di Populonia," *StEtr* XXX: 275–82.

Degrassi, A.

1961–62 "Il sepolcro dei Salvii a Ferento e le sue iscrizioni," *RendPontAcc* XXIV: 58–77.

Dohrn, T.

1961 "Pergamenisches in Etrurien," *RömMitt* LXVIII: 1–8.

1965 "Etruskische Zweifigurengruppe nach Tarentiner Vorbild," *AA:* 377–94.

1968 *Der Arringatore.* Firenze.

Fiumi, E.

1946–47 "Per la cronaca dei ritrovamenti archeologici nel Volterrano," *StEtr* XIX: 349–51.

1957 "Contributo alla datazione del materiale Volterrano," *StEtr* XXV: 367–415.

1959 "Scoperta di due tombe Etrusche e di una tomba romana in Località Poggio alle Croci (Volterra)," *StEtr* XXVII: 251–68.

Gargana, A.

1931 "La necropoli rupestre di S. Giuliano," *MA* XXXIII: 298–467.

Goudineau, C.

1968 "Les fouilles de l'Ecole Française de Rome à Bolsena (Poggio Moscini 1962–68)," *CRAI:* 375–90.

Gros, P.

1970 "Fouilles de l'Ecole Française à Bolsena (Poggio Moscini) 1965–1968," *FA* XXI: 186–87.

Hafner, G.

1965 "Grauen und mädchenbilder aus Terrakotta im Museo Gregoriano Etrusco," *RömMitt* LXXII: 41–61.

1965–66 "Eine Porträtstatue aus Terracotta im Museo Gregoriano etrusco," *RendPontAcc* XXXVII: 105–11.

1966–67 "Männer und Junglingsbilder aus Terrakotta im Museo Gregoriano etrusco," *RömMitt* LXXIII/LXXIV: 29–52.

Hanfmann, G.M.

1945 "Etruscan reliefs of the Hellenistic Period," *JHS* LV: 45–57.

Harris, W.V.

1971 *Rome in Etruria and Umbria*. Oxford.

Haynes, S.

1959 "Etruskische Bronzekopfgefässe aus hellenistischer Zeit," *JRGZ* VI: 115–26.

1965 "Ein etruskischer Bronzekopf von Bolsenasee," *StEtr* XXXIII: 523–25.

Helbig, W.

1963 *Fuhrer durch die öffentlichen Sammlungen klassicher Altertumer in Rom*. Tubingen.

Herbig, R.

1952 *Die jungeretruskischen Steinsarkophage*. Berlin.

Hus, A.

1966 "Réflexions sur la statuaire en pierre de Vulci après l'époque archaique" in *Mélanges d'archéologie et d'histoire à A. Piganiol*, pp. 665–76. Paris.

Kaschnitz von Weinberg, G.

1925 "Ritratti fittili Etruschi e Romani dal secolo III al I av. Cr.," *Atti della Pontificia Accademia Romana di Archeologìa* III: 325–50.

Koch, H., von Mercklin, E., Weickert, C.

1915 "Bieda" *RömMitt* XXX: 161–303.

Laviosa, C.

1964 *Catalogo della Mostra 'Scultura tardo-etrusca di Volterra.'* Firenze.

1969 "Rusellae: relazione preliminare della settima e della ottava campagna di scavo (1963–64)," *StEtr* LXVII: 577–609.

Levi, D.

1931 "Chiusi: La tomba della Pellegrina," *NSc:* 475–505.

Maetzke, G.

1948 "Fiesole: scoperta di antichi avanzi nella chiesa di S. Maria Primerana," *NSc:* 58–60.

1954 "Cortona (Arezzo), Tomba Etrusca a camera in Località 'Il Passaggio'," *StEtr* XXIII: 345–52.

1954a "Tomba con urnetta iscritta trovata in Arezzo," *StEtr* XXIII: 353–56.

1955–56 "Il nuovo tempio tuscanico di Fiesole," *StEtr* XXIV: 227–53.

1957a "Fiesole: Scoperta di tombe etrusche in Via G. Matteotti," *NSc:* 267–82.

Messerschmidt, F. and von Gerkan, A.

1930 *Die Nekropolen von Vulci. EAA* VII. Berlin.

Minto, A.

1943 *Populonia*. Firenze.

1951 "La 'Tanella Angori' di Cortona," *Palladio* I: 60–66.

Paglieri, S.

1959 "Vulci: scavi stratigrafici," *NSc:* 102–11.

1960 "Una stipe votiva vulcente," *RIASA* IX: 74–96.

Pairault, F.H.

1972 *Recherches sur quelques séries d'urnes de Volterra*. Roma.

1972a "Un aspect de l'artisanat de l'albâtre a Volterra quelques visages d'ateliers," *DdA* VI: 11–35.

Pasquinucci, M.

1968 *Le kelebai volterrane*. Firenze.

Phillips, K.

1965 "Papena (Siena)," *NSc:* 6–29.

1967 "Papena (Siena)-Sepoltura tardo etrusca," *NSc:* 23–40.

1967–68 "Late Etruscan tomb Groups from Maligno and Papena," *American Philosophical Society Yearbook*, 617–18.

Pietrangeli, C.

1949 *Il Museo Barracco.*

Renzetti, G.

1950–51 "Carte archeologiche speciali: Vetulonia, carta archeologica della città," *StEtr* XXI: 291–96.

Richardson, E.
1964 *The Etruscans.* Chicago.

Riis, V.P.J.
1934 "The Etruscan city-gates in Perugia," *AArch:* 65–98.

Roma
1973 *Roma Medio Repubblicana. Aspetti Culturali di Roma e del Lazio nei secoli IV e III a.C.* Roma.

Romanelli, P.
1948 "Tarquinia: Scavi e ricerche nell'area della città," *NSc:* 193–270.

Rosi, G.
1925 "Sepulchral architecture as illustrated by the rock façades of Central Etruria (Part I)," *JRS* XV: 1–59.
1927 "Sepulchral architecture as illustrated by the rock façades of Central Etruria (Part II)," *JRS* XVII: 59–96.

Santangelo, M.
1960 *Musei e monumenti etruschi.* Novara.

Structures
1973 *Actes du III Colloque sur les structures sociales dans l'Antiquité.* Bésançon.

Susini, G.
1965 "Sul luogo di rinvenimento dell'Arringatore," *AC* XVII: 141–46.

Talocchini, A.
1963 "La città e la necropoli di Vetulonia secondo i nuovi scavi (1959–1962)," *StEtr* XXXI: 435–51.

Tarugi, G.S.
1960 "La tradizione delle origini etrusche di Montepulciano" *StEtr* XXVIII: 339–45.

Terrosi Zanco, O.
1961 "Ex-voto allungati dell'Italia Centrale," *StEtr* XXIX: 423–59.

1966 "Stipi votive di epoca italico-romana in grotte abruzzesi," *Atti Soc. Tosc. Scienze Naturali:* 268–90.

Thimme, E.

1954–55 "Chiusinische Aschenkesten und Sarkophage der hellenistischen zeit," *StEtr* XXIII: 25–147.

1957 "Chiusinische Aschenkesten und Sarkophage der hellenistichen zeit (Zweiter Teil)," *StEtr* XXV: 87–160.

1959 "Der Porträtwert etruskischer Bildnisse. Probleme antiker Bildniskunst am Beispiel chiusinischer Grabplastik" in *Werke und Wege Festschrift E. Knittel,* 147–63.

Torelli, M.

1968 "Monumenti funerari romani con fregio Dorico," *DdA* II: 32–54 (translated in this volume).

1969 "Senatori etruschi della tarda repubblica e dell'impero," *DdA* III: 285–363.

1970–71 "Contributo dell'archeologìa alla storia sociale: L'Etruria e l'Apulia," *DdA* V: 431–42.

1971 "Per La Storia dell'Etruria in età imperiale," *RFIC* XCIX: 489–501 (translated in this volume).

1974–75 "Tre studi di storia etrusca," *DdA* VIII: 3–85.

1975 *Elogia Tarquiniensia.* Firenze.

Torelli M. and Pallottino, M.

1967 "Terza campagna di scavi a Punta della Vipera (S. Marinella)," *StEtr* XXXV: 331–53.

Torelli, M. and Pohl, I.

1973 "La Stipe Votiva" in Veio-Scoperta di un piccolo santuario etrusco in località Campetti, *NSc:* 40–258.

Turr, E.S.

1963 "Über spätetruskische Tonsarkophage aus Tuscania," *RömMitt* LXX: 68–79.

Van Essen, C.C.

1928 "La Tomba del Cardinale," *StEtr* II: 83–123.

Villa D'Amelio, P.

1963 "San Giuliano: scavi e scoperte nella necropoli dal 1957–1959," *NSc:* 1–76.

Von Gerkan, A. and Messerschmidt, F.

1942 "Das Grab der Volumnier bei Perugia," *RömMitt* LVII: 122–35.

Von Vacano, O.

1951 "Grosseto: Scavi sul Talamonaccio," *NSc:* 251–60.

1960 "Studien an Volterraner Urnenreliefs," *RömMitt* LXVII: 48–97.

1962 "Talamone (Ortebello): Ricerche sul tempio di Talamone," *NSc:* 285–300.

1965 "Die Giebelsima des Tempels von Telamon" *RömMitt* LXXII: 81–92.

1965a "Grosseto: Scavi sul Talamonaccio," *NSc:* 30–39.

Vostchinina, A.J.

1965 "Statua-cinerario in bronzo di arte etrusca nelle collezioni dell'Ermitage," *StEtr* XXXIII: 318–28.

Ward Perkins, J.B.

1961 "Veii: The Historical Topography of the Ancient City," *PBSR* XXIX: 3–39.

Weinstock, S.

1971 *Divus Iulius.* Oxford.

NSc Concordance

1931 = Levi, D.
1948 = Maetzke, G.
1948a = Romanelli, P.
1951 = Von Vacano, O.
1957 = De Agostino, A.
1957a = Maetzke, G.
1959 = Paglieri, S.
1961 = Bocci, P.
1961a = De Agostino, A.
1962 = Von Vacano, O.

1963 = Villa D'Amelio, P.
1965 = Phillips, K.
1965a = Von Vacano, O.
1966 = Balland, A., and Tchernia, A.
1967 = Phillips, K.
1970 *Suppl.* = Colonna, G. et al.
1973 *Suppl.* = Cristofani, M. et al.
1973 = Torelli, M., and Pohl, I.

3

ENTRY INTO THE SENATE AND TIES WITH THE ITALIAN TERRITORY OF ORIGIN: *REGIO VII* (ETRURIA)

IN 1969 I PUBLISHED a study of lists of senators of Etruscan origin.[1] In that study, after a prosopographic analysis, I proposed that there were certain detectable tendencies in the inclusion of the local Etruscan aristocracy in the Roman senate. W.V. Harris's excellent book,[2] published in 1971 with some new prosopographic additions and a section on the Romanization of Etruria, necessitates a review of the new data collected in the last decade or so and a reevaluation of the evidence.

The relationship between Rome and Etruria is as ancient as the *urbs* itself.[3] The phenomenon of the presence of Etruscan *gentes* in the fasti of the early republic is very different in nature from the topic of our present discussion and has its roots in the archaic economic, social, and political situation in which the function of the *gentes* is profoundly different from its function in the fourth century B.C. and onwards.[4]

According to J. Heurgon and others, in the earlier phase from the fourth to third centuries B.C., there were at least three well-known Etruscan plebeian *gentes* in Roman political and military life: the *Licinii*, the *Volumnii*, and the *Ogulnii*. For the first two families a very early integration into the Roman aristocracy can be considered which would tie this inclusion into the Roman aristocracy to the question of the transition from the monarchy to the republic. (In fact, the *Licinii* appear among the tribunes of the *plebs* from the beginning of the republic in 493, and in 481 B.C.). One *P. Licinius Calvus Esquilinus, tr. mil. c.p.* 400 B.C.,[5] is concretely attested to, while the famous *P. Volumnius Flamma Violens, cos.* 307 and 296 B.C., could be among the (plebeian) descendents of *P.*

Volumnius Amintinus Gallus, cos. 461.[6] The case of the *Ogulnii* [7]is more complex. Some of the *Ogulnii* were extremely important in the years between the fourth and third centuries B.C.: they were responsible for opening up the priesthood to the plebs and for significant religious and political activity. *Q. Ogulnius L.f.A.n. Gallus*, the principal figure of the family, was *cos.* 269 while other members (*M. Ogulnius, leg.* 210 and *tr. mil.* 196; *M. Ogulnius Gallus, pr. urb.* 182) were prominent in the second decade of the second century B.C. The family name is most likely central-northern Etruscan (unlike the *Licinii* family): *a vl. uclona la.* is known both at *Perusia* (*CIE*, 4502) and in the matronymic of the Clusine *au. petruni uclnial* (*CIE*, 2571). An inscription from Bolsena *hescnas l. li. uclnas v.* (*CIE*, 5167 = *TLE*, 204) unites the family name to that of the great aristocratic Volsinian family of the *hescanas*. We could consider an extremely early individual concession of citizenship to the Volsinii *principes*, perhaps under the auspices of the *Fabii*, with whom the *Ogulnii* had very close political ties. Additionally, the familiarity of the *Fabii* with Etruria and especially central-northern Etruria is well known.[8] This might explain the singular mission in Etruria of *M. Ogulnius* to obtain a *frumentatio* to send to Taranto in 210 B.C. (Livy XXVII, 3.9). This mission was carried out with the help of one *P. Aquilius*, who had distant Etruscan ancestors.[9] Additionally, we ought not to forget the *cognomen Gallus*, so popular (and *pour cause*) in Etruria. The hypothesis of an older "Etruscan" origin (among the Veians admitted as citizens in 388?) could have equal significance—and thus it is better to let the question hang.

To W.V. Harris we owe a list of Etruscans who had obtained citizenship before the Social War. The list is wholly satisfactory in the majority of cases and I reproduce it here with certain additions and the elimination of the Nigidii whose Etruscan origin does not seem to me to be so certain.

VOLATERRAE	*CARRINATES*	:	*C. Carrinas, pr.* 82 *C. Carrinas, cos.* 43, *procos. Hispaniae* 41, *Galliae* 30
ARRETIUM	*MAECENATES*	:	*C. Maecenas, eq. R.* 91 (Cicero, *Clu.* 153)
SAENA	*SAENII*	:	*C. Cae (nius), mon.* 150 *ca.*—*L. Saenius, cos.* 32

PERUSIA (?)	*PERPERNAE*	:	*M. Perperna, leg.* 168 *M. Perperna, cos.* 130 (*consul ante quam civis:* Valerius Maximus III, 4.5) *M. Perperna, cos.* 92
PERUSIA	*VIBII (PANSAE)*	:	*C. Vibius C.f. Pansa, mon.* 87 *C. Vibius C.f. n. Pansa Caetronianus, cos.* 43
PERUSIA	*VOLCACII (TULLI)*	:	*L. Volcacius Tullus, cos.* 66 *L. Volcacius L.f. Tullus, cos.* 33
TARQUINII	*NUMISII*	:	*C. Numisius, pr.* 177 *T. Numisius Tarquiniensis, leg.* 169
CAERE	*ABURII*	:	*M. Aburius, tr. pl.* 181 *C. Aburius, leg.* 171 *M. Aburius Geminus, mon.* 120 *ca.* *C. Aburius Geminus, mon.* 119–10 *ca.*
CAERE	*TARQUITII*	:	*C. Tarquitius L.f., tr. mil.* 89 *C. Tarquitius P.f. quaest.* 81 *Tarquitius Priscus leg. (Sertorii)* 72
CAERE	*CAMPATII*	:	*C. Camp (atius), mon.* 110 *ca.*
UNCERTAIN	*ANCHARII*	:	*Q. Ancharius, pr. ante* 87

In order to initiate an analysis of this list, we have first to exclude the *Ancharii*, whose Etruscan roots are controversial or at least equally probably Sabine and the *Numisii* who, if of Etruscan origin (at Tarquinii they are known only in the seventh century B.C., cfr. *StEtr* XXXVIII: 325) could be local citizens (cfr. the municipal magistrate of *Tuscana*) enrolled in the colony at *Gravisca*. The picture which appears is extremely interesting. As was expected, *Caere*, a city in close political rapport with Rome from as early as the fourth century B.C. onwards and with *civitas sine suffragio*, had a large number of *gentes* awarded Roman citizenship early on—even if that number was limited to the local aristocracy. This is illustrated by the number of high-quality late classical and Hellenistic hypogaean tombs. Even with an incomplete archaeological record and often absent epigraphic evidence, the *Tarquitii* seem to have had an important family tomb.[10] Other prominent *gentes* from *Caere* of notable lineage such as the *Maclae-Magilii*, the *Matunas*, the *Ursus* do not appear in equestrian prosopography nor in the Roman senate, although by that time they had familial ties with important families of Roman origin (the *Clavtie-Claudii* and the *Luvcilie-Lucilii*). In every case, the late republican Latin family names of *Caere* show an extraordinary continuity with the immediately preceding Etruscan ones. The fact is significant as it documents the stability of the Caeretan property system and social structure. Neither aspect was disturbed by external factors, infiltrations of foreigners, or land assignments, which instead are so evident at Tarquinii.[11]

The relative vacuum at *Tarquinii* and the absolute vacuum at *Volsinii* and *Vulci—a lacuna* confirmed by imperial prosopography—are striking. At *Tarquinii*, where the onomastic innovations have been noted, the Gromatici talk about the Gracchan land assignments (in line with the famous discourse of Tiberius Gracchus) which may also have occurred at *Vulci*. At *Tarquinii* the nucleus of the old aristocracy seems—as we shall see—to pass untouched through the tormented events of the second to first century B.C.: this is not the case at *Vulci*. Conversely, both the earliness and intensity of Rome's relationship with the northern cities is impressive. The consequences of the third century war were less serious for the northern cities than for the southern ones, where land losses were considerable. *Cosa*, the Latin colony (273 B.C.), the *praefectura* of *Statonia* (third century B.C.), the Roman colonies of *Heba* (ca. mid-second century B.C.) and *Saturnia* (183 B.C.) and *Forum Aurelii* (ca. mid-third century B.C.) sprang up on what had once been the territory of *Vulci*. The territory of *Tarquinii*, penalized by the presence of *Gravisca* (181 B.C.), dissolved into a plurality of cities or independent towns—*Forum Cassii*, *Tuscana*, *Blera*, *Axia*, *Surrina*.

In the north, nothing of the sort happened. There, over a longer period of time (at least up to the beginning of the second century B.C.) the archaic forms of dependency were preserved.[12] At *Perusia*, thanks to a close relationship with Rome, three families are inserted early on into the Roman senatorial aristocracy. The relationships of *Arretium* and *Volaterrae* to Rome are more measured while we know nothing of the situations at *Faesulae*, *Clusium*, *Populonia* and *Rusellae*. In fact, the silence from these last cities could be interpreted as a sign of greater weakness in the socio-economic structures with a concomitant attitude of diffidence and closeness in the local aristocracies.[13] The Sullan colonies at *Faesulae*, *Arretium*, *Clusium* and *Volaterrae* (with supplementary penalties vis-à-vis citizenship), the triumviral and then Augustan assignments at *Arretium*, *Florentia*, *Luca*, *Luna*, *Pisae*, *Saena*, and *Rusellae* are not at all casual. *Perusia*, saved until 40 B.C., had to suffer its own particular fate.

The greater initiative of the Perusian *principes* can be tied more to the politically shrewd expansion of their estates in the direction of the nearby and prosperous Umbrian cities of *Asisium* and *Iguvium* than to a presumed difference from other nearby cities in economic orientation. (*Arretium* was earlier and more strongly tied to manufacture than *Perusia*.) The Perusian anxiety concerning land emerges clearly in the critical period in the famous *Vegoia* fragment attributed to a Perusian *princeps* and *haruspex*.[14] It is possible that the political direction taken by *Perusia* may have been inspired by the old supremacy of the dissolved league, broken perhaps in the first half of the third century B.C.[15] Abundant data seem to demonstrate that the prevalent choice of the old Etruscan aristocracy may have been an abstention from the *honores* with a regression into the more comfortable equestrian rank. Several facts illustrate such a behavior: the constant status of *equites* among the Etruscan aristocrats; the prominent equestrian *domi nobiles* recorded in the Tarquinian *fasti* of the *LX haruspices;* the scene on the late Tarquinian Bruschi Tomb with the figure of a horseman; the *argentarius* profession of the Tarquinian nobles *Fulcinii;* the very episode of the *Caesennii* and of the *Caecinae* sketched in Cicero's *pro Caecina;* and lastly the abstentionist behavior of a man like Maecenas, the descendent of *principes* and of *equites Romani*.[16]

All the foregoing allows us to reconsider the Etruscan political behavior in the period of the civil war. In 1969, I attributed a sharply pro-Marian stance to the Etruscan aristocracy (and to the Etruscans in general), and later an even more distinct anti-Caesarian attitude. A recent well-documented study by E. Rawson[17] has taken up the problem again, adding more prudent conclusions to the Caesarian aspect of the question. While E. Rawson has certainly provided irreproachable arguments on certain questions, on other points her methodology is somewhat shaky—as, for example, in her acceptance of absolutely unproven

Etruscan origins for *C. Norbanus cos.* 83 B.C., for the *Volusii* (from *Cingulum*), or for the (hardly) Etruscan *C. Curtius*. There is evident disregard of the archaeological documentation which is provided by the *necropoleis* of the great Etruscan cities. It may be correct not to speak of the Etruscan aristocracy as an organic unitarian entity in political and especially economic terms; however, it is certain that the internal ties of the Etruscan aristocracy which developed with a significant "horizontal" endogamy (e.g., the marriage of *Caecina* of *Volaterrae* with *Caesennia* of *Tarquinii* noted in the *pro Caecina*) found their political cement in the religious practice of the *haruspices*, of which the conservative and anti-monarchic nature cannot be questioned. The discovery of the *Fasti* (of the *summi haruspices* rather than of the whole body) for the *ordo LX haruspicum*[18] with biographical sketches of prominent people going back to the early republican period, all tied to the birth of the mythical child Tages at *Tarquinii*, demonstrates that the *ordo* (*pace* E. Rawson) surely existed in the civil war period and was a body of *principes* (all of equestrian rank) and not a body of *apparitores* as Wissowa would have it. The solemn *lex* of Rome as Cicero recorded it[19] reads *Etruria principes disciplinam doceto* and the names of the known *haruspices* for this period invariably carry the onomastic of the *principes*, from the Perusian *Vulcanius* (MSS. should read *Vulcatius*) to the Tarquinian *Spurinna*.

The partially "abstentionist" attitude of the majority of the northern Etruscan *nobilitas* (excluding *Perusia*) may be explained by the political consequences resulting from the Sullan destructions, by the strong economic crisis, and the abandonment of the coastal strip. It can, however, also (and better) be explained as the instrument of political compensation which gave the local aristocracy an important means of participating in Roman policy effectively but without excessive risks. This also explains the relative indifference demonstrated by this same aristocracy to euergetism in their cities of origin during the second and first centuries B.C. It is possible that this indifference is really a lacuna of epigraphic documentation from urban areas, but there is also a noticeable poverty of pertinent archaeological data and monumental buildings. With the exceptions of the two temples on the acropolis of Volterra, of the walls of Perugia, and the large but unpublished theater-temple complex of S. Cornelio near Arezzo (all unfortunately anonymous and significantly linked to the more lively northern sector) no Etruscan city has provided monuments of the second and first centuries B.C. built *de novo* or reconstructed on a large scale. At the most, there is some redecoration of temples, such as those at Tarquinia, at Caere, at Talamone, at Vetulonia, at Arezzo, and Fiesole. Additionally, there is some construction and monumental activity on the level of substitution with little or limited activity in public construction. A simple comparison with *Cosa*, a Latin colony in the same area, with its numerous second century B.C. monuments or a comparison with the activity of *Ateius Capito* at *Castrum Novum* demonstrates to what extent the socioeconomic and political differences between the Roman colonies and the Etruscan cities. It is these differences which may have determined the manner in which the local elites participated in public building programs or more generally in euergetism.[20]

With Caesar, the senate doors were opened to some Etruscan nobles, an act which led Cicero to announce his repugnance for a curia filled with haruspices, a clear allusion to the Etruscans. Some of the best names of Etruria sat in the Curia of Caesar. If certain *gentes* present in the previous senate (*Perpernae, Aburii, Tarquitii*) had disappeared, the list now enumerated the *Caecinae* of *Volaterrae*, the *Pupii* of *Clusium*, the *Caecinae* and *Iunii Blaesii* of *Volsinii*, the *Caesennii* of *Tarquinii*, the *Coronae* of *Tuscana*, and the *Sanquinii* of *Caere* that sat beside the senators of Latin and Roman colonies. In these last cities the enlistment is modest and chronologically not very homogeneous. To the pre-Caesarian period the *Ateii Capitones* (who go on into the Tiberian age) of *Castrum Novum*, the *Octavii Ligures* of *Forum Clodii*, the *Fidustii* of *Nepet*, and the *Pontii Aquilae* of *Sutrium* are known. No family from a colonial area is honored by a Caesarian *laticlave* except perhaps the *Lartidii*, possibly from *Pistoria*, and the *Appuleii* from *Luna*.

On the whole, however, the Etruscan senators from the Caesarian period are only relatively numerous. The larger number of senators actually belongs to the Augustan and Julio-Claudian periods, but the Etruscan consuls are very much later. Augustan and Julio-Claudian senators include the (*Calpetani*) *Valerii Festi*, the *Cilnii* and the *Martii* of *Arretium*, the *Volasennae* of *Volaterrae*, the *Pompeii Vopisci* of *Volsinii*, the *Vicirii* of *Rusellae*, the *Spurinnae* and the *Fulcinii* of *Tarquinia*, the *Salvii* of *Ferentum*, the *Pullii* and the *Clodii* of *Forum Clodii*, the *Egnatii* of *Caere*, and the *Glitii* of *Falerii*. In the late republican era and up to 32 B.C. only the families already in the senate (*Carrinates, Saenii, Vibii Pansae,*

Volacacii) provided consuls. With the Augustan age these families disappear from the consular fasti and very few names of *gentes* from *Regio VII* are found: the *Caecinae* of *Volaterrae* (1 B.C., A.D. 13), the *Iunii Blaesi* of *Volsinii* (A.D. 10) and the *Appuleii* of *Luna* (29, 20 B.C., A.D. 14). The first *gens* was included because of its political ties to Octavian, the second because of its close relationship to the best Roman aristocracy (the *Cornelii Lentuli*) and the last were close relatives of Augustus. The behavior of Tiberius was only slightly different. Aside from the consuls coming from previous consular families under Augustus (*Caecinae* A.D. 37, *Iunii Blaesi* A.D. 26), the *Sanquinii* of *Caere* (?) (A.D. 21 or A.D. 22), the *Petronii* of *Volaterrae* (?) (A.D. 25), the *Fulcinii* of Tarquinia (?) (A.D. 31) and the *Salvii* of *Ferentium* (A.D. 33) obtained the *fasces* for the first time. For some (*Fulcinii*) a tie with Sejanus was the reason for entry, for others (*Salvii*) a familial relationship to the dynasty provided the means of arrival while for still others (*Sanquinii*) a link to the *partes* of Sejanus may provide an explanation for the admission. In this last category, we should remember the behavior of *Sanquinius Maximus* at the trial of *Fulcinius Trio* (Tacitus, *Ann.* VI, 4).

The Claudian-Neronian period was relatively less favorable to the old Etruscan families. Those consular families which were not yet extinct (*Caecinae, Petronii, Salvii*) kept the fasces while new consuls under Claudius were listed only for the *Valerii Festi* (*Calpetani*) of *Arretium*, circa A.D. 50, and for the *Volasennae* of *Volaterrae* (A.D. 49 and A.D. 54, ca.) and in the year of anarchy for the *Pompeii Vopisci* of *Volsinii* and the *Martii* of *Arretium*. These facts seem to undermine the mythical philetruscanism of Claudius. Nonetheless, there is no doubt that the etruscologist emperor, in addition to showing his own preference for the Etruscan aristocracy by elevating to patrician status several *gentes* (*Salvii:* Suet. *Otho* 1) clearly nourished the preoccupation about future inclusion in the senate. This became quite clear in Claudius' discourse reported by the *tabulae Lugdunenses* and by Tacitus. This speech may have been motivated by actual consideration for the Etruscan situation as is indicated by the remarks on the enlistment for the *ordo LX haruspicum* which itself reveals the heavy loss of rank among the Etruscan *principes.*[21] The intense activity of dynastic exaltation and the *victoria Britannica* as expressed by statues and dedications to the imperial family given by the knights and *flamen Augusti* of *Rusellae*, *A. Vicirius Proculus*, the father of the two future consuls of the Flavian period (see the lists) can be considered an expression of encouragement from Claudius.

The Augustan and Julio-Claudian period is on the whole the most significant for the Etruscan *gentes.* Enthusiasm for the dynasty and for the glorious national past went hand in hand. Statues, buildings, honors, and sacrifices to the dynasty are accompanied by the cult of city memories. The *elogia* of the *Spurinnae* with the fasti for the *LX haruspices* and the statue of Tarchon at *Tarquinii*, the "throne of Claudius" at *Caere* and last, the unique "Corsini throne" a marble reproduction of a throne with circular shoulder finials which was used by the northern Etruscan *principes* in the seventh century B.C. are all part of this cult. The previous conflict between the Etruscans, the Sullan and then triumviral colonies re-emerges now and again. The reproduction of the Forum of Augustus and the altar with stories of the Roman origins at *Arretium* or the reproduction of the Capitoline wolf at *Faesulae* underline the colonial consciousness of their own identity—either *Fidentiores* or *Iulienses*—in contrast with that of the *veteres*, the Etruscans. Of sixty-four senatorial *gentes* from *Regio VII* known for all the late republican and imperial ages, in this period thirty-three—thus half—sat in the senate and seventeen of these held the consulship: this is a very positive picture of co-optation and of selection.

In order to evaluate the local contribution to the senate in light of the Roman colonial senatorial contributions, it is worthwhile comparing the prosopographic lists of the various cities of Etruscan foundation and considering the origin—Etruscan or Latin—of the individual *gentes* in relation to the archaeological documentation.

CITY	GENS	ETRUSCAN GENTILICIAN ATTESTED TO IN THE CITY	EVIDENCE
Arretium	*CILNII*	*kilnei*	
	MARTII		
	VALERII FESTI		
Volaterrae	*CARRINATES*	*carnas*	gentilician tomb
	VOLASENNAE	*velasnei*	gentilician tomb

	ARMINII (?)	*armna*	
	CAECINAE	*ceicna*	gentilician tomb
	PETRONII (?)	*petrna* (*CIE*, 293)	
SAENA	*SAENII*	*seinei*	
PERUSIA	*VIBII*	*vipi*	gentilician tomb
	AFINII	*afuna*	gentilician tomb
	BETUI	*petve*	ceramic stamps
	VOLCACII	*velca*	gentilician tomb
CLUSIUM	*PUPII*		
VOLSINII	*CAECINAE*	*ceicna*	
	SEII	*seie*	
	POMPEII		
	CORNELII (?)		
RUSELLAE	*VICIRII*		
TARQUINII	*CAESENNII*	*ceisinie*	gentilician tomb
	VESTRICII SPURINNAE	*vestricnie*, *spurinas*	gentilician tombs
	FULCINII	*hulcnie*	eponymyn
TUSCANA	*CORONAE*	*curunas*	gentilician tombs
FERENTIUM	*SALVII*	*zalvies*	gentilician tomb
CAERE	*ABURII*	*aparies*	
	CAMPATII	*campanes*	
	TARQUITII	*tarcna*	gentilician tomb
	EGNATII		
	SANQUINII		

The evidence confirms what is shown in the table. The early presence of the Latin family names *(Valerii*, *Martii*) at *Arretium* and at *Clusium (Pupii*) are linked to the Sullan settlements in the area. *Volaterrae*, *Perusia*, *Tuscana*, *Ferentium*, and *Tarquinii* provide only Etruscan names, demonstrating the strong resistance of the local aristocratic element even in the face *(Volaterrae*, *Tarquinii*) of Gracchan and Sullan assignments. *Volsinii* offers both Etruscan and Latin names in almost equal measure: this early

Etruscan mix with the Latin element may be an influence from the neighboring areas (cfr. the *Pompeii*, perhaps from *Interamna Nahars*), *Rusellae* (*Vicirii*) demonstrates very well the effects of the Augustan colony, while at *Caere* the gentilician names certainly attributable to the city (the *Egnatii* and *Sanquinii* are uncertain attributions) provide a picture of conspicuous local solidarity.

As is well known, the year of military anarchy revealed the *arcana imperii*. The new dynasty of Sabine origin emerged from the storm of the Julio-Claudian successions. This dynasty not only rewarded its own partisans but also the residual forces of the Italic aristocracies. Nearly one-third of the total of Etruscan senatorial *gentes* in the Julio-Claudian period were by now extinct: the *Appuleii* of *Luna*, the *Lartidii* of *Pistoriae*, the *Martii* of *Arretium*, the *Carrinates* and the *Volasennae* of *Volaterrae*, the *Saenii* of *Saena*, the *Vibii Pansae*, the *Afinii*, the *Betui*, and the *Volcacii* of *Perusia*, the *Pupii* of *Clusium*, the *Caecinae* and the *Seii-Iunii* of *Volsinii*, the *Fulcinii* of *Tarquinii*, the *Coronae* of *Tuscana*, the *Ateii* of *Castrum Novum*, the *Pullii*, the *Octavii* and the *Clodii* of *Forum Clodii*, the *Campatii* and the *Sanquinii* of *Caere*. There were only ten of the previous thirty-three old *gentes* still in the senate. *Caere* by now was reduced to a village, where the local senate sessions at the beginning of the second century A.D. included only decurions of obscure origins,[22] and had no senators. In this respect, *Caere* followed the destiny of the other more northern coastal cities such as *Castrum Novum*, *Cosa*, *Vulci*, *Vetulonia*, *Populonia*, and other minor hinterland centers such as *Forum Clodii*, *Sutrium*, *Nepet*, *Tuscana*. The fate of southern Etruria and of Maremma had been clear long before. The members of the nine surviving families—except for the *Salvii* and the *Caecinae* who had flickered out under the Flavians—once again hold the office of consul under Vespasian, Titus, and Domitian. For the first time we find the *Vestricii* of Tarquinii (*aet. Vespasiani*), the *Glitii* of *Falerii* (A.D. 79), the *Cilnii* of *Arretium* (A.D. 87), and the *Vicirii* of *Rusellae* (A.D. 89) while the *Caesenii* of *Tarquinii*, the *Petronii* of *Volaterrae*, and the *Pompeii* of *Volsinii* continue to have access to the highest office. To these, the *Flavians* would sometimes add patrician rank (*Glitii*), but contemporaneously they attempted to reinforce the losses of the local aristocracies. Only two families of authentic Etruscan origin entered the senate, the *Ciartii* of *Arretium* and the *Arminii* of *Volaterrae* (?), while the *Venuleii* of *Pisae*, *Cn. Avilius Firmus* of *Arretium*, the *Tullii Varrones* of *Tarquinii* and the very dubious case of *A. Cornelius Palma* of *Volsinii*, had openly Latin origins. Certain clues can tell us something about both the means and the reasons of the selection. *Avilius Firmus* was one of the vice-commanders of the legion in the Jewish wars while the *Tullii Varrones* came from the same city as *L. Caesennius Paetus* who was favored by the imperial house because of his marriage with *Flavia Sabina*, the niece of Vespasian. All of these families, except the *Ciartii* and *Avilius Firmus*, attained the consulship in the Flavian period.

This is the last glorious season for the aristocracy of *Regio VII*. One third of the fifteen known families disappear in the Flavian period (*Glitii*, *Petronii*, *Valerii Festi*, *Avilii*, *Salvii*, *Caecinae*). Another third vanish under Trajan (*Cilnii*, *Vicirii*, *Vestricii*, *Arminii*, *Ciartii*, *Cornelius Palma*). Thus, under Hadrian there are only four surviving families whom we can trace to the Antonine period (the *Pompeii* of Volsinii and the *Venuleii* of Pisae), and the *Caesennii* and *Tullii Varrones* of *Tarquinii* we can follow until the mid-second century A.D. although there was a complex series of adoptions with north Italic and then Spanish families. With Marcus the entire south was taken over by large villas of nonlocal senatorial families such as the Spanish *Fabii Fabiani* on the Tarquinian coast. These villas extended over the region that phenomenon which had already taken place on the beaches of *Lorium*, of *Alsium*, and of *Castrum Novum* between the late republic and the early empire. Only in central and northern areas did the more vital cities produce new senators, all with clear non-Latin but rather Etruscan ancestral families originating from the equestrian class of, usually, the second century. Thus, from *Faesulae* or *Florentia* come the *Umbrici*, the descendents of the first and second century *equites* while the *Vetinae* and the *Petronii* of *Volaterrae* certainly originate from local knights, although they renewed the *fasti* of the first century consuls of the same name. At *Perusia*, the *Vibii Galli* derived from an *eques* of the late second century, at *Volsinii* the *Rufi Festi* and the *Aconii* were also sons of second century knights. These new senators, produced by the rejuvenated economic and politico-administrative importance of the *equites* after Hadrian are the last vestiges of an already highly limited aristocracy. Even if the *Vetinae* and the *Umbrici* do not last beyond the first decades of the third century, the *Vibii* gave to Rome the ephemeral emperor Trebonianus Gallus in the years of military anarchy, while the two Volsinian families carry on into the full fourth century and provide a clear indication of the growing importance of this hinterland city on the threshold of the Medieval period.

This, in brief, is the history of the contribution of *Regio VII* to the senatorial lists of Rome. We have seen the relative scarcity of euergetic activity in the Etruscan municipalities of the second-first centuries B.C. The picture changes substantially in the early imperial age, when there was an impressive public building program in many Etruscan cities. Often these works are known to us without any indication of the donor. Some of them, however, can be attributed by epigraphic evidence to senatorial or equestrian families contesting for the *laticlavius:* the theater at *Volaterrae* built by the already senatorial *Caecinae,* the baths of Pisae given by the consul *L. Venuleius Montanus,* the baths of Tarquinii built by the generosity of the *Tullii Varrones,* the Augustaeum of *Lucus Feroniae* given by the consuls *Volusii Saturnini* (not, however, of local origin) or the baths at *Volsinii,* seemingly built by the knight *Caecina Tuscus* or the statues in the Caesareum of *Rusellae* dedicated by the *eques A. Vicirius Proculus,* father of two Flavian consuls.[23] On the whole, however, it is not really possible to speak of a noteworthy undertaking of euergetism on the part of the local aristocracy. The monuments listed above seem rather to be a kind of propaganda closely tied to the important local historical traditions. For this reason Etruria is rich in unique monuments, such as the *elogia* inscribed by *Vestricius Spurinna* in memory of his own genealogy, or the commemorative epigraph about the restoration of an ancestral *locus sanctus* (perhaps the birthplace of the child Tagete) dedicated by the Tarquinian *Caesennii,* or the fourth century A.D. epigraphical poem to the Volsinian goddess *Nortia,* composed by *Rufius Festus* with precise allusions to his own familial ancestry.[24] Above all, this type of activity characterizes a responsibility felt by all the ruling classes of Etruria, regardless of Etruscan or Latin family origin, to tie the magistracies and connected activity, piously restored, around the rather elusive old league. Senators who were habitually *praetores Etruriae,* knights who were generally aediles—and sometimes even *praetores Etruriae*[25]—exhibited with particular pride the titles of the old magistracies until the fourth century A.D., just as, at least equally and perhaps even more fervidly than the many Italic senators, they did not hesitate to hold magistracies of nearby *municipia* and colonies.

This *pietas* of the local elites was truly without parallel, but the explanation rests in the formidable ideological baggage of the national legacy, an element undoubtedly strongly felt by these *equites* but also an instrument of internal and external propaganda, directed towards the local populations, toward the vestiges of the senatorial circles and towards the imperial court.

PROSOPOGRAPHY LIST

The following prosopographic discussions are based on my two studies "Senatori etruschi della tarda repubblica e dell'impero" (*DdA* 1969: 285 ff.) and "Senatori etruschi della tarda repubblica e dell'impero: qualche addendum" (*Arheološki Vestnik* XXVIII, 1977: 251 ff.; abbreviated *AV* 1977). I have included here an analysis of the Faliscan territory and of the colonies of *Luna*, *Pistoria*, *Luca*, *Florentia*, all part of the Augustan *regio VII*. I will limit myself to discussing the senatorial *gentes* with a summary list of the members for the various cities. In general the prosopographic discussions are to be found in the two articles cited, but if there is new evidence I will include it here.

LUNA *(Gal.)*: Roman colony

APPVLEI

A famous late republican and early imperial family related to the family of Augustus. Originally from the colony Luni, as the tribe and the inscription of SEX. APPVLEIS SEX. F. GAL. SEX. N. SEX. PRON., *ultimus gentis suae* (*ILS*, 935) tell us. The genealogy is well known.

??SVLPICII SCRIBONI

P. SVLPICIVS SCRIBONIVS PROCVLVS, governor in 65–66 of Upper Germany and P. SVLPICIVS SCRIBONIVS RVFVS, governor in 65–66 of Lower Germany (Ritterling 1932: 17 f., n. 10 and 51, n. 9) were the adopted rather than the natural sons of SCRIBONIVS PROCVLVS (*RE* II, A1, col. 882, n. 25): they can hardly be attributed to *Luna* on the basis of *CIL* XI, 1340, dedicated to PROCVLVS.

PISTORIA *(Vel.)*: Roman colony

??LARTIDI

We know of one SEX. LARTIDIVS, *leg. C. Asinii Galli procos. Asiae* in 5 B.C. (*PIR*², L 116), erroneously thought to be the father of M. LARTIDIVS, *[pro] pr.* (Torelli 1980: 160 and *PIR*², L115) and honored to-

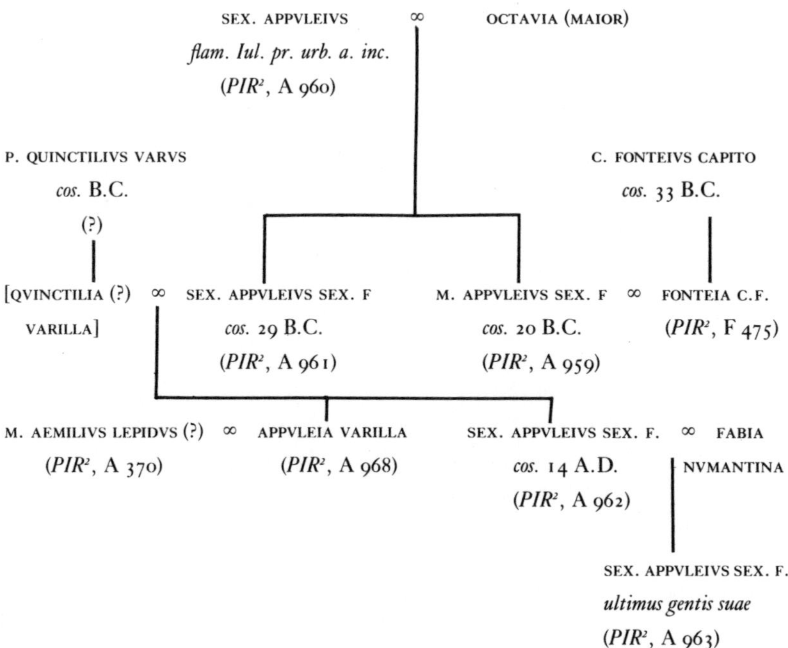

gether with his wife of Umbrian origin, VARENA by the freedman *Diphilus mag. Herculaneus* of *Tibur* in 19 B.C. (and not 13 B.C.). At the time of the dedication *M. Lartidius* and *Varena* were probably already deceased. (*M. Lartidius* is perhaps the same *Lartidius* cited by Cicero (*ad. Att.*, VII, 1.9)). They should be considered the parents of *Sex. Lartidius* who seems to have been *praetorius* in 5 B.C. The family dies out apparently with the daughter of this *Sex. Lartidius*, a LARTIDIA SEX. F. COMINI<A> (*PIR*², L 119), known to have been the wife of T. COMINIVS PROCVLVS, *procos. Cypri* 42/43 (*PIR*², C 1270). The line is reconstructed thus:

The Pistorian origin of the family has been discussed by Syme (1965: 207 = *Roman Papers* I, 328; cfr. Wiseman, n. 222) and is based on the name of the soldier *Sex. Lartidius Sec. f. Vel.* (*ILS*, 2265) of the Augustan period. The chronology of this soldier does not, however, support the hypothesis, especially in the light of the dates of M. LARTIDIVS, who could easily originate from Tibur.

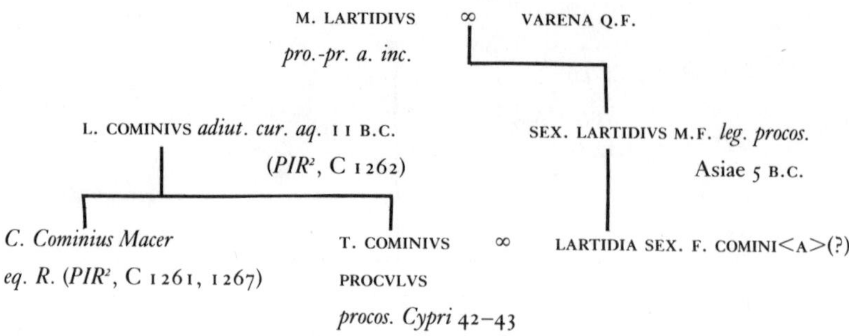

PISAE *(Gal.)*: Roman colony

VENVLEII (*DdA* 1969: 288 f.)

L. VENVLEIVS MONTANVS APRONIANVS, *cos. suff.* 92, was the husband (cfr. *CIL* XI, 1433a: *Venuleior. Mont. et Apron*) of one LAETILIA. Their son, L. VENVLEIVS APRONIANVS OCTAVIVS PRISCVS, *cos. ord.* 123, was the husband of [POMPEIA] CELERINA (*CIL* XI, 1735), who in turn was most likely the daughter of L. POMPEIVS VOPISCVS C. ARRVNTIVS CATELLIVS CELER (see *Volsinii*). Their son L. VENVLEIVS APRONIANVS OCTAVIVS PRISCVS, *cos. ord.* 168, and his daughter (?) was VENV[LEIA---] (*CIL* XI, 1433). A different reconstruction is proposed by Corbier (1981: 1104 ff.).

IVLII LUCANI?? (*DdA* 1969: 288)

L. IVLIVS LARCIVS SABINVS, *tr. pl.* ca. 160, son of IVLIVS LVCANVS, *pr.* 160–70, and of CORNELIA F.F. PRIVIGNA, nephew of (T.) PRIFERNIVS PAETVS, *cos. suff.* 146 (*CIL* XI, 1431).

FAESVLAE *(Sca.)*: Sullan colony

PETRONII (*DdA* 1969: 289 f.)

Q. PETRONIVS MELIOR, *cos. suff.* post 240, husband of DOMITIA MELPIS and son of the knight, *Q. Petronius Melior.*

VMBRICII (*DdA* 1969: 289)

Q. VMBRICIVS PROCVLVS, *leg. propr. Hispaniae Citerioris* (second century A.D.). A knight, *Q. Umbricius Proculus* (*AE* 1951: 181), is known at Florentia: our senator is the descendent of *C. Umbricius Melior*, haruspex in the years of military anarchy (*AE* 1930: 52).

Arretivm *(Pom.)*: Sullan colony

CIARTII (*DdA* 1969: 291)

C. CIARTIUS, *pontifex* 101–2, descendent of the family of *Ciartia L.f. Procule*, wife of the Tiberian knight *Cn. Petronius Asellio.*

CILNII (*DdA* 1969: 291 f.)

C. CILNIVS C.F. POM. PAETINVS, *procos. (praetorius) aet. Tiberii.* His nephew (rather than son) was C. CILNIVS PROCVLVS, *cos. suff.* 87. The son of this man was C. CILNIVS C.F. [PO]M. PROCVLVS, *cos. suff.* 100, was the father (?) of CILNIA PROCVLA and of C. CILNIVS C.F. FEROX, *pontifex, tr. mil. leg. IV.*

MARTII (*DdA* 1969: 292 ff.)

L. MARTIVS C.F. POM. MACER, *procos. Achaiae* ca. 45. His son L. MARTIVS L.F. POM. MACER, *salius palatinus pr.* ca. 50, *cos. des.* 69, was evidently made a patrician by Claudius (contra, see Wiseman, no. 516, 278).

AVILII

[CN. AVILLIVS C]N. F. POM. FIRMVS (?) (*DdA* 1969: 294), *leg. propr. Lyciae et Pamphyliae* ca. 72–74 (Eck 1970: 74 f.). If the identification of the person named in *ILS*, 1000, is correct; his complete name is *Cn. Avillius Celer Fiscillinus Firmus.*

VALERII FESTI (*RE* III, 1, 1363 f.)

The complete name, preserved by *CIL* V, 531 = *ILS*, 989, is C. CALPETANVS RANTIVS QVIRINALIS VALERIVS P.F. POM. FESTUS, *cos. suff.* 71 (*PIR*[2], C 184; *RE* III, 1, 1363, n. 2) and allows us to place this important man of the Flavian period and his natural family at *Arretium.* He is noted as *Valerius Festus* by Tacitus and Pliny, whereas the Tergeste inscription duly notes his origin and tribe with this part of his polyonymy. He was adopted by C. CALPETANVS RANTIVS SEDATVS. His grandfather was among the Arretine colonists of the Augustan period, *C. Valerius A.f. Pom. Festus* (*CIL* XI, 1864), married to a *Crispinia L.f. Firma Valeri Festi* (*CIL* XI, 1863), who repeated the entire onomastic except for the praenomen. His career is known from many texts (Eck 1970: 84, 89, 113, 119 ff., 125 ff., 130). He was born in the Tiberian period, was *leg. Aug. pr. pr. Numidiae* 69/70, *cos. suff.* 71, *cur. alv. Tib.*

72–73, *leg. Aug. pr. pr. Pannoniae* 73–77, *leg. Aug. pr. pr. Hisp. cit.* 78–81, *procos. Asiae* (?) ca. 81. The oldest known member of the adoptive family was C. CALPETANVS STATIVS RVFVS (*PIR*[2], C 236; *RE* III, 1, 1363, n. 4) *praetor* in the period between Augustus and Tiberius (*cur. loc. publ. iudic.* between A.D. 2 and A.D. 24, *cur. alv. Tib.* between A.D. 16 and A.D. 24 (cfr. *ILS*, 5925, 5939), shows a gentilician name known at Rome but also at Histonium (*CIL* IX, 2874) which could be of Etruscan origin, although there are no compelling parallels (cfr., e.g., the hydronymic name of Olpeta in the territory of Vulci). The same is said for another gentilician name of Festus, Rantius, known only at Capua (Schulze 1905: 78, n. 1) which appears in the name of the person adopting Festus and the adopted son of *Statius, Rufus*, C. CALPETANVS RANTIVS SEDATVS. This last person was *cur. tabular. publ.* 46 (*CIL* VI , 31201), *cos. suff.* ca. 50, *leg. Aug. pr. pr. Dalmatiae aet Neronis* (Jagenteufel 1958: 37 ff., n. 10). The end of the family is not known (perhaps it was lost in the Domitianic bloodshed). The VALERIUS FESTUS, *leg. Africae* 194 (Thomasson 1960: 141, n. 41) can hardly be a descendent but may be a provincial offspring from a local family admitted by *Festus* to the citizenship.

ANONYMVS

[---]VS C.F. POM. (*DdA* 1969: 294 f.), *tr. mil. leg. VIII*, [---], *q. pr. pr.*, *tr. pl.*, [---]: is *perhaps C. Cilnius C.f. Paetinus* (?).

VOLATERRAE *(Sab.)*: municipium

CARRINATES (*AV* 1977: 251)

C. CARRINAS, *pr.* 82 B.C., his son was C. CARRINAS, *cos. suff.* 43 B.C. Among the provincial clients of this *gens* is was C. CARRINAS CELER, *senator*, A.D. 54.

CAECINAE (DdA 1969: 295 ff.; *AV* 1977: 251)

A. CAECINA SEVERVS, *cos. suff.* A.D. 1; his brother ought to be the C. CAECINA A.F. LARGVS, titular with the aforenamed of the inscriptions (*CIL* XI, 6689, 54; *AE* 1957: 220). Son of C. CAECINA A.F. LARGVS was C. SILIVS A. CAECINA LARGVS, *cos. suff.* 13, from whom descended the CAECINIA A.F. LARGA (niece rather than daughter), the wife of A. LARCIVS LEPIDVS (*ILS*, 987) and C. CAECINA LARGVS, *cos. suff.* 42 (son? nephew?

note the praenomen *Caius*). From SEVERVS the sons SEX. CAECINA [---], *A. pr. pr.* A.D. 11 and A. CAECINA PAETVS, *cos. suff.* 37, married to the ARRIA *(maior)* from Volterra; son of PAETVS was C. LAECANIVS BASSVS CAECINA PAETVS, *cos. suff.* 64 (adopted by C. LAECANIVS BASSVS), in turn father of C. LAECANIVS C.F. SAB. BASSVS CAECINA FLACCVS *Xvir., stl. iud.*, dead at the age of nineteen.

VOLASENNAE? (*DdA* 1969: 328 f.)

VOLASENNIA C.F. wife of M. NONIVS BALBVS, *procos. Cretae et Cyrenarum aet. Augusti* (*vel Tiberii*), and the nephews C. VOLASENNA SEVERVS, *cos. suff.* ca. 49, and P. VOLASENNA, *cos. suff.* 54, *procos. Asiae* 62, were probably of Volterran origin. No other descendents are known except for the two consular brothers.

??*ARMINII (DdA* 1969: 324 f.)

C. ARMINIVS [-F. STE] L. GALLVS, [---V] *I vir tur*[*mar. equit. Rom., tri*]*b. milit. leg. X* [---, *quaest.*] *prov. Sic*[*iliae, praet. urb*]*anus, leg.* [*leg.*---, *p*]*raef. fr*[*um. dandi, leg. propr. provi*]*nc. Asi*[*ae*---] of the Flavian-Trajanic period. The tribe and provenience of the inscription (*CIL* XI, 7423) are from *Ferentium;* the diffusion of the Etruscan gentilician makes more likely an *origo* from *Volaterra* (where an inscription may link this *gens* to the CAECINAE PAETI). Syme (1962: 96 = *Roman Papers* II, 555) prefers to read *Gall*[*onius*] instead of *Gall*[*us*], tying it to the polyonymy of *Q. Marcius Turbo.*

PETRONII (*DdA* 1969: 298 f.)

Given the inscriptions on the *gradus* of the Volterra theater and the tribe, M. PETRONIVS Q. F. SAB. VMBRINVS, *cos. suff.* 81 (*AE* 1972: 615), could be from Volaterrae, the descendent (nephew or *ex fratre filius*) of PETRONIVS VMBRINVS, *cos. suff.* 25. Certainly from Volaterrae (but not tied to the *Petronii Umbrini*) are the later L. PETRONIVS L.F. SAB. TAVRVS VBOLVSIANVS, *cos. ord.* 261, *praef. urb.* 267–68, and his son (?) L. PVBLIVS PETRONIVS VOLVSIANVS, *cos. suff.* ca. 270.

?*VETINAE* (*DdA* 1969: 299)

L. VETINA PRISCVS, *leg. procos. Asiae* (second century), husband of DIDIA L.F. QVINTINIA. Descendent of this individual is VETINA MAMERTINVS, *XVvir s. f.* 204, perhaps with some kind of tie to the family of M. PETRONIVS MAMERTINVS, *cos. suff.* 150.

SAENA *(Ouf.)*: municipium, triumviral and Augustan colony

SAENII (*DdA* 1969: 299 f.)

L. SAENIVS L.F., *cos.* 32 B.C., perhaps the son of L. SAENIVS, *senator* 63 B.C. (Wiseman 1971, no. 370, 258).

PERVSIA *(Tro.)*: municipium, Augustan colony (?)

VIBII PANSAE (*DdA* 1969: 302 f.)

C. VIBIVS C.F. PANSA, *triumvir mon.* ca. 88 B.C., father of C. VIBIVS C.F. PANSA CAETRONIANVS, *cos.* 43 B.C., and grandfather of C. VIBIVS PANSA, *leg. pro. pr. in Vindolicis* 15 B.C.-A.D. 9.

AFINII (*DdA* 1969: 300)

Perhaps Perugine L. AFINIVS GALLVS, *cos. ord.* 62, on the basis of the onomastic of the emperor C. VIBIVS AFINIVS GALLVS VELDVMNIANVS VOLVSIANVS, son of AEFINIA M.F. GEMINA BAEBIANA.

BETVI

BETVVS CILO (*AV* 1977: 252), *senator* (?) 69.

ANNII (*DdA* 1969: 301 f.)

L. ANNIVS LARGVS, *cos. suff.* 109, father of the *cos. ord.* 147 of the same name, and grandfather of the *salius palat.* 170 of the same name. The ANNII (GALLI) of *Iguvium* are also to be connected with Perugia.

VIBII GALLI (*DdA* 1969: 302)

C. VIBIVS TREBONIANVS GALLVS, *imperator* 251–53, husband of AFINIA M.F. GEMINA BAEBIANA and father of VIBIVS AFINIVS GALLVS VELDVMNIANVS. Their ancestor was *C. Vibius C.f.L.n.Tro. Gallus Proculeianus* (a knight of the the second century).

VOLCACII TVLLI (*DdA* 1969: 303)

L. VOLCACIVS TVLLVS, *cos.* 66 B.C., father of the namesake *cos.* 33 B.C. The senator, *tr. pl.* A.D. 69, VOLCACIVS TVLLINVS perhaps descends from their provincial clients, while C. VOLCACIVS GVRGES, *sen. aet. Neronis*, may be from Perusia.

Clvsivm *(Arn.)*: municipium, Sullan colony

PVPII

A. PVPIVS RVFVS (*AV* 1977: 252), *q. procos. Cretae et Cyrenarum* 30–27 B.C.

GELLII

?? Q. GELLIVS SENTIVS AVGVRINVS (*DdA* 1969: 304), *procos. Achaiae aet Hadriani.*

ANONYMVS

[---] (*DdA* 1969: 305; *CIL* XI, 7114), *procos. (?) Cypri* (second century A.D.).

Volsinii *(Pom)*: municipium

CAECINAE (*DdA* 1969: 306 f.)

L. CAECINA L.<F.>, *quaest.*, *tr. pl. procos.*, at the end of the Republic. To the same family but to the equestrian branch may belong the Volsini *C. Caecina Tuscus* (in connection with IVNIVS BLAESVS (Tacitus, *Hist.* III, 38–39)).

SEII (*DdA* 1969: 308 f.)

Descendent of the *praef. praet.* 14 *L. Seius Strabo,* husband of COSONIA GALLITTA (*PIR*[2], C 1528) daughter of LENTVLVS MALVGINENSIS (*cos.* 10?). Very famous was the adopted son (born of L. SEIUS TVBERO, *cos. suff.* 18) by the name of L. AELIVS SEIANVS, husband of APICATA. Brother of *Strabo* was Q. IVNIVS BLAESVS, *cos. suff.* 10, *procos. Africae* 21–22, father of Q. IVNIVS BLAESVS, *cos. suff.* 26, and grandfather of IVNIVS BLAESVS, *leg. pro. pr. Lugdunensis* 69, with whom the branch of the IVNII BLAESI died out (perhaps with the adoption of the Tarquinian CAESENNII PAETI, q.v.).

CATELLII CELERES

An inscription found at *Volsinii* (Gros 1980: 977 ff.) gives us both the *cursus* and *origo* of [Q. POMPEIVS L.F. POM. VOPISCVS C. ARR]VNT[IVS CATE]LLIVS CELER ALLIVS SABINVS, *cos. suff. a. inc. procos. Africae aet Antonii Pii pr (aetor) Etruriae.* He is the nephew (hardly the son) of L.

POMPEIVS VOPISCVS C. ARRVNTIVS CATELLIVS CELER, *cos. suff.* ca. 77, adopted by L. POMPEIVS VOPISCVS, *cos. suff.* 79. The *cos. suff.* 77 (or perhaps his father) demonstrates in his onomastic to be already adopted earlier by one C. ARRVNTIVS, probably from the *gens* of *Interamna Nahartium*, whence derive the senators [C.AR]RVNTIVS [---t]*r. pl. pro. pr. bis, pr.* [---] and his son [-A]RRVNTIVS C.F. [---] *praet*[*or?*---], the only ones among the *Arruntii* to have the praenomen *Caius*) from the end of the republic or the Augustan period. The last gentilician name found in the new *Volsinii* inscription ALLIVS is probably derived from the connection with the ALLII of nearby *Ferentium* (q.v.). At *Volsinii* Q. POMPEIVS VOPISCVS was already attested to (*CIL* XI, 7284). POMPEIA CELERINA, wife of L. VENVLEIVS APRONIANVS, *cos. ord.* 123 (q.v.), is perhaps the sister of the man honored in the new Volsinian inscription, while the daughter of the *cos. suff.* 77 ought to be POMPEIA CELERINA, wife of M. FVLVIVS GILLO BITTIVS PROCVLVS, adopted son of M. FVLVIVS GILLO, *cos. suff.* 76, from *Forum Novum* (q.v.). On this last person, see Pliny *ep.* I, 4; I, 18.3; III, 19.8; VI, 10.1. (POMPEIA CELERINA was her mother-in-law). On the family and on L. POMPEIVS VOPISCVS, *leg. pro. pr. Thraciae aet. Antonini Pii*, see now Corbier (1981, 1063 ff.).

CORNELII

A. CORNELIVS A.F. PALMA FRONTONIANVS (*DdA* 1969: 309), *cos. II ord.* 109. Descended possibly from [---]*ius A.f. Pal*[---], *quaestor, tr. pl.* [*procos.? leg.?*] *III* of the Augustan period (*CIL* XI, 2679a).

RVFII (*DdA* 1969: 307 f.)

Famous senatorial family known up to the late period; descended from the Volsinian knight (second century A.D.) *C. Rufius Felix:* his offspring are C. RVFIVS FESTVS CAELIVS FIRMVS and RVFIA C.F. PROCVLA, connected to these (perhaps adopted by the TVLLII VARRONES of Tarquinia) is TVLLIA P.F. MARSILLA QVENTINIA ROSSIA RVFINA RVFIA PROCVLA, *c.f.f.* of an inscription from Bolsena (*NSc* 1919: 207). Among the ancestors there was the Neronian philosopher *Musonius Rufus*, also of *Volsinii* (*ILS*, 2944). RVFIVS FESTVS is the father of RVFIVS MARCELLINVS and RVFIVS PROCVLVS (Barbieri, nos. 340–42) of the third century (?; see one RVFIVS FESTVS, *v.c. patronus* of *Cosa* in 236, (Ampolo 1981: 309 ff.) from whom RVFIVS FESTVS, *procos. Africae* 366, descends who in turn is the ancestor of RVFIVS FESTVS, *corr. Lucaniae et Bruttiorum*, and of consuls of the fifth and sixth centuries.

ACONII (*DdA* 1969: 305 f.)

Descended from a knight *L. Aconius L.f. Pom. Callistus*, the Christian senator of the fourth century L. ACONIUS GALLISTUS, *signo Cynegii*. Other ACONII (pagan) are known from the fourth century aristocracy.

ANONYMVS (*DdA* 1969: 309 f.)

The inscription (*CIL* XI, 2699 = *ILS*, 5013 = *CIL* XI, 7287) reveals to us a [*leg. Aug. pro. pr. Pannoniae inferioris... cos.... procos. Beticae? pr.... tr. p*]*l. cond*[*id., quaest., patronus*] *in Italia Volsiniensium patriae suae, item Ferent. et Tiburtium, item colon. Ialicens. in prov. Betica, praet. Etrur. XV populor., sacerdos Caeninensium*. Perhaps C.RVFIVS FESTVS LAELIVS FIRMVS (see above), son of the knight and perhaps himself a knight at the beginning of his career.

RVSELLAE *(Arn.)*: municipium, Augustan colony

ANONYMVS

[---]VS Q.F. AR[N---]NVS. Named in a fragmentary *cursus* from the baths of *Rusellae* (Saladino 1980: 193). The text in two fragmentary joining parts reads:

> [---]*o Q.f. Ar*[*n*---]
> [---]*no, cos.* [---*po*]*ntif.*
> [---*leg. exe*]*rcitus Br*[*itannici*---]
> [---*procos. prov.*] *Narbone*[*nsis*---]
> [---*leg. leg. XX Vale*]*riae Vi*[*ctr. (?)* ---]
> [---]*o* [---]

Certainly of Rusellan origin (whence the tribe *Arnensis*, now securely the one of *Rusellae* (Saladino 1980: 193)), the anonymous senator was probably one of the participants in the Claudian expedition to Britannia in 43, as a *legatus* of the *exercitus Britannicus* (up to now an unknown formula) under the command of *A. Plautius*, along with other senatorial colleagues of the better Italic aristocracy (including Vespasian and *Hosidius Geta* (*ILS*, 971)) and possibly *A. Didius Gallus:* (s.v. *Histonium* or *Larinum*). All the *legati* obtained the consulship in the years immediately after the expedition, if the identification of the expedition is correct; the entirety of the onomastic elements (origin and remains of the *cognomen*) would allow us to consider *Q. Sulpicius Camerinus, cos. suff.* 46. The Narbonese proconsulship is dated to the last years of Caligula's reign or to the initial years of Claudius' (ca. 39–42) and not too distant from that should be the command of the *legio XX Valeria Victrix* in Germany which would have guaranteed him a command in the *exercitus Britannicus*, to which the legion has been attached since the invasion of the island. (Birley 1981: 434 f., cautiously suggested that the name could be *Q. Caecilius Q.f. Arn. Marcellus.* This, however, is difficult to accord with the name in the new inscription, certainly of the first century). An alternative is offered in line 5 by the editor, [*---pr. Etru*]*riae, VI [vir turm*(*arum*) *eq*(*uitum*) *Rom*(*anorum*)] because in the text (in which we do not have the African proconsulship of A.D. 56) there is not enough space for the entire *cursus* successive to the youthful office of *VI vir turmarum equitem Romanorum*. We should also remember the local echo of the *victoria Britannica* which the *flamen Augusti A. Vicirius Proculus* publicized and who was the father of two future consuls of Rome (Saladino 1980a: 229 ff.); the scanty remains of the local onomastic do not attest to the *Sulpicii*.

VICIRII (*AV* 1977: 252 f.)

We know of an *A. Vicirius A. f. Arn.*, [---] *tr. mil. leg. IV Scythicae* and *aed. Etruriae*, from the early imperial period (the inscription (*CIL* XI, 1806) comes from the territory between Saena and Rusellae). He ought to pertain (Saladino 1980a: 230) to the family of *Rusellae*, whose most ancient member known to us would be VICIRIA A.F. ARCHAIS, wife of M. NONIVS BALBVS, *tr. pl.* 32 B.C., and mother of M. NONIVS BALBVS, *procos. Cretae et Cyrenarum aet. Augusti* (*vel Tiberii*). He is probably identical to *A. Vicirius Proculus, tr. mil. e flamen Augusti* in the Claudian period (Saladino 1980a: 229, 232 f.) and father of A. VICIRIVS PROCVLVS, *cos. suff.* 89, and A. VICIRIVS MARTIALIS, *cos. suff.* 98. What happens to the *gens* in the second century and after is not known.

TARQVINII (Stel.): municipium

CAESENNII (*DdA* 1969: 312 f.)

A branch of the family of Tarquinian *principes* joins the senate in the late republic, with L. (?) CAESENNIVS LENTO, *leg. Caesaris in Hispania* 45 B.C., *VII vir agr. div.* 44 B.C. A second branch (unlikely the same LENTO) includes L. CAESENNIVS PAETVS, *cos. ord.* 61, husband of FLAVIA T.F. SABINA (perhaps the daughter of FLAVIVS SABINVS, *cos. suff.* 44, *praef. urb.* 62–69, brother of Vespasian) and father of L. IVNIVS CAESENNIVS PAETVS (adopted from the BLAESII? or from the IVNII PASTORES?), *cos. suff.* 79, *procos. Asiae* ca. 92; brother of the *cos. ord.* 61, may be A. CAESENNIVS GALLVS, *cos. a. inc. leg. Aug. pro. pr. Galatiae Cappadociae* 80–82. The separation of this branch with that of the CAESENNII SOSPITES, attested to at Tarquinia in the equestrian rank in the Julio-Claudian period (Torelli 1975: 133) is difficult to trace: in fact, A. IVNIVS PASTOR L. CAESENNIVS SOSPES, *cos. suff.* 114, carries in his name the evidence of a tie with the IVNII PASTORES, perhaps the same man who was *cos. suff.* 79; also important is the presence in the *fasti* of the following years of IVNIVS PAETVS, *cos. suff.* 127, of d. (?) IVNIVS PAETVS, *cos suff.* 145 and of IVNIVS PAETVS, *cos. suff.* 154. There are a number of CAESENNII between the second and third centuries (*PIR*², C 169, 171, 175; cfr. L. CAESENNIVS ANTONINVS, *cos. suff.* 128), but there are no clear genealogical ties with the family under discussion.

VESTICII SPVRINNAE (*DdA* 1969: 316, 5; Torelli 1975: passim).
Descendents (nephew?) of the *Spurinna haruspex* of Caesar by the way of adoption or by the marriage of a *Vestricius* with a *Spurinna*, T. VESTRICIVS SPVRINNA, *cos. II suff.* 98, was the husband of one COTTIA (in turn the daughter or niece of A. COTTIVS, *procos. Hispaniae Ulterioris aet. Augusti* (*PIR*², C 1548)) and father of VESTRICIVS COTTIVS. Nothing certain about continuity of the *gens* in the second century.

?NVMISII (*DdA* 1969: 314)
T. NVMISIVS TARQVINIENSIS, *leg.* 169, 167 B.C.

??FVLCINII (*DdA* 1969: 313)
C. FVLCINIVS TRIO, *praet. per.* 24; his brother L. FVLCINIVS TRIO, *cos. suff.* 31. May belong to the family *Fulcinius Priscus*, jurist of the mid-first century.

TVLLII VARRONES (*DdA* 1969: 314 ff.)
P. TVLLIVS VARRO, *procos. Macedoniae aet. Vespasiani vel Domitiani*. His son was P. TVLLIVS P.F. STEL. VARRO, *cos. suff.* 127; his nephew (Groag) adopted by L. DASVMIVS HADRIANVS, *procos. Asiae aet. Traiani*, would be P. DASVMIVS RVSTICVS, *cos. suff.* 119, or else L. DASVMIVS P.F. STEL. TVSCVS, *cos. suff.* 152 (if he is not the son of RVSTICVS as Groag considers

him). Son of TVSCVS is M. DASVMIVS L.F. STEL. TVLLIVS VARRO an adolescent before 161. TVLLIA MARSI F. MARSILLA QVENTINIA ROSSIA RVFINA RVFIA PROCVLA of *Volsinii* is to be connected with these (nephew of DASVMIVS VARRO? or perhaps a parallel branch?).

FABII FABIANI (*AV* 1977: 253)

Probably of Spanish origin, they acquire property at Tarquinia by adopting *Vetilii* and *Lucilii*. A *Fabius Fabianus* (and possibly a senator) of the second century is attested to at Tarquinia: C. FABIVS LVCILIANVS, *mag. sod. August. Claud. II* 213, and his son C. FABIVS FABIANVS VETILIVS LVCILIANVS, *cos. des. aet. Severi Alexandri*. A possible tie may exist with C. FABIVS CILO, *cos. II ord.* 204, *cur. r. p. Graviscanorum*, again of very likely Spanish origin.

TVSCANA (Stel.): municipium

CORONAE (*DdA* 1969: 327 f.)

In the late republican period one C. SELICIVS (SELIVS?) CORONA is known as *tr. pl.* 44 B.C. From him we have L. CORONA L.F. PRO[---], *procos. Cretae et Cyrenarum aet. fere Augusti* (known by an epigraph found recently (Reynolds 1976: 306, n. 26) and L. CORONA RVFVS, *leg. pro. pr. aet. fere Augusti* (if this person is not the same as *procos. Cretae et Cyrenarum:* (Panciera 1982)). Almost certainly of Tuscanian origin (the great Etruscan aristocratic family of the fourth-third centuries B.C.: *curunas*).

FERENTIVM (Stel.): municipium

SALVII (*DdA* 1969: 311 f.)

M. SALVIVS OTHO, *praetorius* of the Augustan period, son of a knight; his son L. SALVIVS OTHO, *cos. suff.* 33, *procos. Africae* 40, *adlectus inter patricios* 47, married to ALBIA TERENTIA. Their sons were L. SALVIVS OTHO TITIANVS, *cos. II ord.* 69, married (?) to one COCCEIA and M. SALVIVS OTHO, *imper.* 69, married to STATILIA MESSALINA. The son of TITIANVS was M. SALVIVS OTHO COCCEIANVS, killed by Domitian.

ALLII

L. ALLIVS L.F. STEL. VOLVSIANVS (*DdA* 1969: 310; *AE* 1972: 179), *tr. mil. leg. XII Fulm. cert. const.*, *quaest. prov. Baeticae*, *aed. Cer.* The *gens* of this person is tied to one of the *Catellii* of *Volsinii* (q.v.). Less certain is the link with the [*L. Allius*---], *III vir a.a.a. f.f. tr. mil. leg. III Cyr. quaest.* [---] of the third century, son of *L. Allius F*[*lavius*---] and husband of a woman of the noble family of Ephesus, the *Vedii Antonini*.

?? *ARMINII* (See Volaterrae.)

CASTRVM NOVVM (Ani.? Pap.?): Roman colony

ATEII CAPITONES (Wiseman, nos. 52–53, 215)

L. Ateius Capito, a Sullan centurion, father of two sons: C. ATIVS (L.F. ANI.) CAPITO, *tr. pl.* 55, *leg. Caesaris agr. dand.* 44 B.C., and L. ATIVS L.F. ANI. CAPITO, *pr. aet. Caesaris*, whose son was C. ATIVS L.F.F.N. CAPITO, *cos. suff.* A.D. 5, and a very famous jurist. *L. Ateius M.f. Capito, duovir* of *Castrum Novum* (*CIL* XI, 3583–4) is also tied to this family and may even be the Sullan centurion. A fragmentary inscription published by Petrucci (1982) could also pertain to the *cos.* of A.D. 5.

FORVM CLODII *(Ste.?)*: praefectura, municipium

PVLLII

CN. PVLLIVS [-F.] POLLIO (*DdA* 1969: 317), *procos. Narbonensis, comes Augusti in Gallia Comata et Aquitania* (?) (*CIL* XI, 7553 = *ILS*, 916).

OCTAVII LIGVRES? (Wiseman, nos. 290–91, 247)

At *Forum Clodii*, one *A. Octavius A.F. Ligus II vir* (5 B.C.) is known: two senators in 75 B.C., M. OCTAVIVS LIGVS and L. OCTAVIVS LIGVS, are attested to. The sister of the two senators, *Octavia M.f.*, wife of the famous *duovir* of Ostia *P. Lucilius Gamala* belongs to this family, according to the brilliant reconstruction of Cebeillac (1973: 517 ff.). The date of *P. Lucilius Gamala* is in the first half of the first century B.C.

CLODII VESTALES (*PIR*[2], C 1191–92)

Of local origin, as the gentilician name also seems to announce, are C. CLODIVS C.F. VESTALIS, *procos. Cretae et Cyrenarum aet. Augusti vel Tiberii* (may be the same person or the son of C. CLODIVS C.F. *triumvir a.a.a. f.f.* ca. 40 B.C.) and his son of the same name who was *X vir stl. iud.*

SVTRIVM (Pap.?): latin colony, municipium

PONTII

L. PONTIVS AQVILA (*DdA* 1969: 318), *tr. pl.* 45 B.C. (Cfr. *CIL* XI, 3254; II, 13).

NEPET (Ste.?): latin colony, municipium

FIDVSTII

M. FIDVSTIVS (*DdA* 1969: 318; Wiseman 1971, no. 175, 231), *senator* 43 B.C.

AURELII

? M. AVRELIVS PROPINQVVS (*DdA* 1969: 318), *C.v.* (third-fourth century).

CAERE (Vot.? Ste.): municipium sine suffragio, municipium

ABVRII (*DdA* 1969: 319 f.)

Family of the republican period. M. ABVRIVS, *tr. pl.* 187 B.C., father of C. ABVRIVS, *leg.* 171 B.C. and grandfather of the twins and *triumviri monet.* C. ABVRIVS GEMINVS (119–110 B.C.) and M. ABVRIVS GEMINVS (120 B.C.). It is hard to tie D. ABVRIVS BASSVS, *cos. suff.* A.D. 85, to this family.

CAMPATII (*DdA* 1969: 321 f.)

? C. CAMP(ATIVS), *triumvir monet.* ca. 110 B.C., possibly the great-grandfather of SEX. CAMPATIVS M.F. M.N., *triumvir cap.*, *tr. mil.* in Augustan period.

TARQVITII (*DdA* 1969: 320 f.)

Among the *Tarquitii* from *Caere* (Etruscan *tarchna*), one can place, with relative certainty: TARQVITIVS PRISCVS, *leg. Q. Sertorii* 72 B.C., M. TARQVITIVS PRISCVS, *procos. Bithyniae* A.D. 58. At *Caere*, there may also be C. TARQVITIVS P.F., *quaest.* 81 B.C. (if he is not the same Sertorian legate: the praenomen *Publius* is not, however, attested to at *Caere* among the *Tarquitii*). Possibly not Caeretan but from *Veii* originally (but the *Manlii* are well known at *Caere:* perhaps the person who adopted him was from *Caere?*) Q. MANLIVS ANCHARIVS TARQ[VITIVS SATVRNI]NVS, to tie in with *l'equs* of *Veii M. Tarquitius T.f. Tro. Saturniunus.* To the other branch of the family we should attribute TARQVITIVS RVFVS who adopted [P. SEX]TVIS [- F.] SER. TARQVITIANVS, *q. propr. Macedoniae* A.D. 14, *leg. Tiberii;* the brother of these is P. SEXTIVS P.F. SER. LIPPINVS TARQVITIVS, *q.*, *praef. fr. d.*

EGNATII (*DdA* 1969: 320 f.)

Separate from the other branch, possibly deriving from *Capena*, the branch at *Caere* plausibly includes M. EGNATIVS RVFVS (*PIR*[2], E 32) *aed.* ca. 26 B.C., and is descended from the *eques L. Egnatius Rufus*, cfr. *T. Egnatius T.f. Vot. Rufus, dictator Caerit., aed. Etruriae*, and *A. Egnatius M.f. Ae*[---] of *Caere.*

?*SANQVINII* (*DdA* 1969: 326 f.)

Q. SANQVINIVS Q. F. STE., *q.*, *tr. pl.*, *pr. procos* (mid-first century B.C. ca.), is perhaps the father of M. SANQVINIVS Q.F., *triumvir monet.* ca. 17 B.C. Son (or nephew on the part of the brother) of this man was Q. SANQVINIVS MAXIMVS, *cos. II ord.* 39, *praef. urbi* 39–41. At *Caere*, a *Sanquinia C.f.* is known: the tomb of the first *Sanquinius* is at *Lorium* near *Caere* (but note also that it is the location of many famous *otium* villas.

FALERII *(Hor.):* Gracchan colony, municipium

GLITII

The branch of the *gens* which gave to the senate at least two representatives is definitely Faliscan in origin. The first we know of is dated to the beginning of the first century and probably was already a senator, L. GLITIVS GALLUS, patron of the freedman *L. Glitius Gliti Galli lib. (CIL* V, 5345), and possibly the husband of the well known VISTILIA, who Pliny (*N.H.* VII, 39) first married one *Glitius clarissimus civis* (cfr. *PIR*[2], G. 180). His son was P. GLITIVS L.F. GALLVS (*PIR*[2], G 184), *tr. mil. leg. I* (?), *III vir cap.* [*quaest. prov. Baeticae?*], took part in the Pisonian conspiracy (Tacitus, *Ann.* XV, 56) and was exiled to Andros with his wife EGNATIA MAXIMILLA (cfr. Dittenberger, 1915–1924: 811, 812). The wife derived from the Capena line of C. EGNATIVS MAXIMVS, *III vir mon.* ca. 73 B.C. (*PIR*[2], E 40). Their son was P. GLITIVS P.F. GALLUS (*PIR*[2], G 185), *III vir a.a.a.* [*f.f.*] *quaest.* [*Titi C*]*ae* [*s*]*aris, praet.*, *hasta pura don. per censuram cos.* ca. 79 (cfr. Cebeillac 1972, 74). The Faliscan origin is practically certain thanks to the dedications to two of the principal members of the family, the Flavian consul and his father (*CIL* XI, 3097; XI 3098 = 7492 = *ILS*, 999).

CAPENA (Stel.): municipium

EGNATII (*DdA* 1969: 320 f.)

The attribution at *Caere* on the grounds of the tribe (*Stellatina*) is uncertain and more likely (unpublished inscription at *Lucus Feroniae*) to be at *Capena* for CN. EGNATIVS C.F. STELL., *senator* 165 B.C., *procos. Macedoniae*, author of the *Via Egnatia* (*AE* 1973: 492); grandfather of CN. EGNATIVS, *senator ante* 70 B.C., and of C. EGNATIVS CN. F. CN. N. MAXIMVS, *triumvir monet.* 73 B.C. (son of the former man).

INCERTAE ORIGINIS

Here is a list of some senators (or families of senators) which for various reasons are originally of *regio VII* (with varying degrees of certainty), but the cities to which they belong cannot be specified.

ANCHARII

? Q. ANCHARIVS (*DdA* 1969: 327 f.; Wiseman 1971, no. 25, 212), *pr.* 88 B.C. Attribution on the basis of the onomastic.

FIDICVLANII

Q. FIDICVLANIVS FALCVLA (*DdA* 1969: 325; Wiseman 1971, no. 174, 231), *senator* 74 B.C. His Etruscan origin is dubious.

PERPERNAE (*DdA* 1969: 325 f.)

M. PERPERNA (l.f), *leg.* 168 B.C., father of M. PERPERNA M.F.L.N., *cos.* 130 B.C., and grandfather of M. PERPERNA M.F.M.N., *cos.* 92 B.C., *cens.* 86 B.C. and of C. PERPERNA (?), *pr.* 91 B.C. Perhaps from the *cos.* 92 B.C. deriving from M. PERPERNA VENTO (VEIENTO?), *pr.* 82, *leg. M. Lepidi* 77 B.C., *leg. Q. Sertori* 77–72 B.C. The daughter of this man is PERPERNIA, *virgo vestalis* 69 B.C. The family seems to die out at that point. Possible city of origin: *Perusia*, *Veii*.

ANONYMI

[---]VS C.F. STEL. [---]a., [*leg.*] *leg. XV Apollin.*, [*---cur viar. Clodiae*], *Ciminiae, Cassiae, IV vir i.d. ter. quinq.* (*CIL* XI, 3008: Viterbo). Tarquinia, Ferentium or Tuscana—dated to the second century.

[---]CVS MODESTVS PAVLINVS. *Cv.*, *praef. urbis feriarum Latinarum quaest. urbanus, aed. Cer. praetor eodemque tempore praetor Aetrur.* [sic] *XV popul*[*or*], *cur. r*[*ei*]*p. splendidissimae civita*[*tis*] *Mars. Marr. eodem t*[*e*]*mpore et cur. viar. Tib. Val. et alim.* (*CIL* XI, 3667). Of Etruscan origin because he held the *praetura Etruriae*, possibly an *Arrius* or a *Caesennius*.

NOTES

1. Torelli 1969: 285 ff.
2. Harris 1971.
3. Torelli 1977: 251 ff.
4. *Romanization* 1975.
5. Sordi 1960: 76 f.; Torelli 1974–75: 62 f.
6. Heurgon 1958: 151 ff.; Cassola 1962: 202 f.
7. Cassola 1962: 151; *RE* 1937: c. 2063 ff., *s. v.* Ogulnius.
8. Ampolo 1975: 410 ff., and 1981: 45 ff.
9. Harris 1971: 319 ff.
10. Cristofani 1965.
11. Torelli 1975: 189 ff.
12. Torelli 1974–75: 67 ff.
13. Gaggiotti and Sensi 1982.
14. *Arruns Velthymnus* is the haruspex who received the *Vegoia* prophesy: his name is to be put in connection with the cognomen *Veldumnianus* which is known among the Perusian *Vibi Galli*, cfr. Heurgon 1955–56.
15. Torelli 1981: *passim*.
16. Torelli 1975: 129 and 191.
17. Rawson 1978: 132 ff.
18. Torelli 1981: *passim*.
19. Cicero *leg.* II, 9.21.
20. On the problem of euergetism in Etruria before and after 90 B.C. see Torelli 1981a.
21. Tacitus, *Annales* XI, 5.
22. Torelli 1975: 191 ff.

23. *CIL* XI, 3614 = *ILS*, 5918a.
24. Torelli 1981a.
25. *CIL* VI, 537 = *ILS*, 2944.
26. Liou 1969, cfr. Torelli 1971: 499 ff.

BIBLIOGRAPHY

Ampolo, C.

1975 "Gli Aquilii del V secolo a.C. e il problema dei Fasti Consolari più antichi," PP: 409–16.

1981 *Gli Etruschi e Roma*. Roma.

Bendinelli, G.

1919 "Bolsena-Silloge epigrafica," *NSc:* 206–9.

Birley, A.

1981 *The Fasti of Roman Britain*. Oxford.

Cassola, F.

1962 *I gruppi politici romani nel III sec. a.C.* Trieste.

Cebeillac, M.

1972 *Les "Quaestores principis et candidati" aux Ier et IIeme siècles de l'Empire*. Milan.

1973 "Octavie epouse de Gamala et la Bona Dea," *MEFRA* LXXXV: 517–53.

Corbier, M.

1981 "La *tavola marmorea* de Bolsena et la famille senatoriale des Pompeii," *MEFRA* XCIII: 1063–1112.

Cristofani, M.

1965 *La Tomba delle Iscrizioni a Cerveteri*. Firenze.

Dittenberger, W.

1915–1924 *Sylloge Inscriptionum Graecarum*³. Berlin

Eck, W.

1970 "Die Legaten von Lykien und Pamphylien unter Vespasian," *ZPE* VI: 65–75.

1970a *Senatoren von Vespasian bis Hadrian: prosopographische Untersuchungen mit Eischluss der Jahres-und-Provinzialfasten der Statthalter*. München.

Epigrafia

1982 *Epigrafia e Ordine senatorio: Tituli V*. Roma.

Gaggiotti, M. and Sensi, L.

1982 "Ascesa al senato e rapporti con i territori d'origine. Italia, Regio VI (Umbria)," *Epigrafia:* 245–74.

Groag, E.

1933 *Prosopographia imperii romani saec*. I, II, III. Berlin.

Gros, P.

1980 "Une dedicace Carthaginoise sur le forum de Bolsena," *MEFRA* XCII: 977–89.

Harris, W.V.

1971 *Rome in Etruria and Umbria*. Oxford.

Heurgon, J.

1955–56 "Traditions étrusco-italiques dans le monnayage de Trebonien Galle," *StEtr* XXIV: 91–105.

1958 "A propos du cognomen Violens et du tombeaux des Volumnii," *AC* X: 151–59.

Jagenteufel, A.

1958 *Die Statthalter der römischen Provinz Dalmatia von Augustus bis Diokletian*. Wien.

Liou, B.

1969 *Praetores Etruriae XV populorum*. Bruxelles.

Panciera, S.

1981 *Supplementa Italica*. Roma.

Rawson, E.

1978 "Caesar, Etruria and the Disciplina Etrusca," *JRS* LXVIII: 132–52.

Reynolds, J.
1976 "The Inscriptions of Apollonia" in R. Goodchild et al., *Apollonia, The port of Cyrene (Suppl. Libya Ant. IV)*, 293–334.

Ritterling, E.
1932 *Fasti des römischen Deutschland unter dem Prinzipat*. Wien.

Romanization
1975 *Studies in the Romanization of Etruria*. Rome.

Saladino, V.
1980 "Iscrizioni Latine di Roselle I," *ZPE* XXXVIII: 159–202.
1980a "Iscrizioni Latine di Roselle II," *ZPE* XXXIX: 215–36.

Schulze, W.
1904 "*Zur Geschichte der lateinischen Eigennamen*" (Abhandlungen Kon. Akad. Göttingen). Berlin.

Scott, R.
1981 "A new inscription of the emperor Maximinus at Cosa," *Chiron* XI: 309–14.

Sordi, M.
1960 *I rapporti romano-ceriti e la civitas sine suffragio*. Roma.

Syme, R.
1956 "Missing Persons," *Historia* V: 204–12.

Thomasson, B.
1960 *Die Statthalter der römischen Provinzen Nordafrikas von Augustus bis Diokletian*. Lund.

Torelli, M.
1969 "Senatori etruschi della tarda repubblica e dell'impero," *DdA* III: 285–363.
1971 "Per La Storia dell'Etruria in età imperiale" *RFIC:* 489–501 (translated in this volume).
1974–75 "Tre studi di storia etrusca," *DdA* VIII: 3–78.
1975 *Elogia Tarquiniensia*. Firenze.
1977 "Senatori etruschi della tarda repubblica e dell'impero: qualche addendum," *Archeoloski Vestnik* XXVIII: 251–54.

1980 "Innovazioni nelle tecniche edilizie romane tra il I sec. a.C. e il I sec. d.C." in *Tecnologia, economia e società nel mondo romano*, 139–61. Como (translated in this volume).

1981 *Storia degli Etruschi*. Bari.

1983 *"Edilizia Pubblica in Italia Centrale tra Guerra Sociale ed Età Augustea: Ideologia e Classi Sociali" in Les Bourgeoisies municipales aux IIe et Ier siècles av. J.C.* 241–50. Naples (translated in this volume).

Wiseman, T.P.

1971 *New Men in the Roman Senate 139 B.C.–A.D. 14*. Oxford.

NSc Concordance

1919 = Bendinelli, G.

4

TOWARDS THE HISTORY OF ETRURIA IN THE IMPERIAL PERIOD

STUDIES OF THE CONSTITUTIONAL HISTORY of the peoples of ancient Italy have had to consider the epigraphic evidence of the Roman period belonging to those regions, since frequently the magistracies of the conquered Italic peoples were conserved in a more or less integral form by the Romans. Thanks to those studies, initiated by Mommsen and his followers and continued in this century by the classic works of Rosenberg, Kornemann, Leifer, and Rudolph, today we have a general if controversial picture of the Etrusco-Italic and Latin constitutional situation which the literary sources alone would never have revealed.

There is an increasing tendency to forget that the original context of that evidence is and remains Roman. Bernard Liou's book opportunely reminds us of that with regard to the *praetores* and *aediles Etruriae.*[1] This book addresses two lists, arranged in chronological order (unfortunately not very rigorous) of important men who held the office of *praetor* or of *aediles Etruriae.* For every entry the epigraphic data with the *cursus honorum* is given: nearly every existing text has been reproduced photographically.

Before discussing Liou's conclusions, I would add to selected entries a few additional prosopographical and archaeological remarks.

1. IMP. CAES. TRAIANUS HADRIANUS AUG.

   The "neo-Augustan" political structure was not a discovery of Hadrian but was actually commonplace under Claudius, Vespasian, and all of the Antonines. The coins and medallions of Antoninus Pius[2] are noteworthy for both the topography and legends of the archaic history of Latium. Hadrian propagated a political structure of the local offices of the magistracies (12–14), but the attitude of the ruling classes towards the municipal and colonial public offices is a problem that merits more study. The behavior of the emperor, of the senatorial class, and of the higher equestrian bureaucracy, period by period and region by region, concerning this type of *pietas* toward the older sites and cities of origin is of critical importance. In the absence of such a study I can share only in the most general form Liou's statements about the Hadrianic choice of cities to honor.

As for the philetruscanism of Hadrian (which ought to be understood as merely an "archaizing" attitude), I would add and emphasize that there is an unparalleled case in the late Republican and Imperial consular *fasti* of a pair of consuls who took office together, on the Kalends of April 127, Tullius Varro and Iunius Paetus: both were Tarquinian either by birth or ancestry.[3] This singular occurrence (I am not acquainted with any other examples of similar distinction given to two representatives of the aristocracy who were of Etruscan origin) coincides with the presence of Hadrian in Rome and in Italy, as well as with the celebration of the first decade of his reign (to which, possibly, the coins and, less securely, a well-known relief in the Uffizi refer).[4]

Nonetheless, it is possible that those displays of devotion towards the venerable Latin and Italic institutions to which *SHA. Hadr.* 19 refer may have taken place in such circumstances and at such a time.

As for C. Cilnius Proculus, a new fragment of the *Fasti Ostiensi* (kindly brought to my attention by F. Zevi) notes a consul of this name for A.D. 100. In light of this new information the Arezzo inscription[5] and *CIL* XI, 1833, together with *CIL* XI, 1835, should be reconsidered.

It is probable then that the "philetruscan" behavior of Hadrian goes back to the mysterious Plutia,[6] while I would insist even less than Liou does (16) on the possible Etruscan *ultima origo* of Cn. Pedanicus Fuscus and still less on an Etruscan *origo* for the Dasumii, whom Syme has justifiably placed in Apulia and whom I would locate more precisely at Canusium.[7]

2. P. TULLIUS VARRO

The *stemma* of the Tulli is a *crux interpretum*. Liou takes up the thesis of Saria and of Pflaum against the identification of P. Tullius Varro as the *cos. suff.* 127[8] who is named with his friend in the *Testamentum Dasumii*. He supports instead the identification of Tullius Varro as the otherwise unknown *cos. suff.* c. 100 named in *CIL* XI, 3366. It is a seductive idea but in the absence of any knowledge of this presumed *cos. suff.* c. 100 I would prefer to stick to the traditional hypothesis put forward and documented by Stein.[9] Stein proposed the identification of P. Tullius Varro with the father (and not the uncle) of Dasumius Tullius Tuscus, *cos. suff.* 152, and thus with the son (and not the nephew) of the man named in *ILS*, 1002. Liou missed an inscription from Bolsena of one TVLLIA P.F. MARSILLA QVENTINIA ROSSIA RVFINA RVFIA PROCVLA, *clarissima foemina*,[10] which attests to ties between the Rufi Festi (the sister of Rufius Festus of *CIL* XI, 2698, the first senator of the family, went by the name of Rufia Procula) and the Tarquinian Tulli. It is likely that a Rufia Procula may have been adopted by M. Dasumius Tullius Varro, son of the *cos.* 152, who was connected to that Quintinius who co-owned with Tullius Varro a goodly portion of the Viterban land crossed by the *aqua Vegetiana* (*ILS*, 5771 and add.). I cannot, in the final analysis, follow Liou's statement (22, n. 4) regarding the scarcity of traces of the family at Tarquinia. To the three freedmen which Liou cites one can add the P. Tullius Callistio named in both *CIL* XI, 3366 (and perhaps 3365) as well as another inscription from Centumcellae[11] but which is surely tied to the Tarquinian family.

3. L. VENULEIUS APRONIANUS OCTAVIUS

I completely agree with Liou's careful analysis of *CIL* XI, 1432.[12] The reading given below, as has already been proposed by Groag and Kahrstedt, removes any uncertainty regarding the difficulty of "localizing" the *praetura Etruriae* or of supposing a representation in every city by the president of the league in function of his annual office as many scholars had interpreted it.[13] The interpretation of Liou is fundamental for a unified comprehension of the juridical and political structure of the league of the *XV populi*.

It would be very useful to have a less schematic diagram than that given by the author for the reconstruction of the important texts *CIL* XL, 1432–33.[14] It was the opportune moment to provide a more elaborate edition than that, largely inaccurate, given by the *Inscriptiones Italiae*, and especially to demonstrate in a clearer manner the oddity of these two texts in light of the fragment *Inscr. It.* VII, 1 n. 18. This last fragment could, I believe, be pertinent to the titular of *CIL* XI, 1525, and thus, according to Groag,[15] be that of Venuleius Apronianus, *cos.* 123. On this point it would have been better for Liou not to relegate to a footnote Groag's reconstruction in which he inserts into *CIL* XI, 1525, the mention of *praetura Etruriae.* A clearer graphic reconstruction would have eliminated every hesitation regarding Pflaum's hypothesis in which *CIL* XI, 1433, may have also mentioned a connection to the *sodales Antoniniani Veriani:* Liou (31) does not share this opinion.[16]

A final consideration concerns instead the inscription of Corliano, *CIL* XI, 1735, where Liou (31) in the text seems to accept the traditional reading of . . . *Laetilia et Celerina uxo(res),* consecrated by the authority of Mommsen and Bormann. In a footnote, however, he refers neutrally to the correction (rather than the reading) of Donati . . . *Laetiliae Celerinae uxo(ri).* This textual modification by the eighteenth century scholar constitutes actual violence to the original transcription which I prefer to read . . . *Laetilia L.f. Celerina uxo(r).* This reading takes into account that the gentilician names of the two people previously mentioned follow the lacunae in which their respective patronymic would have been contained. This correction would have the advantage of eliminating the textual difficulty which derives either from the reading of the *CIL* or from the correction of Donati.

4. Q. PETRONIUS MELIOR

To this man and to his son of the same name Liou dedicates some of his best remarks (32–35 and appendix 97–103). His conclusions about the chronology of the younger of the two Petronii seem very plausible and judicious.

Archaeologists should take note of the important data gathered by Liou (101–103) for the dating of the sarcophagus of Q. Petronius Melior junior—especially important for a period such as this one in which the chronology of sarcophagi seems to be so controversial. Equally, or even more important, is that they now also know how to deal correctly with the fanciful graphic additions by Gori which Liou rightly considers spurious. This point has not been clear to all those who have studied the sarcophagus.

5. C. BETUUS CILO MINUCIANUS VALENS ANTONIUS CELER P. LIGUUIUS RUFINUS LIGUUIANUS

It may be precisely with this inscription that the problem of the chronology of *praetura Etruriae* comes into clearer focus. In a concise analysis (37–43) Liou identifies this man, who seems to have had a totally municipal *cursus* (*aedilis* five times, *duovir* and patron of Perugia as well as *sacerdos trium lucorum*) to finally reach the *praetura Etruriae*, with Betuus Cilo mentioned by Tacitus (*Hist.* I, 37) who was a victim of the Galban repressions. Liou is surely correct to maintain that this second Betuus Cilo was a member of the senatorial order and perhaps the legate of Aquitania anonymously referred to by Suetonius (*Galba* 9)—in connection with the Vindex revolt. He is consequently forced to suppose that the ruler of the Perugian inscription may be a descendent of the man involved in the civil war events of 69. This is possible; however, if the Betuus Cilo of Perusia is to be considered related to the probable senator of the same name from the Neronian period, logically he may be rather the ancestor of the Neronian senator involved in the revolt of Vindex since a kind of withdrawal by the family from the senatorial *fasti* of Rome into the obscurity, however comfortable it may have been, of the Perugian forum is unthinkable. To justify that position of abstention hypothesized by Liou it is necessary to find parallels—and these, unfortunately, do not exist. The criterion of the use of polyonymy for the late dating of the Perugian inscription is not worth much, as Liou himself concedes it to be "bien incertain." In fact, many examples of polyonymy just as multiple and just as ancient do exist. We should think about the recent documentation[17] concerning the full name of the *cos. ord.* 13, C. Silius A. Caecina Largus, and also about L. Pompeius Vopiscus C. Arruntius Catellius Celer, and important people in the Neronian and Flavian periods as well as the famous informer A. Didius Gallus Fabricius Verento or, for a more ancient example between Augustus and Tiberius, L. Aquillus Florus Turcianus Gallus. It is thus easier to demonstrate that the Perugian polyonym may be a (very close) ancestor of the Neronian senator than to demonstrate the reverse. With these elements in hand it becomes very problematic to sustain the basic assumption of Liou's book: that the *praetura Etruriae* is of Hadrianic creation.

6. SEX. VALERIUS PROCULUS

This is another bothersome element in Liou's thesis. The block from Bettona bearing the inscription of this *praetor Etruriae* was found in a collapsed tomb of the Republican period.[18] In the tomb there was Etruscan and Roman material dating up to the first century A.D. (not only the cameo, but also the majority of the ring bezels are datable to the Augustan-Tiberian period). At this point, Liou's reasoning becomes capricious. As it is difficult for him to date the inscription to the period dictated by the archeological data, he overcomes the problem with these words (44): "La présence même d'une inscription relative à un *praetor Etruriae* nous rendra sceptique: quand bien même elle serait la plus ancienne de notre série, il n'est guère pensable qu'elle remonte au début du I siècle. On peut fort bien, dans un tel contexte, commettre une erreur d'une siècle; mais nous serions plutôt porté à croire que le contexte archéologique ne nous est d'aucun secours, s'agissant d'une tombe trouvée effondrée et pillée, et qui fut ouverte semble-t-il, à tout venant . . . l'inscription est vraisemblablement du II siècle." It is not necessary I believe to underline the *petitio principii* of Liou, who, before examining all the evidence, had already concluded that *praetores* of the beginning of the first century could not exist. That inscriptions may "travel" from one tomb to another seems to me a bit difficult to believe, even admitting that the excavation does not seem to have been conducted with particular precision. Additionally it would still need to be shown what type of tomb the inscription (which in fact attests to *duoviri* for Vettona) belonged: the presence of *duoviri*, perhaps a good hint to the date of the inscription, is slipped into a footnote. Liou, who is so accurate in the unearthing and pulling together of documents scattered all over, should have been able to go to the tomb itself to check whether the tombs of the second century A.D. do (or do not) exist there. And finally, one can note that the author himself, on the dating of this person to the second century A.D. (and thus dating the tomb to the first and the praetorship to the second century A.D.) affirms that "une seule inscr. nous plonge, a vrai dire, dans un certain embarras, celle de Sex. Valerius Proculus."

7. ANONYMOUS

The person named in the inscription *CIL* XI, 2699 = *ILS*, 5013, is a high-ranking person of Volsinii from the time of Severus Alexander, most likely *leg. pr. pr. Pannoniae Superioris.* I doubt that it could be an Aconius as Liou thinks (49): the dedicant *tr. mil. leg. XIV Geminae* is a L. Aconius Callistus who is well known from other Volsinian inscriptions. It is much more probable that the inscription refers to one Rufus Festus, in light of the two *CIL* XI, 7287, fragments attributed to Rufus Festus which commemorate either the reconstruction or redecoration of the temple of the goddess Nortia. Nortia was particularly venerated by precisely the Rufi Festi.[19] The manner in which Liou treats (50) the relationship between *CIL* XI, 2686 = *ILS*, 4036 (*Dis deabusq. Primitivus dea Nort. ser. act. ex voto*) and *CIL* XI, 2714 (*Rufiae Primitivae contubernali sanctissimae Primitivus r.p. ser. act. b. m. fec*) is significant: he does not seem to want to draw the obvious conclusions for the identification of our *ignotus.*

8. . . . CUS MODESTUS PAULINUS

This man comes from a well-known senatorial family to judge from the cursus including the praetorship mentioned in *CIL* IX, 3667, which also tells us that he served as *praetor Etruriae.* Liou does not attempt an identification, since he limited his research to the *index cognominum* of the *CIL* XI. It could refer to either the family of the Areii or to that of the Caesennii, both of Etruscan nobility,[20] on the basis of *CIL* XV, 838, a lead water pipe of one Arria Caesennia Paulina, of a senatorial family. The same *cursus,* with a *praefectura urbana feriarum Latinarum,* the *quaestura urbana* and the absence of military offices allows us to deduce, as Liou notes, that this inscription refers to a gens of the highest rank, not implausibly patrician, of the first quarter of the third century A.D.

9. ANONYMOUS

Nothing can be added to Liou's observations (53) on such a fragmentary text.

10. L. TIBERIUS MAEFANAS BASILIUS

Liou's discussion (54–57) regarding this man and that on successive Anonymous, Liou's number 11, are convincing, particularly on the formula *ex-praetoribus XV pop(ulorum).* The proposed identification for the anonymous person of *CIL* XI, 5170, as one of the Turcii Aproniani who are very well known from early imperial prosopography seems quite likely. I would add that the existence of a late imperial haruspex, whose name has been incorrectly transmitted to us, Apruncullis Gallus[21] belongs undoubtedly to this family which was certainly from Etruria.

The *aediles* list follows (68–78) that of the *praetores.* Since the list deals exclusively with people possessing municipal careers, my observations are briefer.

11. [Not commented on in original article. Eds.]

12. [C.] METELLIUS C.F.

The inscription from Cortona, *CIL* XI, 1905, deserves an accurate graphic reconstruction as I believe, against Liou (69), that at line five it is easier to integrate [pr] than [*aed.*]. The consequences of such a change to the respective lists is obvious. The reconstruction would have justified a reading as follows:

[C.(?) M]etellius C.f. Stel. Gal[lus]
IIII vir aed.
[C.] Metellius C.f. St[el.]
IIII vir. aed., q.,
[pr.] Etruriae, III vir. i.d. [(bis?)].

It is evident that the second name refers to the father of the first man (perhaps he died at an early age) since he did not have—unlike his son—a *cognomen*. As a result, as Liou admits, lines two and four are complete (the photograph clearly shows this) and imposes an evident and rigorous construction of the epigraphic text on the part of the *quadratarius.* In turn, this leaves in the lower left line five, sufficient space for only two letters and not three, thus for *PR(aetor)* and not *AED(ilis)*. Bormann[22] first refused to accept the supplement [*pr(aetor)*] because it did not accord with his reconstruction of the Etruscan league in the *CIL.* Instead, when freed from the cares of the previous article and having the inscription at hand, he chose the latter supplement. Liou, freeing himself too abruptly from an awkward situation, says parenthetically "nous ne croyons pas à l'éventualité de *praetor*, *PR.*" The absence of the *cognomen* and the splendid working of the text force us to date the inscription to the first half of the first century A.D.: here, then, is another probable *praetor* before Hadrian.

13. A. VICIRIUS A.F.
Liou provides very little scope for argument in this case, although I cannot easily accept the hypothesis that we are dealing with an ancestor of A. Vicirius Proculus, *cos. suff.* 89 and A. Vicirius Martialis, *cos. suff.* 98. Liou (73, note 1) opportunely reminds us of Viciria A.f. Archais (*CIL* X 1440), mother of M. Nonius Balbus of Nocera. One should note that M. Nonius Balbus married an Etruscan Volasennia C.f. Tertia, possibly of Clusine origin. The example of Urgulania, who "forced" a policy of "Etruscan" marriages on the Plautii Silvani, from Trebala Suffenas, could provide a chronological terminus for parallels. The only great difficulty is the excessive chronological gap between the Viciria of the Herculaneum inscriptions and the obscure Flavian consuls. In effect, I find it difficult to imagine such a slow career progression for this equestrian family from Chiusi.

14. L. ALFIUS QUIENTUS
It is difficult to argue with Liou's analysis (73 note 2) of this inscription pertaining to this man from Chiusi (*CIL* XI, 2116 = *ILS*, 6610). The observations concerning the praefectura fabrum are especially sensible.

15. T. EGNATIUS RUFUS
The inscription (*CIL* XI, 3615 = *ILS*, 3257) is one of the key points in the study of the ancient Italic and Etruscan magistracies, and Liou's discussion (75–77) is limited to the single federal magistracy held by Egnatius Rufus. Nearly all of the problems raised by the text about the magistracies of Caere are confined to a note where important references are scattered throughout: this treatment creates difficulties for the reader. It is sufficient to consider the controversial identification of the tribe of Caere often held, on the basis of this very inscription, to be the Voturia.[23] Liou does not seem to realize (77) that the design incised below the text is modern. The "bulle suspendue a un ruban..." is in reality a coat of arms of the

1600–1700s as is the basket with grapes below it. The coat of arms was probably cut when the stone was moved as it was also completely reworked from a quadrangle to a hexagon and hollowed out in back. Furthermore, the entire argument about the Etruscan *raufe* in relation to the unequivocal Roman *cognomen* of Egnatius is superfluous. On the other hand, Liou does not note the assignment of Cn. Egnatius C.f. Stell., *senator*, circa 165 B.C. and of his descendents (Cn. Egnatius Cn.f., *senator*, 100 B.C. and C. Egnatius Cn.f. Cn.n. Maximus, *tr. monet* 73 B.C.) to Caere made by Badian.[24] Furthermore, Badian identifies both the group around this person and the Caere tribe with the Stellatina. The first century A.D. date for the inscription is possible, but I would not accept without argument a Claudian date[25] nor the first century chronology as Liou would have it.

16. . . . POMP[---]

On this Clusine inscription (*CIL* XI, 2120) Liou's comments are a bit too concise. In particular, it is necessary to demonstrate that the first line, where the onomastic element [---] *o Pompo* [---] is, should be more or less in connection with the mention of the *aedilitas Etruriae*, preceded by the remains of a desinential word [---]*NO*. This might force us to consider whether it refers to the cognomen of a second and different person. Even more problematic is the silence on the chronological aspects of the inscription. To judge from the *CIL* transcription, the *hederae distinguentes* in the place of the usual punctuation seem to assign the inscription to a not particularly ancient period. It is in any event difficult to date it to the first century B.C.: this is not without consequence for the general conclusions of Liou's book.

In the conclusions (79–96), Liou gives the *praetores* and *aediles* lists, dividing them by urban functions, chronology, titularity, place of origin, and municipal offices eventually held. From these lists, one can only extract, in spite of all the subtle argumentation of the author, that these offices of the old Etruscan league were honorifically bestowed on senators, equestrians and local *nobiles*. This, of course, is exactly what happened for the municipal magistracies which came to be offered to persons of rank connected to the city in question by birth or function (*curatores rei publicae, curatores viarum,* etc.) or because of economic interests (ownership of *fundi*). We should not forget that municipal and colonial offices were offered to the emperor himself or to members of the imperial house and that these offices were often administered by praefects. The situation of the Etruscan league is no different: it is impossible to demonstrate that the *praetura* was the prerogative of the senatorial rank (four of eleven individuals are of exclusively local fame) while it seems very likely that the aedilitas may have been reserved for individuals of modest rank. Of the four listed *aediles* (another can be added from a Tarquinian inscription)[26] which are securely *aediles* (no. 12, in my opinion, is a *praetor*), two are *equites* and two are—as far as we know—only local magistrates.

These remarks justify only partially the conclusions of our French colleague. Certainly there was a distinction of rank between *praetores* and *aediles.* We have no senators who held the office of *aedilitas Etruriae* but this circumstance does not have chronological importance, in that the *aedilitas* existed earlier than the *praetura* and was then abolished by the *praetura.* At least two men (nos. 5 and 6), if not three (with no. 12) are *praetores* of the first century A.D. and still another was aedile no earlier than the second century A.D. Therefore, it is inexact to affirm that "à aucun moment, nous n'avons la preuve d'une coincidence, d'une interférence chronologique entre les deux séries d'inscriptions." The other *argumentum e silentio* suggested to Liou by Pflaum, not that a federal *cursus* did not exist, in that someone could successively be *aedilis* and then *praetor*, does not have any validity as these fictitious magistracies were based on importance: *praetura* to someone of rank, *aedilitas* to a more obscure figure. If we were not well informed about the municipal structures and if we had to base our knowledge only on the offices mentioned by the usual *cursus* of noteworthy individuals, we could conclude that in some cities a *cursus* and hierarchy simply did not exist as, for example, among *aediles duoviri* and *quinquennales*, finding senators who had taken exclusively *quinquennalitas* and individuals of local note who had only been *duoviri.* It is thus possible that a true and clear-cut *cursus* in the League may not have existed, but it is certain that the two magistracies, of different levels and thus held by persons of diverse rank, may have coexisted. The diverse importance of the two offices in a certain way is demonstrated by the unequal number of examples, twelve for the *praetura* against four for the *aedilitas.*

Thus the announced purpose of Liou's book, which had occasionally forced the author into awkward assessments (nos. 5 and 6) and as it seems even Liou is willing to admit (82, note 6; 83, note 2), becomes difficult to sustain. It is truly difficult to suppose a reorganization of the league on Hadrian's part, to whom (at the limit) one can attribute a *pietas* for the older institutions of Italy, but this *pietas* was not on the same level as his interest in Hellenic institutions and even this *pietas* is no greater than that of his predecessors, such as Domitian or Trajan himself. It is, therefore, an error of historical perspective to attribute this presumed interest in the *priscae institutiones* of Etruria to an increased importance of the true Etruscan families (at that time probably only the Caesennii of Tarquinia and the Caecinae of Volterra existed). On the other hand, it may be that the explosion of affection for their natal land by aristocrats of Etruscan origin was a generic and universal archaizing tendency as well as an imitation of imperial trends. The period of Hadrian is quite separate from that of Claudius when the authentic local Italian traditions (and here I am thinking about the *elogia Tarquiniensia*) were not just erudition but actually played a more or less significant part in determining political lines or influencing ideological positions.

Liou's pages on the league in the late empire are very welcome, especially in light of the ingenious but over elaborate theories of De Dominicis[27] on the edict of Spello, even if many of his arguments cannot really be countered.[28] Only the discovery of new documents can tell us something more concrete about the relationship between the *sacerdos-coronatus Tusciae et Umbriae* and the *praetor Etruriae*, although I prefer the thesis first proposed by Kornemann and then taken up by Liou and Gascou. The other problems of the *praetura Etruriae*, such as the Latin name (89–92) and its connection to the ancient federal structure (92–94), Liou sticks to the more widely held and orthodox opinion: on such a difficult subject, this approach is laudable. For the corresponding office of *zilaΘ meχl rasnal* even in light of the Pyrgi inscription, Liou translates the office as *praetor Etruriae populorum* (and why not as *praetor populorum Etruriae* which would be verbatim from the Etruscan?).[29] As for the question of the XV populi, Liou does not take a position on whom they may have been, and limits himself to cite Pisae, Faesulae, or Florentiae, or Saena as possible new members of the federal alliance. He also correctly rejects the hypotheses of Bormann which were based on the Plinian list. A study of this question would be opportune and with new knowledge in hand, one could return profitably to the consideration of the problem, which is closely linked to the Romanization of Etruria. The subject should not be treated exclusively by literary source work[30] but should be looked at in a new way, uniting topographic, archaeological, epigraphic, and literary data. The understanding of the phenomenon of the league's restoration in the Roman period must necessarily begin from here since any single point of view—archaeological, epigraphic, etc.—can only be of limited scope and thus erroneous. The league in the Etruscan period, known to us only by three inscriptions (*TLE*², 87, 137, 233) fell into oblivion, at least as far as we know after the mid-third century B.C.[31] and thus after the fall of Volsinii and the sack of the Fanum Voltumnae in 264 B.C. It is likely, then, that the league may have dissolved and then have been reconstructed only in the imperial period. When? Here too Liou is prudently cautious: although he does not reject the hypothesis of an act of political restoration by Augustus, he seems to prefer the necessary alternative, so to speak, of Claudius. I find the Augustan hypothesis, which was dear to Bormann, more suitable. The Claudian reforms (Suetonius *Claud.* 22, 1) to which Liou turns to justify his inclination for a Claudian restoration are generally of very limited significance, and furthermore, to be seen in direct association with the *caerimoniae* of Rome. The *LX haruspices* interested Claudius only for the ancient Roman customs of using them in the *procuratio prodigiorum* and he initiated the reconstitution of the *collegium* in the year of the census. In order to sustain the Claudian hypothesis, some examples of wide-ranging and deep intervention in local affairs—which is what the reorganization of the league is—are needed. Unfortunately, these examples are absent for the Claudian age, while in the Augustan age they are abundant throughout ancient Italy. In Etruria alone, one could cite the foundation of the Municipium Augustum Veiens, in addition to the instances already cited by Bormann. In this respect, Liou's book is a first and very helpful contribution, to which many other contributions on the municipal structure of ancient Italy should follow. From such works important data on the little-known Augustan political constitutional reorganization of the peninsula could emerge. As an example, from my work[32] on the *octoviri* of Trebula Mutuesca one can easily extract that an older magistracy was either resurrected or readapted in the transformation of Trebula from a *vicus* to a *municipium*. This older magistracy should be linked to the presence in the area of Roman colonists from the viritane deductions of Curius Dentatus. It may be that this magistracy was considered "Sabine" (cfr. the *octoviri* at Amiternum) by those who had conceived the reorganization of the territory. These archaizing tendencies under Augustus occur frequently in the constitutional progress of ancient Italy, as the recent example of the attribution of *Luna* to *Regio* VII proves (Pliny, *N.H.* 3, 5, with Livy, 41, 13, 3–5). The so-called throne of Claudius (a monument in some respects to be compared to the Tiberian base at Sorrento)—is it really of Claudius?—from Cerveteri perhaps may be linked with the particular Claudian ties to the Etruscan senate but to Cerveteri itself in particular. For example, we should remember the marriage with Plautia Urgulanilla, descendent of Urgulania, probably Caeretan, and now the presence of *Clavtie-Claudii* at Cerveteri in the fifth century B.C.,[33] even if this last event is rather remote in time and very likely unknown to Claudius himself.

In a sense, the problem is bound to remain open at least until one can reexcavate the theater at Caere and new discoveries, at Cerveteri as elsewhere, can provide us with a richer and broader picture than the one we now possess of the municipal life of the Etruscan cities: consider the building of the Augustales at Rusellae with its rich sculpture of the Julio-Claudian family and new important Latin inscriptions. Regardless of the need for more information and the detailed observations made here, Liou's *Praetores Etruriae* remains an important book for all scholars of Etruscan and Roman antiquity. The diligence and care of the author, the sagacious prosopographic research, up-to-date and exact, the collection of a dispersive and poorly known body of material are laudable. It is these aspects which will certainly stimulate new studies which, in the light of what Liou has shown, should not be deferred indefinitely. Surely stimulating further research is the principal hope of those who undertake scholarly research.

NOTES

1. Liou 1969.
2. Cfr. *BMC Emp.*, IV, pl. LV., pls. 6, 5; 29, 5; 30, 4, 10; 31, 2, 6, etc. The thesis of Strack 1931: 233, n. 984, accepted by Liou 1969: 13, n. 9, about a presumed tie between Ariccia and Nerva is without foundation.
3. Torelli 1969: 312–16.
4. *BMC Emp.*, III, Hadr. nr. 324, pl. 52, 15 for the coins. For the Uffizi relief, Ryberg 1955: 132 f., pl. XLVI, fig. 71.
5. *NSc* 1925: 224. Liou 1969: 15, n. 3, strangely omits the reference to *AE* 1926: n. 123.

6. Syme 1957: 309.
7. For the Dasumii in Apulia, Syme 1957: 791, and on Canusium, Torelli 1969: 298.
8. Liou omits a reference to the text edition in *Inscr. It.*
9. Stein 1940: 43.
10. *NSc* 1919: 207.
11. *NSc* 1940: 189.
12. *CIL* XI, 1432 = *Inscr. It.* VII, 1, n. 16: *praetori Etruriae (quinquies) Pisis [quinquennali].*
13. Pallottino 1955–56: 67.
14. *CIL* XI, 1432 = *Inscri. It.* VII, 1 nn. 16–17.
15. Groag 1931: 157.
16. Pflaum 1966: 154.
17. Panciera 1963–64: 94 ff.
18. *NSc* 1916: 3.
19. Cfr. *CIL* VI, 537 = *ILS*, 2944.
20. Torelli 1969: 345, n. 6 and 352 ff., n. 79.
21. Thulin 1907: 47.
22. Bormann 1887: 114, n. 14.
23. Taylor 1960: 89.
24. Badian 1963: 133.
25. Cristofani 1967: 616.
26. An inscription from Tarquinia provides another possible *aediles*, Torelli 1975.
27. De Dominicis 1949: 67 ff.
28. Gascou 1967: 609 ff.
29. Olzscha 1969: 290 ff.
30. As in Pfiffig 1966.
31. Lambrechts 1959: 72.
32. Torelli 1963: 262 ff.
33. Pallottino 1969: 79ff.

BIBLIOGRAPHY

Badian, E.

1963 "Notes on the Senators of the Roman Republic," *Historia* XII: 129–43.

Bastianelli, S.

1940 "Civitavecchia," *Nsc:* 183–98.

Bendinelli, G.

1919 "Bolsena-Silloge epigrafica," *NSc:* 206–9.

BMC

1927 *British Museum Coin Collection. A Guide to the Exhibition of Roman Coins in the British Museum.* London.

Bormann, E.

1887 *Inscriptiones Aemiliae Etruriae Umbriae Latinae.*

Cristofani, M.

1967 "Un *cursus honorum* di Cerveteri," *StEtr* XXV: 609–18.

Cultrera, G.

1916 "Tomba a camera etrusco-romana scoperta in Bettona," *NSc:* 3–29.

De Dominicis

1949 "L'Umbria nell'ordinamento della Diocesis Italiciana," 67–98, 1949. *Università di Perugia, Annali della Facoltà di Giurisprudenza,* 59.

Fronzaroli, P.

1969 "Studi sul lessico comune semitico," *RendAccLinc* XXIV: 285–320.

Gascou, J.

1967 "Le rescrit d'Hispellum," *MEFR:* 609–59.

Groag, E.

1931 "Prosopographische Bemerkungen," *WienSt:* 157–60.

Lambrechts, R.

1959 *Essai sur les magistratures des républiques étrusques.* Bruxelles.

Liou, B.

1969 *Praetores Etruriae XV populorum.* Bruxelles.

Olzscha, K.

1969 "Etruskischer Litteraturbericht," *Glotta* XLVII: 279–323.

Pallottino, M.

1955–56 "Nuovi spunti di ricerca sul tema delle magistrature etrusche," *StEtr* XXIV: 45–72.

1969 "L'ermeneutica etrusca tra due documenti chiave," *StEtr* XXXVII: 79–91.

Panciera, S.

1963–64 "Ancora sui consoli dell'anno 13 d.C.," *BCAR* LXXIX: 94–98.

Pfiffig, A.J.

1966 *Die Ausbreitung des römischen Stadtewesens in Eturien*. Firenze.

Pflaum, H.

1966 *Les sodales antoniniani de l'époque de Marc Aurèle*. Roma.

Ryberg, S.

1955 *Rites of the State religion in Roman Art MAAR* XXII. New Haven.

Saria, B.

1970 *Antike Inschriften aus Jugoslavien*[2]. Amsterdam.

Stein, A.

1940 *Die Legaten von Moesian*. Budapest.

Strack, P.L.

1931 *Untersuchungen zur römischen Reichspragung des zweiten Jahrunderts*. Stuttgart.

Syme, R.

1957 "Ceionii and Vettuleni," *Athenaeum* XXXV: 306–15.

Taylor, Lily Ross

1960 *The Voting Districts of the Roman Republic*. Roma.

Thulin, C.O.

1907 *Die etruskische Disciplin*. Goteborg.

Torelli, M.

1963 "Trebula Mutuesca. Iscrizioni corrette ed inedite," *RAL* XVIII: 230–84.

1969 "Senatori etruschi della tarda repubblica e dell'impero," *DdA* III: 285–363.

1975 *Elogia Tarquiniensia*. Firenze.

NSc Concordance

1916 = Cultrera, G.

1919 = Bendinelli, G.

1940 = Bastianelli, S.

5

A *TEMPLUM AUGURALE* OF THE REPUBLICAN PERIOD AT *BANTIA*

In 1962 at Banzi (ancient *Bantia*) six small rectangular inscribed *cippi* were found during the construction of the heating system for the community nursery school. The sides of the *cippi* are barely worked except for the rounded top side which carries the inscriptions: the thickness of this rounded top varies from two to six centimeters. Unfortunately, I do not know the precise circumstances concerning the actual discovery: from the municipal secretary, Sig. G. Labriola, and the urban policeman of Banzi, Sig. S. Cantiani, I understand that the six *cippi* were found at a depth of 2.44 meters from the modern ground level and were stuck in virgin soil so that only the rounded inscribed face projected above the ancient ground level. Furthermore, they were arranged in two lines of three *cippi* each, equidistant (3.30 m) from each other. That the *cippi* were oriented in a north-south direction, as reported by those present, is extremely important. Unfortunately, we do not know the order in which the *cippi* were arranged: this would be crucial to our understanding of the complex. The municipal secretary maintains that *cippus* no. 6 was placed so that the inscription was oriented obliquely in a north-south direction. One of the workmen with whom I spoke said that during the excavation he saw an apparently regular very large stone west of the two rows of *cippi* (Fig. 5.1).

The six *cippi*, all in local limestone, are:

1. *cippus*, ht. 41 cm, top diam. 35 cm, inscription: letter ht. 8 cm
CAEN (Plate 5.1a)

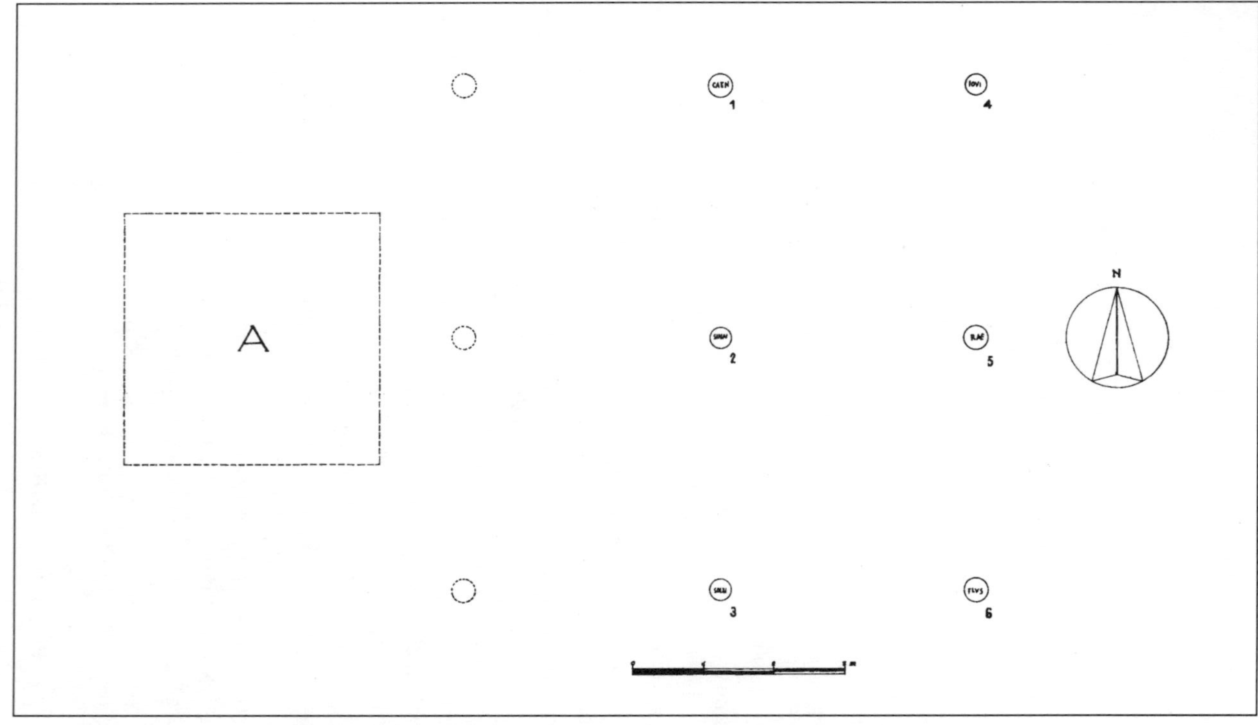

Fig. 5.1—Reconstruction of the Augural temple of Bantia
The numbers indicate the cippi in the same order as they are presented in the text. The letter A indicates the "large stone" to the west of the *Templum* (imaginary size).

2. *cippus*, ht. 44 cm, top diam. 29.8 cm, inscription: letter ht. 6.9 cm
SINAV (Plate 5.1b)

3. *cippus*, ht. 45.5 cm, top diam. 31 cm, inscription: letter ht. 6.3–6.7 cm
SOLEI (Plate 5.1c)

4. *cippus*, ht. 56 cm, top diam. 29 cm, inscription: letter ht. 5.6 cm
IOVI (Plate 5.2a)

5. *cippus*, ht. 37 cm, top diam. 34 cm, inscription: letter ht. 8 cm
RAVE (Plate 5.2b)

6. *cippus*, ht. 37 cm, top diam. 34 cm, inscription: letter ht. 6.5–6.8 cm
FLVS (Plate 5.2c)

The letters are the same on all the *cippi*, except for *cippus* no. 4. The other five have regular letter forms that are fairly wide for the *L*, *F*, *E*, *N*, *A*, *V* while the *S* and *C* are rounded. *Cippus* no. 4 is distinguished by its rather small letters and its dimensions: the height is noteworthy. Additionally, the inscription on *cippus* no. 4 seems to have a slightly less archaic flavor: it may have been a replacement for a *cippus* destroyed or damaged earlier.

The date of the stones is within the first century B.C. on the basis of the archaic dative form '*ei*' (*Solei*) and for the inclusion of a divinity (and perhaps more than one) who belongs to the Oscan pantheon (*Flusa; Rave?*)

The six *cippi*—along with three other *cippi* almost certainly still *in situ* and outside of the excavated area—belong to a unique monument which up to now we know of only by literary testimony: an augural temple. I hope to demonstrate that such an identification provides the most appropriate explanation for the inscriptions themselves and their significance. Of these inscriptions, two are fully written out and thus easily understood. No. 3, *Solei*, is the dative of the divinity *Sol*, and no. 4, *Iovi*, is clearly the dative of *Iuppiter*. The text of no. 6 *Flus(ae)* or *Flus(ai)* is the name of a goddess in the central Italic pantheon, cited in several Oscan inscriptions and alluded to in the name of a month found in Osco-Latin sources.[1]

The mere identification of this divinity allows us to understand that

Plate 5.1a—Cippus no. 1.

Plate 5.1b—Cippus no. 2.

Plate 5.1c—Cippus no. 3.

Plate 5.2a—Cippus no. 1.

Plate 5.2b—Cippus no. 2.

Plate 5.2c—Cippus no. 3.

the portion with the favorable (certainly *Iuppiter* in this case) divinities of the augural temple was in the eastern section while *Sol* implies a southern placement. In brief, of this augural temple with eight seats, we have the north-south line with a central *cippus* which is the central point for all four axes as well as the diagonals of the *templum*. The three *cippi* which refer to the *pars familiaris* are the northeast, the east and the southeast. Now we can attempt to interpret the other three *cippi*. The passage of Martianus Capella I, 45 which has long been recognized as an important fragment of a text referring to the Etruscan augural discipline helps us to read *cippus* no. 1 as *Cae(lus) N(octurnus)* and thus to place it at the extreme north of the *templum*. *Cippus* no. 2, however one plays with the abbreviation, is not plausibly the name of a divinity nor of a pair of divinities.[2] I see no other possible interpretation than *s(edes) inau(gurationis)*.

A clear reading of no. 5 is not possible, although I will suggest a reading based essentially on the position of the *cippus* in the monument.

With these premises, we should now examine the sources on the form and origin of the augural temple. S. Weinstock has addressed the problem in two different and exemplary studies;[3] now the monument at *Bantia* sheds new light on the question.

The passage of Varro (*Ling*. VII, 6) is critical: "*templum tribus modis dicitur, ab natura, ab auspicando, a similitudine: a natura in caelo, ab auspiciis in terra, a similitudine sub terra*." These distinctions are only partially comprehensible: we have a *templum caeleste* which is the natural *templum*: the sky. Then we have a *templum in terra* (from which *auguria* and *auspicia* are drawn) and lastly a *templum a similitudine*. For this last *templum* we can only think of objects considered pertinent to temples by assimilation or resemblance (for example, *exta* of animals), a significance, however, contradicted by its being "*sub terram*."

Festus and Servius go even further and describe for us how the *templa in terra* were constructed. Festus (P. 157 M, 146 L) says in fact "*minora templa fiunt ab auguribus cum loca aliqua tabulis aut linteis sepiuntur, ne uno amplius ostio pateant, certis verbis definita. Itaque templum est locus ita effatus aut ita septus, ut ex una parte pateat angulosque adfixos habeat ad terram*." Servius (*ad. Aen*. IV, 200) less organically instead states "*alii templum dicunt non solum quod potest claudi, verum etiam quod palis aut hastis aut aliqua tali re et linteis (lineis, Mss.) aut loris aut simili re saeptum est, quod effatum est, amplius uno exitu in eo esse non oportet, cum ibi sit cubitururs auspicans*." Varro, in another famous passage (*Ling*. VII, 8) gives us the definition and the inaugural formula of a *templum* in the earth: "*in terris dictum templum locus augurii aut auspicii causa quibusdam conceptis verbis finitus. Concipitur verbis non [h]isdem usque quaque; in arce sic: [i] tem<pla> tescaque † me ita sunto quoad ego † easte lingu[m] noncupavero. Ullaber arbos quirquir est, quam me sentio dixisse, templum tescumque[m] † festo in sinistrum. Ollaner arbos quirquir est, quod me sentio dixisse te<m>plum tescumque[m] † festo dextrum. Inter ea corregione conspicione cortumione utique ea erectissime sensi.*" E. Norden[4] and S. Weinstock[5] have both amply commented on the parallels with sacred formulaic language, and Weinstock has also corrected, as Seowasser earlier, the *me ita* in the manuscript tradition to "*metata*" or the like. I would add that "*tescumquem festo*" could be corrected to *tescumque m(ihi) f(initum) esto* rather than to *m(eum) f(initum)* as Bergk proposed.[6]

Varro continues (*Ling.* VII, 9) to explain this formula, probably little understood even in his own time: "*in hoc templo faciundo arbores constitui fines apparent*," that is, the boundaries of the *templum in terra* are trees. Festus returns to this same point in his *templum minus* for which it is proscribed that *angulos adfixos habeat in terra*, namely, the *palis aut hastis aut aliqua tali re* of Servius. Not only does this agree with the etymology of *templum*,[7] but it also corresponds extremely well to our *cippi* which represent the ends of the *cardo*, of the *decumanus*, and the four corners of the *templum*.[8] The *cippi* were stuck in the earth with only their rounded faces visible and are worked so as to represent trees, the original boundaries of the temple. Nor are they unlike archaic milestones and the *cippi* of Gracchan divisions.[9] This is a further demonstration that urban subdivisions, field measurements, and procedures for auspices derive from the same sacral-juridical source and used analogous methods,[10] just as the Gromatics explicitly tell us.[11] The same relationship is unequivocably established by the sequence in the Gubbio Table VI-a. The *templum minus* (as opposed to the *templum maius*, the celestial one) or if one prefers, the *templum in terra* had its corners indicated by *pali* or *hastae* and its walls indicated by wooden boards or strips of linen or by leather straps and its function, as already noted, was tied to the *auspicia* and the *auguria*.[12] The augur performed his prayers using *arcani sermones*[13] or *concepta verba*[14] in order to *effari* and *liberare* the place when the auspicant, entitled to the *spectio*, awaited the omen. At this point the work of the augur, requested by the auspicant with a *stipulatio*,[15] was limited to a prayer and the *nuntiatio* of the portents.[16] The new monument at *Bantia* perhaps clarifies another obscure element in the augural ceremony, the *tescum*. Modern scholars have variously understood this unclear word because, first, it had been given the same importance as the *templum*,[17] and second, one wanted it to be a particular technical term, probably of Sabine origin,[18] used in the augural formula. The sources actually seem to support both hypotheses. In every instance the original significance of the word seems to be "rock, stone" and not "earth freed from evil spirits" as Latte would have it.[19] A very corrupt passage in Festus (P. 356 M, 488 L, cf. *exc.* 48 L) distinguishes precisely all the external elements which enter into the augural act when he says "*<Tesca sun>t loca augurio desig<nata. . . . . ? termino finis in terra auguri. Op[p]illus . . . >lius loca consecrata ad. . . . . . sit. Sed sancta loca undique <saepta? doce?>nt pontifici[s] libri, in quibus* <scriptum est? templum>*que sedemque tescumque. . . . . . dedicaverit, ubi eos (scil. deos) ac<cipiat volentes> propitiosque.*" Clearly the priestly text delineates a *templum*, the space where the auspices are taken, a *sedes*, the place where the auspicant sits, and a *tescum*. The word also appears in the augural formulae outlined by Varro and discussed above. In that formula, however, there is no word for *sedes*, simply because the auspicant has yet to participate, but *tescum* is mentioned. The *tescum* is either the bedrock, the stone on which the augur sits (cfr. Livy I, 18.7) which is distinct from the auspicant's *sedes* (*infra*) or, if we give greater weight to Varro,[20] the stone or rock that the augur had consecrated to a divinity, in our case the *cippi* and thus the boundaries. Of the two explanations I prefer the first, not only because of its adherence to the sources but also because it is probable that the "large stone" seen during the excavation to the west of the *cippi* could be the '*tescum*' of the Bantian *auguraculum*. This stone, placed to the west but with respect to the *templum* in *terris* which are the *cippi* oriented to the east is exactly the direction that the augur should be facing during the augural ceremony. If we interpret *tescum* thusly, we would have the advantage of resolving the not insignificant problem of the *lapides augurales* of the Gubbio Tables.

The documentation presented by the Gubbio Tables is fundamental to our discussion for its intrinsic value as well as for what it tells us about the spread of the concepts of augural science.[21] We are told that *auspicium* precedes all ceremonies of public propitiation (I-a, 1–2; I-b, 8; I-b, 10–14; VI-a, 16–18; VI-b, 48–49) and in one case of a private ceremony (II-a, 17): at Rome where were both *auspicia publica* and *auspicia privata*. We also have a description of the *auspicium* itself (VI-a, 1–7). The description closely connects[22] the guidelines for the *limitatio* of the augural temple (VI-a, 8–11) and those of the *pomerium* (VI-a, 12–16) and the *nuntiatio* of the augur (VI-a, 16–19). Shortly I shall present the points of comparison between the ceremony at Gubbio and the Roman augural rite. Clearly the *auspicium* ceremony is performed by two people using real and formal *stipulatio*,[23] between the augur, the interpreter of the *oscines*, the divine signs, and the auspicant. If the auspices are favorable, the *stipulatio* reinforces the sacerdotal authority (and the magisterial authority since it includes a *lustratio populi*), just as we gather from the Roman sources. The petitioner sits (VI-a, 2. . . . *eso; tremnu serse* . . . ; (VI-a, 5). . . . *sersi, pirsi sesust* . . .) in a *tabernaculum* (VI-a 2 and 16) . . . *tremnu* . . .) while the augur is in an established position (VI-a, 5: *esmei stahmei stahmeitei* . . .):[24] this too is found in the Roman sources.[25] The whole procedure obviously unrolls according to the norm and formula of the *stipulatio* (VI-a, 1–5) with the necessary clause of ceremonial *silentium* (VI-a, 5–8).[26] Next come the explicit descriptions of the ceremonial place the *templum* (VI-a, 8–11). The *templum* must be within well-established pomerial limits (VI-a, 10–11 . . . *todcome tuder ---bis------;* . . . *todceir tuderus* . . .) and in connection with the *ara divina* placed near the *angulus imus* of the *templum* (VI-a, 8–10: *agluto hondomu porsei nesimei asa deueia est* . . . ; *agluto hondomu asame deueia* . . .), and with the *lapides augurales* where there is the *angulus summus* (. . . *anglome somo porsei nesimei uapersus auiehcleir* . . . ; *angluto some uapefe auiehclu* . . .) In the next lines the Table mentions the *pomerium* whose line is critical to the definition of the augural *templum*. Even though most of the topographic notations are largely unintelligible because they are tied to the toponymns used in Umbrian Gubbio, the sense is that the *sedes augurales* (and thus the *arae divinae* are in the center of the *pomerium* and that within the whole *pomerium* it is permissible to perform the appropriate auspices (VI-a, 15–16). The connection between this pomerial line and the one of Romulus is, from a conceptual point of view, certain.[27] The passage about the *templum* is much discussed and controversial.[28] The only way to unravel this complex knot is to suppose that the *uapefe auiehclu* are the two augural *sedes*, that of the augur (thus that of the *arsfertur*) and the one of the auspicant,[29] and that these two seats are on the same line as the divine altar, and that line, in turn, is parallel to the *pomerium*, more or less as Vetter suggested.

In this way, an augural temple can be either quadrangular or square, which is logical and which conforms to the new monument from Banzi.

It is not logical to presuppose triangular and circular constructions with which the discussions on the problem abound.[31]

There is an old antinomy in the sources about the orientation: for some (Varro, *Ling.* VII, 7; Festus, P. 339 M, 454 L; Pliny, *N.H.* II, 143) the orientation should be towards the south but according to others (Livy I, 18.6; Dionysius Halicarnasseus, II, 5.2–3; Plutarch, *Quaest. Rom.* 78; Servius, *ad Aen.* II, 693; Isidorus, *Etym.* XV, 4.7) it should be towards the east. In fact, it is possible that such an antinomy may derive from a confusion between the direction in which the augur and the auspicant should be facing.[32] The augur should be facing east and the auspicant south as is obvious from the very important passage in Livy concerning Numa's inauguration. If we had had more precise information about what was found at Banzi we might have resolved the controversy.

The *templum* at *Bantia* confirms F. Brown's intuition about the monument which he found on the *arx* of the Latin colony of Cosa.[33] He termed the structure the "Square" and identified it as the *auguraculum*, created when the colony was founded. The coincidences are extraordinary: the Cosa *templum* and the Bantia *templum* are both on the *arx*,[34] with a similar orientation. From the quadrant (the πλινθίον of Plutarch, *Rom.* 22 and *Cam.* 32) which lies between the northeast and northwest you get a complete view of the city and the axes of the "Square" are on a north-south and east-west line: at Cosa the axes have a slight twelve-degree shift towards the east from the north side. The measurements are also similar: the sides of the platform at Cosa measure 7.40 meters (25 feet), while at Banzi the distance between the single *cippi* (taken from the outside edge of each *cippus* by those present at the excavation) is equal to 3.30 meters which results in a total measure (including the *cippi*) of 7.50 meters, practically identical to that of Cosa. Additionally, the distance between the centers of the *cippi* are 3.60 meters circa, equal to 12 feet, a number sacred to all theological and theosophic speculations of the ancient world in general and the Etrusco-Italic world in particular.

Another important point is the much discussed (and much denied) relationship between the augural *templum* and "Himmelsteilung."[35] We have proof that the transposition of the celestial sphere (Varro's *templum in caelo*) was divided by astronomical-theological criteria into a number of *sedes* occupied by divinities of diverse character and spheres of influence, all on one surface, one space, one *locus.* This was not only known to the augural science but was actually a fundamental element in the entire procedure of *auspicia*.[36] This is not the place to examine when and under what impulse this may have entered into the Etruscan-Italic world but it will suffice to note that there was a deep common mediterranean interest in oionoscopy in which the various favorable and unfavorable signs are classified by the quality of the *signum* (type of bird, type of cry, etc.) and the provenience.[37] From this, one can pass to a hermeneutic of *signa* (not just birds but lightning, etc.) based principally on provenience. We can say that in all probability these astrological conceptions are widespread in the Etruscan world (from whence they passed to the Roman-Italic world) already by the late sixth century B.C. if, as I believe, the "stars" mentioned in the Punic text of Pyrgi are to be understood in the sense transmitted to us by Festus.[38] The star, which Ateius Capito (and his source the augur P. Servilius) in a euphemistic manner interpret as a symbol of *laetum et prosperum loci inaugurati*, of that same "Himmelsteilung," is the kind of compass which the augur traced out to achieve the division of space. Now, even if it does not seem that the Roman augural ritual included divinities other than Jupiter,[39] we have evidence that in the *libri augurum* of Rome reference was made to other divinities.[40] This could mean that the *signa* were connected to various divinities, at least from a certain period onwards, although when and how this may have happened is difficult to establish. Orphic literature certainly recognized an *ogdoas*,[41] and it is likely that the Etruscan—and Roman—speculation on the division of the templum *in caelo* originates from this sort of religious and philosophical conception. In any event, the crucial incentive for this decisive transformation of augural doctrine ought to derive from the Etruscan fulgural discipline which elicited the interest of Roman antiquarians in the second-first century B.C., who probably had access to translated texts starting from the second century.[42] The diffusion of these concepts, however, should probably go back to at least the third century B.C.,[43] the period to which the inscription from Ardea, *CIL* I², 455 = Vetter 364 b,[44] is dated. The influence on the "Himmelsteilung" of the *fulguratoria* quickly must have reached also the haruspicine, to judge from the Piacenza Liver usually dated to the third century B.C., if this science is not also derived from models inspired or coming directly from the Orient.[45] The haruspicine discipline always was, up to the very latest periods, considered a national Etruscan one.[46] The fulgural science instead was known at Rome from the most archaic times: the "Blitzlehre" has always had a major role in Roman augural science.[47]

To examine the significance and position of the individual *cippi* in the *templum*, I will make continual reference to the fragment of the Etruscan discipline quoted by Martianus Capella (I, 14 ff) and to the famous Piacenza Liver.[48]

The *Cae(lus) N(octurnus)* of *cippus* 1 constitutes at the outset a major difficulty. Martianus puts a *Nocturnus* in seats one and sixteen: this is obviously an unfavorable divinity located (as the name indicates) in the north. *Nocturnus* appears in four dedications (*CIL* III, 1956 = *ILS*, 4887, 9753, 14243^{2}, *CIL* V, 4287 = *ILS*, 4888) found in Dalmatia and in Italy. The name of the god as it appears in the Bantian text seems to be a ἅπαξ. Luckily, Plautus, *Amph.*, vv. 271–84 clarifies the situation. His verses contain a clear allusion to the sky and thus we can uderstand *Nocturnus* as an adjective: the substantive *Caelus* is omitted. In Plautus, the god is placed in opposition to another divinity, *Sol*, who also is in our *templum* and, I believe, opposite *Cae(lus) N(octurnus).* In the verses Sosia complains about the length of the famous night:

Sosia: "*certe edepol, si quicquamst aliud quod credam aut certo sciam,*
credo ego hac noctu Nocturnum obdormivisse ebrium.
nam neque se Septentriones quoquam in caelo commovent,
neque se Luna quoquam mutat atque ut exorta est semel,
nec Iugulae neque Vesperugo neque Vergiliae occidunt.
ita statim stant signa, neque nox quoquam concedit die."
Mercurius: "*perge, Nox, ut occepisti; gere patri morem meo:*
optimo optime optimam operam das, datam pulchre locas."
Sosia: "*neque ego hac nocte longiorem me vidisse conseo:*
nisi item unam, verberatus quam pependi perpetem;
eam quoque edepol etiam multo haec vicit longitudine.
credo edepol equidem dormire Solem atque adpotum probe;
mira sunt nisi invitavit sese in cena plusculum."

It is obvious that Sosia is speaking about the god of the night-time sky and its starry face (and thus *Nocturnus* is not to be confused with *Lucifer-Vesper).*[49] With this identification, we can turn to Varro (*Ling.* V, 58): "*Terra enim et Coelum, ut Samothracum initia docent, sunt dei magni. . . . . . : sic pater magnus, mater magna, his sunt Caelus* <Tellus>": I will return to the connection with the *di magni* of Samothrace in another identification.[50]

The epigraphic evidence for *Nocturnus* is marked by an extraordinary circumstance already noted by others but variously interpreted. Two dedications come from Salona (*CIL* III, 1956 = *ILS*, 4887, 14243²). Of the two one was found in the same place as three other fascinating dedications, on the land of one Anton Grgic-Barko. Of the three found together, one was to a *Liber pater* (*CIL* III, 14224 1) and the other two are to a *Deus Magnus conservator loci* <h>uius (*CIL* III, 14242, 1–2 = *ILS*, 7310). It is curious that there are dedications to such diverse divinities in one place. All the divinities, however, are found together in the astrological cycle of Martianus.

This fact becomes even more interesting when we note that again from Salona (no more precisely than that) we have other dedications to a *Liber pater* (*CIL* III, 1951), to *Silvanus* (*CIL* III, 1957–60) and to *Consen[ti]o deorum* (*CIL* III, 1935 = *ILS*, 4005). These must be compared to Martianus VII *Liber*—Liver 7 *fufluns*, and Martianus VIII *Veris fructurs* (*Silvanus?*)—Liver 8 *selva*, and Martianus I *Di consentes penates*—Liver 16 *tin*/*θvf.* I wonder whether the Salona dedications were not part of a monument similar to that at Bantia or at least inspired by the well known astrological precepts. The situation could gain further credence in the fact that in the late period augural science found a welcome reception in the Illyrian-Pannonian regions as did many other characteristics of *prisca romanitas.*[51] In the third century A.D. the *augures pannoniaci* were quite famous (*SHA Sept. Sev.* 10.7; *Alex. Sev.* 27.6) as the recently discovered tomb at Brigetio demonstrates (dated to the third century A.D.) with its contents, the characteristic *lituus* and the ritual *prefericolus.*

Cae(lus) N(octurnus) must be absolutely to the north, as Weinstock[52] and Pallottino[53] read the Piacenza Liver and Martianus. Pallottino actually has proposed a displacement of two seats in Martianus's text, thereby beginning with north between seat fourteen of the Liver (*cilen*) and seat fifteen (*tinc-cilen*). Whatever it may be, the orientation of the Liver and thus the order of the gods in Martianus must not be fixed by locating the cardinal points between one divine seat and the other but rather by making the cardinal points coincide with the seats, which among other things on the basis of the new document are all the same size, as Biedl noted some time ago.[54] *Nocturnus-cilen* and north coincide: this is one of the more relevant conclusions to be drawn from the new monument.

The interpretation of *cippus* no. 3 *Solei* is clear. The cult of *Sol* is said to go back to a very ancient period, indeed to the "Sabine" kings.[55] There was a cult of *Sol* at Rome on the Quirinal, the hill traditionally linked to the "Sabine cults"[56] and *in Circo,* with distinct festivals. Near Lavinium there was a sanctuary tied to an ancestral cult of Aeneas[57] where *Sol Indiges* was worshipped along the banks of the river Numicus. Perhaps this god should be identified with *Lar Aineias,* as has been recognized recently by more than one scholar.[58] The god is much venerated but the sequence of the inclusion in the *templum* at *Bantia* is owed not so much to the recognition of the antiquity of the cult but rather to the belief that the *templum* was an earthly projection of the heavenly sphere through which the sun passed. To *Cae(lus) N(octurnus),* the face of the starry sky (in which the *Septentriones* shine, to quote Plautus)[59] was without sunshine and thus wholly northern. The sun, the solar disc at the zenith, the perfect midday, was placed in opposition to *Caelus:* thus *Cae(lus)* and *Sol* represent the two extremities of the *cardo.* As we will see, this solar (and astrological) theology is at the core of the *templum* partition and is repeated in the other seats of the Bantian monument. The correspondence between the list of Martianus Capella and the Piacenza Liver seems correct: in seat six Martianus puts a *Celeritas Solis filia,* while the Liver, in opposition to 14 *cilen* (identified with *Caelus Nocturnus*), puts at 6 *caθ* and in the sixth internal seat *caθa* which is identified with the sun or more specifically with a particular aspect of the sun.[60] Thus, I think that what Pallottino suggested for the displacement of seats in Martianus has been demonstrated.[61]

Now let us examine the *cippus* with the dedication to *Iovi.* This seat, undoubtedly, goes at the northeast of the *templum,* it seems to me, and thus constitutes an *angulus. Iuppiter* appears in the first three seats of Martianus and in frames 14 *tin/cilen* and 15 *tin/θvf* of the Liver. The importance of the divinity in the Etruscan and Italic pantheon, perhaps combined with the fulgural discipline, makes it possible that he should appear in more than one seat.[62] Once it is established that *cilen* is the north, then the position that he holds in the Liver is north-northeast and northeast. This is an orientation which, as Pallottino observed,[63] corresponds to the orientation of the axes of most Etruscan temples and to the temple of Jupiter Capitolinus in Rome.[64] It is clear from the sources that the quadrant with its center at the northeast was considered the most favorable.[65]

The other angulus is *Flus(ae).* She was a very popular Oscan divinity in the areas around *Bantia* and is known to us from numerous sources.[66]

She is identified with the Roman *Flora*, who, the ancient authors uniformly agree, had an extremely ancient Sabine or Italic origin.[67] Her origin is certainly Italic, and she is assimilated with the Greek divinity Demeter rather than Aphrodite 'Ανθεία, as is widely held.[68] This identification is the only one that accords with historical data, given the immense popularity of Demeter in the Italiote Greek cities. *Flusa-Flora*, for her very nature, as Demeter, was associated with *Ceres*.[69] It is not accidental that *Ceres* and *Flora* festivals are so close together in the Roman calendar.[70]

That the Oscan divinity is present in the Bantian *templum* is explicable only by the popularity the goddess must have enjoyed locally: in this respect she should be considered in the category of "*municipalia sacra.*"[71]

Bantia after the Social War was then elevated to a *municipium*. It is not possible that, if Bantia had been a colony, in a monument so important to public life such as the *auguratorium* a divinity foreign to the Roman pantheon should appear. Only the Roman pantheon was permitted in centers of purest Roman culture—which colonies were. Additionally, Bantia was that particular type of *municipium* in which *duoviri* were the highest magistrates, if the observation is correct.[72]

How can we place the *cippus* in accord with Martianus and the Liver? In the fourth position Martianus puts *Lynsa silvestris* (?) and *Mulciber* and in the fifth, *Ceres Tellurus, Terrae pater Vulcanus.* The two seats immediately preceding that of *Celeritas Solis filia* mentioned above are earth-goddesses, the mysterious *Lynsa*, who is connected by the adjective *silvestris* to the forests, *Ceres, Tellus, Terra* and *Vulcan* in the double aspect of *Vulcan* and of *Mulciber*. In the Liver we have instead in seat II *uni/mae*, in the third *tec/um* and in the fifth *eθ*. A theoretical identification with *Minerva*[73] *eθ* is possible for *tecum* which seems both to be completed into *eθ(ausva)* and to be identified with the Greek goddess *Eilytheia*.[74] In seat two *Uni* appears (latin *Juno*) and has a chthonic character equal to that of *Menerva-Minerva*.[75] We should also bear in mind the *interpretatio graeca* of *Uni Pyrgensis* with *Eilytheia*.[76] The argument carries even more weight when we consider that the divinity *Mae* accompanies *Uni* in seat two. This divinity must be identified with the *Maius* of Macrobius' passage (Sat. I, 12.17ff) which is strongly influenced by the Etruscan discipline:

> *sunt qui hunc mensem ad nostros fastos a Tusculanis (Tuscis? as a lectio facilior?) transisse commemorent, apud quos nunc quoque vocatur deus Maius, qui*

est Iuppiter, a magnitudine scilicet ac maiestate dictus. . . . . . Cingius mensem nominatum putat a Maia, quam Vulcani dicit uxorem, argumentumque utitur, quod flamen vulcanalis Kalendis Maiis huic deae rem divinam facit. . . . . auctor est Cornelius Labeo huic Maiae, id est terrae, aedem Kalendis Maiis dedicatam sub nomine Bonae Deae, et eandem esse Bonam Deam et terram ex ipso ritu occultiore sacrorum doceri posse confirmant.

The same idea reappears in a fragment of Lydus (*de mens* IV, 80) recently attributed to Fonteius Capito:[77] ". . . Καθ'ἕτερον δὲ ἱερὸν λόγον ὁ Φοντήιος χρῆναι τιμᾶσθαι τὴν γὴν ἐν ταῖς καλένδαις Μαίαις λέγει. . . . . ."

Maius-Maia is the Earth and is associated with *Vulcanus* not only in late sources but also in the *libri sacerdotum populi romani* (*ap.* Gellius XII, 14) where *Maia Vulcani* is an explicit connection. (Some think that like *Pomonus* and *Pales* there may be a sex change for *Maius-Maia*, but a Lucanian inscription with *Florus Iovus*, Vetter, no. 183, makes this dubious.) An analogous situation is also found in Martianus Capella where all the divinities connected with the earth or with chthonic cults appear together one after the other. In both the Liver and Martianus the position is between east and south: thus the southeast position that I have assigned to the Banzi *cippus* is probable although not mathematically certain.[78] I would add that the identification of *Flus(a)* with *Terra* finds additional support in the Varronian doctrine on the *dei magni*.

Now we can reexamine the most problematic *cippus*, no. 5, with the inscription *rave*. There are three possibilities: First, that it stands for one or more gods of the Roman pantheon as do *cippi* 1, 3, 4; second, that it may be the abbreviation of one or more gods of the Oscan pantheon as is *cippus* no. 6; third, that, as *cippus* no. 2, it may be the abbreviation of a Roman or Oscan term connected to the augural act. As for the first possibility, I see no other logical solution than *R(obigo) Ave(rrunco)*.[79] The god *Robigus* (after his transformation into a goddess *Robigo*) protected the harvests from *robigo*, that is, the grain from developing rust. On April 25 a she-dog and an ewe were sacrificed to him at the fifth mile of the via Claudia in celebration of the ancient feast of *Robigalia*. Radke, who has recently demonstrated the connection between this goddess and *Averruncus*,[80] wanted to see the name of the god in a passage of Gellius (V, 12.14) and has also correctly connected the name to the rare word *averruncare* = *avertere* (Varro, *Ling.* VII, 102). Can we insert this divine couple, conceptually one god only, into our temple? On the one hand it is true that a close interdependence between the *auguria* and harvests[81] existed and at Rome an *augurium canarium* involving the sacrifice of a red she-dog was celebrated.[82] On the other hand *vineta virgetaque inaugurare* does not necessarily imply their insertion into our *templum*, apparently dominated by philosophical-astrological speculation based on the great gods whereas this god is really a rather minor figure by the time the temple was created.

Even if the *Robigalia* were regular celebrations, the day of the *augurium canarium* was a *dies conceptivus*, a moveable celebration, and the two rites were performed in different places so that an attempt to link the augural ceremony to the harvests is a long shot. The greater difficulty, however, in sustaining this identification is that we would lose all the concordances so far found with the sources pertaining to the "Himmelsteilung." For this reason it seems futile to push forward this hypothesis although it is not to be definitively discarded.

The grounds for maintaining the second possibility are even more difficult. No Oscan documents refer to divinities that we can possibly put in relation to the text from Banzi: nonetheless, one possibility exists. On a bronze litra from Nuceria Alfaterna[83] (there are many known examples in London, Paris, and Berlin) the obverse carries the head of *Ceres* wearing a crown of grain and the legend *Nuvkrinum Alafaternum* (and variants). On the reverse, there is the figure of a Dioskouros carrying a lance and standing beside a horse with the legend (the reading is controversial):

ḍegvinum raṿạlanum.

With the exception of the nineteenth century scholars of Oscan (including Cavedoni and Corssen),[84] all modern authorities do not actually interpret the legend although they leave us to understand that we have a genitive plural.[85] It seems possible that the formula designates the god represented by the accusative singular just as the head of *Vulcan* on a roughly contemporary coin from Isernia is indicated by the accusative singular.[86] If my reasoning is correct, we would have the name of the Dioskouroi, elsewhere in the Oscan territory known as *iouieis pucleis* (Vetter, nos. 202 and 225) which translates Διὸς κοῦροι, although in our example probably they are called by another name. On the Bantian *cippus* partially or completely the name on the coin—and better still the second part of *ravalanum*—is kept. In this light, our comprehension of the Bantian *templum* can be pursued along new and important lines of development. After the discovery of a new bronze strip with an archaic Latin inscription from Lavinium it has been almost universally accepted that the Dioskouroi are to be identified with the *Penates.*[87] The *Penates* had a very famous cult at Lavinium, which probably should be identified with the sanctuary excavated by the University of Rome near Pratica di Mare.[88] The *Penates* are listed by Martianus Capella in the first region—in fact, he explicitly mentions the *Di Consentes Penates.* In the Piacenza Liver the divine name of *θufłθas* (seat sixteen/one) abbreviated as *θvf* (seats sixteen and one/one) and in this case associated with the name *tin* appears repeatedly in the most favorable areas near the *caput iecinoris* or *lobus pyramidalis* or directed towards the center of the *pars familiaris* of the object. As Thulin thought and as Pallottino was able to demonstrate on linguistic grounds *θufłθas* translates in all likelihood as *Consentes.* In fact, Martianus associated them with the Samothracian θεοὶ δυνατοί as we have seen above. Furthermore, the doctrine of Etruscan origin attributed to Nigidius Figulus (*ap.* Arnobius III, 40) lists four types of *Penates:*[89] *Iovis, Neptuni, inferorum, mortalium hominum.* A final theory of Etruscan origin and attributed to Caesius includes in the *Penates* group (even if not all are identified) *Fortuna, Ceres, Genius, Iovalis* (?), and *Pales.*[90] Of these hypotheses, that closest to the Etruscan discipline is the *Penatenlehre* quoted anonymously in Arnobius III, 40: "*hos (scil. Penates) Consentes et Complices Etrusci aiunt et nominant, quod una oriantur et occidant una, sex mares et totidem feminas, nominibus ignotis et miserationis parcissimae; sed eos summi Iovis consiliarios ac partecipes.*" The relationship to the gods on Samothrace is really part of a pseudophilosophic construction which is certainly older than Varro and very dear to him. We should reconsider the Varronian passage (*Ling.* V, 58) because from his remarks we will have a clear picture of the origin of the augural act: "*Terra enim et Caelum ut Samothracum initia docent, sunt dei magni, et hi quos dixit multis nominibus, non quas Samothracia ante portas statuit duas virilis species aeneas dei magni, neque, ut volgus putat, hi Samothraces dii, qui Castor et Pollux, sed hi mas et femina et hi quos Augurum libri scriptos habent sic "divi potes"; pro illo quod Samothraces* θεοὶ δυνατοί." This speculation about the *initia* of Samothrace has a stoic overtone according to Weinstock.[91] I have reason to believe that it is even older, if these concepts make their way into the *libri augurum* (almost certainly earlier than 300 B.C., date of the *lex Ogul-*

nia) and acquire such authority. As Weinstock himself noted, it is probable that in the construction of the eight-seat Etrusco-Italic *templum*[92] the oldest component is anti-zodiacal, namely the orphic *ogdoai* which are composed of the four elements Sun, Moon, Day and Night (fr. 300 K). It is important to note that the discovery at Lavinium can provide points of comparison. In fact, the Lavinium sanctuary (if truly of the *Penates*) is composed of twelve altars while the thirteenth was almost certainly out of use by the time the other twelve altars existed as they are on higher platforms that the thirteenth altar.[93] The platforms were erected before the fourth century B.C. according to recent information. Thus we can suppose that the identification of the *Consentes* with the *Penates* goes back to at least that period. The identification also precedes that of the *Consentes* with the δώδεκα θεοί known in Rome by the time of Ennius (*Ann.* fr. 62, Vahlen) and consecrated by the famous *lectisternium* of 217 B.C. (Livy XXII, 19.9) reformed by the *decemviri sacris faciundis* who took office in ceremonies *Graeco ritu*.

The eastern seat of the *Consentes Penates* thus accords perfectly with Arnobius' words "*. . . qui oriantur una et occidant una. . . .*"[94] These are the gods of the rising sun who function collectively and whose power was extraordinary. In this way the two *cippi* of the *cardo* and the only surviving *cippus* on the *decumanus* are tied together because they represent the path of the sun, from its zenith in the south to its nadir in the north and its rising in the east. Instead the two *cippi* of the *anguli* refer to an important divinity connected with primeval elements, in this case of the sky and of the earth: the logic of the situation seems almost to impose the proposed interpretation of the *cippus*. We should not exclude the possibility that the word *rave* may be from *ra-*, discussed above, and *ve-*. This last syllable would constitute the abbreviation of *Vesta*: the fact that the relationship between *Vesta* and the *Penates*[95] was very close only corroborates these hypotheses.

As for the third possibility, that *rave* might be an Oscan or Latin word tied to the augural ceremonies (as an equivalent of *tescum*) there is simply no evidence to sustain that argument. If the reconstruction proposed is correct, the *cippus* ought to be at the perimeter of the *templum* and in all the other cases of such placement a divinity is named. There is no alternative other than to accept the second theory until other arguments or new evidence regarding the other three *cippi* and the *pars hostilis* bring confirmation or modification of what has been suggested above.

Cippus no. 2 ought to be at the center of the *templum*. In my opinion the text should be read: *s(edes) inau(gurationis)* and indicates the center of the *templum*, the crossroads of the *cardo*, *decumanus* and diagonals in the direction of the *anguli*. An incomplete passage of Festus (347 M, 436 L) technically defines as *solida sella* this *sedes*.[96] The *sedes* of the inauguration was a stone[97] where the auspicant sat, with his face turned toward the south. This stone had, as far as one can deduce from another incomplete passage of Festus,[98] a sacred physiognomy distinct from the temple, even though it was part of it.[99] Nonetheless, the seated position is rather that of the auspice, as all the sources agree. The relationship between the *sedes* or *solida sella* and the *tabernaculum* is unclear. In every case, if the correspondence between the *lapides augurales* of the Gubbio text and the *sedes* of the auspicant and the augur, then the stone *sedes* and *tabernaculum* coexisted but they have not been identified. Furthermore, the *tabernaculum* could be moved when *vitium* existed during the act of taking possession.[100]

I can only hope for the reopening of the excavations which the Superintendent of Antiquities, D. Adamesteanu, tells me will begin again as soon as possible. From the new excavations we can certainly hope to recover at least a portion of the information lost four years ago and hope as well for other elements, above all topographic and archaeological elements, which can be added to the epigraphic and literary data gathered here.

NOTES

1. Vetter 1953: no. 21, altar in the House of the Faun, Pompei: *Fluusai;* no. 1475, line 24 in the Agnone Tablet: *Fluusai Kerriiai.* On the name of the month *flusaris,* Vetter 1953: no. 227, from Scoppito (near Amiterno): *meseneflusare; CIL* I², 756 = *ILS*, 4906 = *ILLRP*, 508, *lex Furfensis* of 58 B.C.: *mense flusare.* On the interpretation of the month, Radke 1963 and *infra* note 68.
2. E.g., dividing *S-INAV* or *SI(lvano)-NAV* does not occur as the second part of any divinity's name.
3. Weinstock 1932 and in *RE* (1934) s.v. '*Templum*'; Latte 1948 and von Blumenthal 1934.
4. Norden 1939: 16 ff.
5. Weinstock 1932: 95–100.

6. I prefer *m(ihi)*, also paleographically possible, to *m(eum)*, which is accepted by Norden 1939: 33 ff. because there is a parallel with the augural formula pronounced by the *arsfetur-augur* in the Gubbio Tables (VI-a 5: cfr. examples of this *dativus commodi* in prayers, Devoto 1940²: 148.
7. Da **tem-lo-mı* (wood) cut, according to Weinstock 1932: 102 ff.
8. *CIL* I², 21 = *ILS*, 5801 = *ILLRP*, 448 from the first half of the 3rd century B.C. and *NSc* 1953: 343 = *AE* 1955: no. 191 = *ILLRP*, 454 a.
9. *CIL* I², 639 = *ILLRP*, 470; *CIL* I², 640 = *ILLRP*, 467; *CIL* I², 643–4 = *ILLRP* 473; *ILLRP* 471 with bibliography.
10. Castagnoli 1956: 67. Cfr. Mansuelli 1965, *cippi* used for the orientation of the streets of Marzabotto.
11. Hyginus. *Grom.* 131 Th.; Frontinus 10 Th. The continued references to auspicial traditions on the part of the *Gromatici* is probably only intellectual, but it is clear that in the more ancient period, when the augural groups were the only ones to have a tried experience in astronomic observation and when culture—also the technical one—way a long way from being 'lay,' one had to go to the augural science for all the necessary operations in land division, regardless of whether it was an urbanistic or agrarian division.
12. In the *templum* both *auspicia* and *auguria* took place. According to Mommsen 1887–88, II, 1, 9 *auspicium* and *augurium* are synonyms. Cfr. Servius *ad Aen.* III 20: "*sed auspicia omnium rerum sunt, auguria certarum; auspicari enim cuivis etiam.*" Against this, Wagenvoort 1947: 38 and De Francisci 1959: 517 ff.
13. *Festus exc.* 16 M 110 L: evidently prayers said secretly in order to preserve their magical value.
14. *Varro Ling.* VII, 8 and VI, 53; Cicero *de leg.* II, 21; Servius *ad Aen.* I, 446; the term corresponds to the *arcani sermones* in note 13.
15. In Cicero *de leg.* II, 8.20 and II, 34.71 this refers to the formula used by the auspicant to ask for intervention by the augur, cfr. Gubbio Tables VI-a, 1–5. The intervention of the augur was not obligatory although it seems to have been necessary in earlier times to judge from the inauguration of Numa (Livy I, 18.6; Plutarch *Numa* 7) for people who did not have priestly authority as for example Romulus, Mommsen 1887–88, I, 105, n. 5.
16. Festus 333 M, 423 L (in parentheses, the corrections made by Mommsen): "*spectio in auguralibus ponitur pro aspectione. Et nuntiatio, quia omne ius sacrorum habent, auguribus competit (spectio, Mss.), dumtaxat quod eorum (quorum Mss.) consilio rem gerent magistratus, hos (non, Mss.) ut possent impedire nuntiando quaecumque vidissent. At his (satis, Mss.) spectio sine nuntiatione data est, ut ipsi auspicio rem gererent, non ut alios impedirent nuntiando.*" Cfr. Cicero *Phil.* 2.32.81 "*nos (scil. augures) nuntiationem solum habemus, consules et reliqui magistratus etiam spectionem.*" Cfr., also the *nuntiatio* in the Gubbio Tables

VI-a, 17: *Combifiatu* (Id. 14: *kumpifiatu*). For all the tasks of the augur, see Cicero *de leg.* II, 8.20. Cfr., also Varro *de r. r.* III 2.2 and III, 71 and *Ling.* VI, 95.

17. Weinstock 1932: 107. Bloch's suggested integration of *[t]esco* in an inscription of Lucus Feroniae *ILLRP* no. 93 is most unlikely: it may be possibly *[p]esco* (cfr. Vetter 1953: 225)?
18. Flink 1921: 56.
19. Latte 1948: 156.
20. Varro, *Ling.* VII, 10: "*loca quaedam agrestia* (and thus *deserta et difficilia*, Pseud. Acr. *ad* Hor. *Ep.* I, 14.19) *quod alicuius dei sunt, dicuntur tesca . . . tesca aiunt sancta esse qui glossas scripserunt*" Norden's interpretation 1939: 20 ff. ἱερὰ ὀργάς is unfounded either in the sources or in reality, but is based on a generic analogy which is contrary to historical logic. For a criticism of Norden's interpretation, Latte 1948.
21. Critical edition with ample apparatus is found in Devoto 1940^{2}. More recently, see Vetter 1953: 170 ff., and Pisani 1964: 126 ff.
22. The logical order of VI-a is very odd but clear. The principal argument is the *lustratio populi*, but the *lustratio* had to be performed by someone who was *inauguratus:* one begins from the auspices. But the auspices took place in the temple and thus, ruining the logical order, this becomes the topic at hand. The *templum* in turn is connected to *fines publici* and that is why the delineation of the *pomerium* is explained at this point. Only after this does the actual argument about the *lustratio* begin.
23. See Luzzatto 1934: 69 ff.
24. Vetter's translation "*huic stationi stabilitae*" (cfr. Pisani "*huic statui statuto*" but this carries another meaning) seems to me to stick more closely to the augural practices than the translation of Devoto "*in hac superficie extensa*"; von Blumenthal 1934 prefers a translation of the "die Beobachtungsgrenze" type.
25. Rose 1923 whose conclusions are not completely convincing, *infra*.
26. Ritual silence (cfr. Festus P. 348 M, 438 L, s.v. *silentio surgere* ". . . *qui post mediam* <noctem auspic>andi causa ex lectulo suo si<lens surr>exit et levatus a *lecto in solido (se posuit se) detque . . .* " and P. 351 M, 439 L s.v. *sinistrum*) occurs in many other Roman ceremonies as well as in the auspices, Latte 1960, *passim*.
27. Lugli 1952: chap. 2. The pomerium Romuli passed for all the *loci inaugurati* (Tacitus, *Ann.* XII, 24); the pomerial line is established by the *collegium augurum* (Varro, *Ling.* V, 143; the augur Messala in Gellius XIII, 14). This is also confirmed in later epigraphic sources (*CIL* VI, 1235).
28. See Devoto 1940^{2}: 161 and bibliography. The remarks by Goidanich 1934 are not particularly reliable.

29. Also the augur sat: Livy I, 18.7: "*Augur ad laevam eius (scil. Numa) capite velato sedem cepit. . . .*" The *lapides augurales* of Gubbio cannot be the stone (?) where the birds were set free as Goidanich 1934: 256 proposed.
30. Vetter 1953: 234 ff. Cfr. Tacitus, *Ann.* II, 13: "*structam ante augurale aram.*"
31. E.g., the speculations in Frothingham 1914 (circular *templum*), and 1915 (triangular *templum*), and 1917. On prehistoric connections, Rose 1931, but his hypotheses are without foundation.
32. Already proposed by Bouche-Leclerq 1882: 188 ff., and countered by Rose 1923 on the basis of a famous passage in Cicero *de off.* III, 66 (cfr. Valerius Maximus VIII, 2, I) in which he tells the story of the augurs who forced the destruction of Ti. Claudius Centumalus' house on the Caelian Hill (south of the Capitol) because it disturbed the aupices on the *arx*. Rose's objections are not particularly valid as the augurs, in accord with the *ius augurale*, were also safeguards of the *spectio* of magistrates (towards the south).
33. Brown et al., 1960: 11 ff.
34. The *arx* and the *auguraculum* are very closely tied: cfr. Varro *Ling.* VII, 8 "*. . . in arce sic.*" (cfr. also V, 47) and the note (probably confused in the source) in Festus, *exc.* P. 18 L: "*Auguraculum appellabant antiqui quam nos arcem dicimus, quod ibi augures publice auspicarentur.*" The augural rite in the Gubbio Tables occurred on the *arx* (and not in the forum as Goidanich 1934: 244 ff. has it). But what was the connection with the *auguraculum* (Varro *Ling.* VII, 8) on the Quirinal (cfr. *CIL* VI, 976 = *ILS*, 317)?
35. The correspondence and relative transposition of the *templum caeleste* and *templum in terris*, defended energetically by Müller and Deecke 1877: 124 ff. and recently reconsidered, Deubner 1925: 457 ff. is not supported in any of the numerous ancient sources (Regell 1882) nor in any monuments which are clearly defined *templa auguralia*.
36. As De Francisci 1955–56: 27 ff. with bibliography.
37. Cfr. for example Plautus, *Poen.* vv. 48 ff., *Asin.* vv. 249.
38. P. 351 M, 479 L; cfr. *Grom. vet.*, ed. Lachmann, Vol. I, p. 303, 22 ff.; Pugliese Carratelli 1965.
39. Cfr. Cicero *de leg.* II, 20: "*Interpretes . . . Iovis Optimi Maximi publici augures . . .*" and in *de div.* II, 34.72: "*. . . Interpretes Iovis.*"
40. "*Divi potes*" (or the *Penates*): Varro *Ling.* V, 58; Mani: Festus P. 157 M, 274 L: "*Manes di ab auguribus invocantur, quod hi per omnia aetheria terrenaque ma*<nare *credantur. Idem di su*> peri atque inferi <dicebantur . . . > augures, quod sanctis <. . . ?o> minis."
41. *Infra*, note 92.
42. See the fragment of Vegoe (Mazzarino 1966: 171 ff. and Colonna 1966) which dates most likely to the period of Gracchan reforms.

43. See the assimilation of the *di novensides* (evidently from *novem* and *sedes*, thus gods with nine seats in space) and the gods capable of hurling thunderbolts: Pliny, *N.H.* II, 138: "*Tuscorum litterae novem deos emittere fulmina existimant*"; Arnobius III, 38 "*Novensiles putat . . . deos noven Manilius, quibus solis Iuppiter potestatem iaciendi sui permiserit fulminis*"; cfr. Wissowa 1892 and Weinstock in *RE* XVII, I coll. 1185 ff. (against Vetter 1953 and Wagenwoort 1947: 83 ff.).
44. The same gods in addition to a Marsian inscription Vetter 1953: no. 225, 159, are also represented in a series of *cippi* from Pesaro (*CIL* I^2, 375 = *ILS*, 2977 = *ILLRP*, 20). The series deserves to be restudied in the light of other evidence such as the six altars from Veii (*CIL* I^2, 2628–32 = *ILLRP*, 27–31) and the Agnone Table.
45. There is much dissent concerning the links between the Etruscan haruspicine and oriental hepatoscopy, see Furlani 1936 and Contenau 1940: 274 ff.
46. See the sources collected by Thulin 1909: 131 ff. which confirm the national Etruscan character of the discipline in contrast with the official practices of the Roman state which goes back to the Etruscan haruspicine (Cicero *de leg.* II, 21).
47. Cicero *de leg.* II, 21: "*caelique fulgura regionibus ratis temperanto.*" Lightning bolts were considered *auspica maxima* (or *optima*) Servius *ad Aen* II, 693: "*hoc auspicium cum de caelo sit, verbo augurum maximum appellatur*"; cfr. Dio Cassius XXXVIII, 13; Cicero *de div.* II, 35.73; Dionysius Halicarnasseus II, 5; *ILS*, 9337. The origin of the *fulguratoria* for the doctrine of the divine seats was already noted by Biedl 1931: 212 ff. in particular.
48. On the connection between Martianus and the Liver, cfr. Thulin 1906, Weinstock 1946 and Pallottino 1956: 223 ff.
49. Stewart 1960.
50. We should note the oath of the Paflagones (Cumont 1901: 27 ff. = *ILS*, 8781) of 3 B.C. in the name of Zeus, Gea, Helios, and all the gods (including Augustus) on 6 March, the anniversary of the *inauguratio* of Augustus as *pontifex maximus* (*Inscr.It.* XIII, 2: 420 ff.). Cfr. the judgement of Drusus in Diodorus XXXVIII, II and the *devotio* of Mure in Livy VIII, 9.6 and in Silius Italicus X, 435 ff.
51. Barkcóczi 1965: 219 ff., fig. 5 See also the *lituus* from a Cerveteri tomb dated to the beginning of the sixth century B.C. (*Kunst* 1966: 25 ff. and fig. 2.) Here is another demonstration of the common origin of Etruscan ritual traditions and Roman ritual traditions of which the Bantia *templum* is an example.
52. Weinstock 1946.
53. Pallottino 1956: 226.
54. Biedl 1931: 211.

55. Varro *Ling.* V, 74; Dionysius Halicarnasseus II, 50. 3.; Augustine *de civ. Dei* IV, 23; Quintilian *Inst.* I.7.12.
56. Santangelo 1941: 77–214 esp. 123 ff. We should be aware of the singular reduplication of cults *in colle*, among which is *Sol*.
57. Pliny *N.H.* III. 5. 56 and Dionysius Halicarnasseus I, 55. 2. Cfr. Koch 1933: 107 ff.
58. Recently, Alföldi 1963: 252 ff. The chthonic character of the god (Dionysius Halicarnasseus I, 55.2 "... πατὴρ θεος χθόνιος ...") accords well with the position in the *templum* at Bantia.
59. As already noted by Frothingham 1917. See also the passage of Festus, *exc.* p 220 L, s.v. *Posticum* where the phrasing is almost identical to Cicero *de div.* I, 22.45.
60. Probably *Sol* as a chthonic divinity (cfr. the gloss of Dioscorides in *TLE2*, 823: καυτάν = *solis oculus* = *majoran*). This god in the epigraph of *Laris Pulenas* (*TLE2*, 131, line 5) is connected to Liber-*fufluns* and with the funerary destination of the Magliano *defixio* (*TLE2*, 359) where *Sol* appears together with an underworld divinity like *calu.* Another aspect, if really a divinity, would be that of *usil*, the rising sun as seen in the Perugia mirror Gerhard-Körte 1974, no. 78 (cfr. De Simone 1965: 537 ff.).
61. *Supra*, note 53.
62. Following Pallottino 1956.
63. To Pallottino's remarks about the placement of *Iuppiter*, I would add the verses of Silius Italicus X, 435 ff.: "*Tarpeia, pater, qui templa secundam/incolis a caelo sedem*" which can be compared to the passages of Varro (ap. Festus, P. 339 M, 428 L: "*A deorum sede cum in meridiem spectes*..." and in Servius (*ad Aen.* II, 693) already cited by Pallottino.
64. Cfr. Pallottino 1956 and Enking 1957.
65. From Servius *ad Aen.* II, 793 ("*Sinistra autem partes septentrionales esse augurum disciplina et ideo ex ipsa parte significativa esse fulmina, quoniam altiora et viciniora domicilio Iovis*") and thus the point of view is toward the east of the augur (see also the playful verses reported by Cicero *de nat. deor.* I, 28, 10: "*Constiteram exorienten Auroram forte salutans cum subito a laeva Roscius exortius. / Pace mihi liceat, Caelestes; dicere vestra; / mortalis visus pulchrior esse deo)*" with the point of view towards the south of the auspicant: to the left of both can only be northeast.
66. *Supra* note 1. An inscription to *Florus Iovius* (Vetter 1953: 120 ff., no. 183) was found in the Lucanian area.
67. Sources collected by Radke 1965: 129 ff.
68. Wissowa 1912^2: 197 thought it to be Aphrodite Ἀνθεία. The identification with Demeter was made by Altheim 1956: 197 and then followed by Radke 1965: 129.

69. Cfr. the Agnone Table, Vetter 1953: no. 147, 104 line 24: *fluusai kerriiai.*
70. The *Cerialia* take place on April 19, the *Florialia* on 28 April: *Inscr. It.* XIII, 2, 442 ff., and 449 ff., (with sources). See also the fragment of Fabius Pictor (Huscke 1, 6) where a *sacrum Cereale* to *Ceres* and *Tellus* is mentioned: from the context it seems to be an extremely ancient ritual. On the connection between *Cerere* and *Flora*, cfr. Le Bonniec 1958: 195 (with earlier bibliography). On *Ceres* and *Tellus*, see Altheim 1931: 123 where the *Ceres Tellurus* of Martianus Capella is discussed.
71. Festus, P. 157 M, 273 L: "*Municipalia sacra vocantur quae ab initio habuerunt ante civitatem Romanam acceptam. Quae observare eos voluerunt pontifices, ut eo more facere, quo adsuessent antiquitus.*"
72. Degrassi 1949: 281 ff. = Degrassi 1962: 99 ff and Degrassi 1960: 141 = Degrassi 1962: 185 ff. This deduction is based on a better reading of *CIL* IX, 418 that I saw at Banzi and hope to discuss in print shortly.
73. *As Thulin 1909: 42 on the escort in the mirror in ES* V, 146; cfr. Clemen 1936: 27.
74. The name is complete on the mirror, *ES* V, 6 (cfr. Thulin 1909: 48). Camporeale 1960: 247 implicitly accepts the identification.
75. Colonna 1966: esp. 91 ff. I thank my friend G. Colonna for both this information and for suggestions made in discussions on the problem.
76. Strabo V, 226.
77. Weinstock 1950: 44 ff.
78. *Supra* p. 000. (p. 76 in the October draft version)
79. It is also possible to identify the divinity (or divinities) on the *cippus* with *Rau(dus)*, a lesser-known god to whom a gate in the 'Servian' wall of Rome was dedicated (*porta Rauduscalana:* cfr. Lugli 1952, Vol. III: 271–76). It is also mentioned in an inscription in *Fulginiae* (*CIL* XI, 6206), Radke 1965: 207 with earlier bibliography.
80. Radke 1965: 72 .
81. Latte 1960: 66 ff. treats the problem with abundant data.
82. On the *Robigalia*, cfr. *Inscr. It.* XIII, 2. 448 f. On the *augurium canarium* (Festus P. 285 M, 386 L; Pliny *N.H.* XVIII, 14) see Latte 1960: 68 for an argument against a connection between the two celebrations.
83. Sambon 1906: 381 no. 1006; Head 1911[2]: 41, who note a type with the Dioskouroi on galloping horses (bronze litras?).
84. Cavedoni 1839: 138 ff.
85. As Vetter 1953: no. 200 A9 = Pisani 1964: 44, XIX.
86. Vetter 1953: no. 200 B6 *b* = Pisani 1964: 44—I: the text cannot be in the genitive plural.
87. Castagnoli 1959–60 = *AE* 1961, no. 286 = *ILLRP*, no. 1271a. For the identification of the Dioskouroi with the *Penates*, cfr. Weinstock 1960;

Alfoldi 1965: 265 ff.; Masquelier 1966. Arguments against this association are found in Peyre 1962: 461–62.

88. Many thanks are owed to Prof. Castagnoli for many useful suggestions and for permission to cite the results of the recent excavations at Lavinium. I want to thank my friends C. Giuliani, A. Mura, and P. Sommella for having provided precise information of the data and problems concerning the discovery spot.

89. Thulin 1909: 34 ff.; Pallottino 1948–49: 254. Two marginal but interesting facts support the identification *θufl θas* = *Consentes Penates* = *Dioskouri*. The first is the existence of a dedication to *θuflθas* on a bronze point, perhaps a spear point (*TLE2*, no. 149) a weapon associated with the Castori and the second is the existence of a pair of divine twins in an architectural terracotta from Bolsena (Andrén 1940: 209 II: 3, pl. 78, 268) with the name *θuluter* (*TLE2*, no. 208). In the same group of terracottas from Volsinii other divinities are named (*Mera-Menerva-Cilen*).

90. That *Pales* should be present among the *Penates* is interesting since that divinity was also worshipped on the foundation day of Rome. For Fortune among the Penates there is an inscription from Veii, (*AE* 1927: 36, no. 122; cfr. Vitucci 1953: 259 and Servius Dan. *ad Aen.* II, 325.

91. Weinstock 1946: 118.

92. *This is a very elaborate construction, and for its type, coherent. But the discussion of the templum* of sixteen seats is full of contradictions and does not hold up to a logical analysis, despite the feeble possibility of some agreement and correspondence between the various seats. The *templum* of eight seats is more ancient and more solid as the famous passages of Pliny *N.H.* II, 143 and Cicero *de div.* II, 42 demonstrate.

93. Castagnoli 1959–60: 3 ff. There is another source regarding the altars which actually ties in with the Etruscan discipline: a fragment reported by Lydus (*de mens.* IV, 2) from the περὶ ἀγαλμάτων of (C. Fonteius?) Capito defines Janus as the god of time (cfr. Liver I; *ani*) and explains the *twelve* altars dedicated to him as symbols of the twelve months. Macrobius says the same thing, attributing it to Varro, cfr. Weinstock 1950.

94. This phrase may be a translation from the Etruscan, given the equivalence proposed for *θu* (cfr. *θu-flθas*) = *unus* (and thus *una*).

95. *Macrobius II, 4.11* "... *Vestam, quam de numero penatium aut certe comitem eorum esse manifestum est.*" On this question, cfr. Brelich 1949. On *Vesta* and *Ianus*, Brelich 1949: 28 ff.: this should be compared to note 93, *supra*.

96. Festus, P. 347 M, 436 L: "*Soldia sella At*<eius Capito ait ... sedere>iubetur, cum *mane surg*<ens auspicandi gratia evigi>lavit, quod antiqui expres<s>e <nec *superiore nec inferi*>ore parte excavat<as ad auspiciorum usum fa>ciebant sedes. *Quas s*<edes ab eam causam quod> in[h]is nihil erat constr<uctum? ... appella>

bant, inquit Verrius, quod <solidum idem quod totum>, absurde, ut mihi videtur, <si quidem omne quod> sit totum, ait dictum solidum." Cfr. Festus P. 348 M, 438 L and *supra*, note 29. The auspicant had to sleep in the *templum* (cfr. Serv. *ad Aen.* IV, 200). Many auspices were taken at night, including the censorial ones, Mommsen 1887–88, I, 102, note 1.

97. Cfr. the *sedile lapideum* of the Feronia sanctuary at Terracina (Altheim 1956: 44 ff.). We should bear in mind that in augural language '*sedere*' meant to "*captare auspicia*" (Servius, *ad Aen.* IX. 4; cfr. Statius, *Theb.* III, 459). To perform a rite seated meant to establish magical contact with the earth, cfr. Wagenvoort 1947: 25, note 1 (with biblio.).
98. P. 356 M, 483 L cited in the text, above.
99. Cfr. the anecdote about the sow of Attus Navius who was found in the center of the vineyard-*templum* (Cicero *de div.* I, 17.31). According to Dionysius (III, 70) she was seated and Sch. Ver. *ad Aen.* X, 241 (suppl. Keil): "... *in tabernaculo in sella* <sed>ens auspicabatur... pullis e cavea *libe*<r>atis <immissisque in lo>cum circum sellam suam..."
100. *Supra* note 99 in which *tabernaculum* and *sella* coexist. On the displacement of the *tabernaculum* cfr. Serv. *ad Aen.* II, 178.

BIBLIOGRAPHY

Alföldi, A.

1963 *Early Rome and the Latins.* Princeton.

Altheim, F.

1931 *Terra mater.* Giessen.

1956 *Römische Religiongeschichte II.* Berlin.

Andrén, A.

1940 *Architectural Terracottas of the Etrusco-Italic Temples.* Lund-Leipzig.

Barkcóczi, L.

1965 "New data on the history of the late Roman Brigetio," *Acta Antiqua* XIII: 215–57.

Biedl, A.

1931 "Die Himmelsteilungung nach der disciplina Etrusca," *Philologus* LXXVI: 199–241.

Bouche-Leclerq, A.
1882 *Histoire de la divination dan l'antiquité IV.* Paris.

Brelich, A.
1949 *Vesta.* Zurich.

Brown, F.L., Richardson, E.H., and Richardson, R., Jr.
1960 *Cosa II: The Temples of the arx MAAR* XXVI. Roma.

Camporeale, G.
1960 "Thalna e scene mitologiche connesse," *StEtr* XXVIII: 233–62.

Castagnoli, F.
1956 *Ippodamo di Mileto e l'urbanistica a pianta regolare.* Roma.
1959–60 "Sulla tipologia degli altari di Lavinio," *BCAR* LXXVII: 145–72.
1961 "Dedica arcaica lavinate a Castore e Polluce," *StMatStRel* XXX: 109–17.

Cavedoni, C.
1839 *Indicazione dei principali monumenti antichi del real Museo Estense del Catajo.*

Clemen, R.
1936 *Die Religion der Etrusker.* Bonn.

Colonna, G.
1966 "Nuovi elementi per la storia del santuario di Pyrgi," *AC* XVIII: 85–102.
1966a "Selvans sanχuneta," *StEtr* XXXIV: 165–72.

Contenau, G.
1940 *La divination chez les Assyriens et les Babiloniens.* Paris.

Cumont, F.
1901 "Un serment de fidélité à l'empereur Auguste," *RevEtGr* XIV: 26–45.

De Francisci, P.
1955–56 "Intorno all'origine etrusca del concetto di imperium," *StEtr* XXIV: 19–43.

1959 *Primordia Civitatis*. Roma.

De Simone, C.
1965 "Etrusco *usel-sole," *StEtr* XXXIII: 537–43.

Degrassi, A.
1931 *Inscriptiones Italiae*. Roma.
1949 "Quattuorviri in colonie romane e in municipi retti da duoviri," *MemAccLinc*: 281–345.
1960 "Sul duovirato nei municipi italici" in *Omagiu lui C. Daicoviciu*: 141–45.
1962 *Scritti vari di Antichità*. Roma.

Deubner, L. (ed.)
1925 *Chantepie de la Saussaye*, Pierre Daniel. *Lehrbuch der Religionsgeschichte*. Tübingen.

Devoto, G.
1940 *Tabulae Iguvinae*². Roma.

Enking, R.
1957 "Zur Orientierung der etruskischen Tempel," *StEtr* XXV: 541–44.

Flink, E.
1921 "Auguralia und Verwandtes" in *Commentationes in honorem Fridolfi Gustafsson*. Helsinki.

Frothingham, A.L.
1914 "Circular Temple and Mundus. Was the Temple Only Rectangular?" *AJA* XVIII: 302–20.
1915 "Grabovius Gradivus, Plan and Pomerium of Iguvium," *AJPh* XXXVI: 314–22.
1917 "Ancient Orientation Unveiled," *AJA* XXI, part I: 55–76; II: 187–201; III: 313–36.

Furlani, G.
1936 "Mantica hittita e mantica etrusca," *StEtr* X: 153–62.

Goidanich, P.F.
1934 "Rapporti culturali e linguistici tra Roma e gli Italici: del templum augurale nell'Italia antica," *Historia* VIII: 237–69.

Head, A.
1911 *Historia nummorum*². Oxford.

Huske, E.
1959 *Die Gubischen Tafeln*. Liepzig.

Koch, C.
1933 *Gestirnverherung im alten Italien*. Frankfurt.

Körte, G.
1974 *Etruskische Spiegel*. Berlin.

Kunst
1966 *Kunst und Kultur der Etrusker (Cat. Mostra di Vienna)*. Wien.

Latte, K.
1948 "Augur und templum in der Varronischen auguralformel," *Philologus* XCVII: 143–59.
1960 *Römische Religiongechichte*. München.

Le Bonniec, H.
1958 *Le culte de Cérès à Rome*. Paris.

Lugli, G.
1952 *Fontes ad topographiam veteris urbis Romae pertinentes*. Roma.

Luzzatto, G.
1934 *Per un'ipotesi sulle origini e la natura delle obbligazioni romane*. Milano.

Mansuelli, G.A.
1965 "Contributo allo studio dell'urbanistica di Marzabotto," *PP* XX: 314–25.

Masquelier, N.
1966 "Penates et Dioscures," *Latomus* XXV: 88–98.

Mazzarino, S.
1966 *Il pensiero storico classico*. Roma.

Mommsen, T.
1887–88 *Römisches Staatsrecht*³. 3 vols. Stuttgart.

Muller, K.O., and Deecke, W.

1877 *Die Etrusker II.* Stuttgart.

Norden, E.

1939 *Aus altrömischen Priestbüchern.* Lund-Leipzig.

Pallottino, M.

1948–49 "Rivista di Epigrafia Etrusca," *StEtr* XX: 251–65.

1956 "Deorum sedes" in *Studi in onore di A. Calderini e R. Paribeni,* 223–34, Milano.

Peyre, C.

1962 "Castor et Pollux et les Penates pendant la période républicaine," *MEFR* LXXXIV: 433–62.

Pisani, V.

1964 *Le lingue dell'Italia Antica oltre il latino.* Torino.

Pitimada, L.

1953 "S. Onofrio (Catanzaro) Rivenimento di cippo militare," *NSc:* 343–44.

Pugliese Carratelli, G.

1965 "Le stele di Pyrgi," *PP:* 303–5.

Radke, G.

1963 "Beobachtungen zum römischen Kalender" *RhMus* CVI: 313–15.

1965 *Die Götter Altitaliens.* Münster.

Regell, P.

1882 *Fragmenta auguralia.* Hirschberg.

Rose, H.J.

1923 "The Inauguration of Numa," *JRS* XIII: 82–90.

1931 "De templi Romani origine," *Athenaeum:* 3–14.

Sambon, A.

1906 *Les monnaies antiques de l'Italie.* Paris.

Santangelo, M.

1941 "Il Quirinale nell'antichità classica," *MemPontAcc* III, V: 77–214.

Stewart, Z.
1960 "The God Nocturnus in Plautus' Aphitruo," *JRS* L: 37–53.

Thulin, C.
1906 *Die Götter des Martianus Capella und der Bronzeleber von Piacenza.* Giessen.
1909 *Die etruskische Disciplin*. Göteborg.

Vetter, E.
1953 *Handbuch der italischen Dialekte I.* Heidelberg.

Vitucci, G.
1953 "I Cicutii e la Fortuna Penate," *RivFil:* 259–62.

Von Blumenthal, A.
1934 "Templum," *Klio* XXVII: 1–13.

Wagenvoort, H.
1947 *Roman Dynamism*. Oxford.

Weinstock, S.
1932 "Templum," *RömMitt*. XLVII: 95–121.
1946 "Martianus Capella and the cosmic system of the Etruscans," *JRS* XXXVI: 101–29.
1950 "C. Fonteius Capito and the Liber Tagetici," *PBSR* XVIII: 44–49.
1960 "Two Archaic inscriptions form Latium," *JRS* XL: 112–18.

Wissowa, G.
1892 *De dis Romanorum indigetibus et novensidibus.* Marburg.
1912 *Religion und Kultus der Römer*[2]. Munich.

NSc Concordance
1953 = Pitimada, L.

6

A NEW INSCRIPTION FROM BANTIA AND THE CHRONOLOGY OF THE BANTIAN MUNICIPAL *LEX OSCA*

IN THE PRODUCTIVE ONGOING EXCAVATIONS in the area between Venosa and the boundary of Apulia directed by A. Bottini for the Archaeological Superintendency of Basilicata, the main focus has recently been the ancient Frederician abbey complex of S. Maria di Banzi, for a long time recognized to be at the center of the Lucanian and then the Roman city of *Bantia*. The investigations which I conducted in 1967 around the adjacent nursery school had brought to light the remains of a *templum augurale* (Chapter 5) and confirmed earlier topographic hypotheses. Now, the new excavations have allowed us to define more precisely that the abbey complex in the general abandonment of the city in the late antique period actually continued to be used and was destined to perpetuate in its name the name of the ancient city.[1] In the excavations below the pavement level of the actual church, substantial remains of an earlier ecclesiastical structure have been discovered. An *in situ* fragment of a splendid mosaic permits us to date this basilica to the Norman period, presumably successive to a third and earlier building of the late antique or Lombard periods.[2] In turn, this structure incorporates earlier material. Inserted into the wall, which may be the facade of a building that existed before the actual church, the excavators found an inscription on a fragmentary block (ht. 18 cm length 20.5 cm, thick 58 cm). The thickness, easily visible because of the corner position of the block in the wall, is totally preserved as its measurement equal to two Roman feet proves. The height of the stone is also fully preserved. The block is rough on its base and not perfectly smoothed on the lower part of the inscribed side: these two facts, coupled with the perfectly smooth upper surface indicate that

Plate 6.1

the original block placement was in a paved surface. The block is incomplete only on the right side, on the length. As a result, the inscription is preserved at the beginning (note the accurate finishing of the left border on the inscribed face) while the left part of the text is lost to us.

The inscription is accurately cut, with very distinct letters (the cutting is 3 mm deep and 6–7 mm wide): in particular, the *Z* in line 1 is extremely long, the *o* shows traces of a compass, the *V* is very open. In line 2 the *T* is very tall and large, the *R* shows archaic details (the round part is practically angular, the tail is open and doesn't actually join the straight leg), the *P* is completely open with little straight strokes. The only trace surviving between the second and third letter of line 2 is a deep circular form. At line 1 the vestiges of an *S* are visible at the break.

The text then is as follows:

Zoves [---]
tr. pl. [---]

Despite the *lacunae*, the text can be easily understood as an indication of possession sacred to Iuppiter. Let us now try to establish whether it is a dedication or a boundary cippus (line 1) attributed, bestowed, or established (line 2) by a *tri(bunus) pl(ebis)* or by *tri(buni) pl(ebis)*.

The first problem we encounter is that of the language in which the inscription is written: whether it is Oscan or Latin. Unfortunately, the mention of the *tribunus plebis* is not indicative. From the time when the abbreviation for the magistracy, tr. pl., becomes common, it appears in both the Latin and Oscan formulae at *Bantia*. The identical formula is found in the *Tabula Bantina Osca* (henceforth *TBO*) and can be taken as another clear example of the Latinization of the local language. The name of the divinity, Zoves, in which the initial Z reveals the existence of the contraction *di* (well-known at Rossano di Vaglio in Ζωϝηι[3] and in the *TBO* as for example in *zicolo* from *diicolo* here attests to a genitival form which seems at variance with the common Oscan usage. The Oscan form is constantly characterized by the termination *-eis*, and in particular is frequently used with the name of the divinity mentioned both at Pompeii and at Rossano di Vaglio.[4] Nonetheless, it is the *TBO* which illustrates the weakening of the genitival termination *-eis* into *-es* as in *pantes*—Latin *quanti* (gen. value)[5] to the more correct and diffuse genitive in *-eis* (for example *senateis, carneis, aceneis*, etc.). If the linguistic observations are correct, we can conclude that we have an Oscan text in the Latin alphabet which is absolutely contemporary to the *TBO* and which is of considerable historical importance.

If the dedication is expressed in the genitive, the stone can be nothing other than a *terminus* of the property of a sanctuary of Jupiter. The formulaic tradition of dedications in Oscan as in Latin is clear. In fact, I do not know of texts—either in Oscan or in republican Latin inscriptions—with a pure and simple dedication in the genitive, unless the name of the god is preceded, or somehow accompanied, by the indication of the object or thing possessed (for example, *pocolum vel sim.*)[6] or by the reference to things possessed by the divinity (for example, *de stipe*, *castud*, *vel. sim.*). The text seems to signify ownership or a connection to the possessions of the god.

Secondly, the form itself of the stone, left rough on the lower surface, indicates that the block may have been stuck in the earth. The accurate finishing (1.4 cm) of the left corner of the inscribed face would be incomprehensible in a dedicatory inscription for a statue or altar. Both the rough lower surface and the finished left corner are, however, perfectly compatible with a boundary stone of a sacred building. The finished corner is, in fact, necessary to preserve the corner since a boundary stone is subject to deterioration and destruction.

Unfortunately, we do not have clear examples of sacred *termini* from the Republican period.[7] Nonetheless, comparisons with *cippi* which delimit public domain, such as those between the Sardinian tribes[8] or those used as private boundary markers, both notoriously common, are sufficiently convincing and strengthen the hypothesis that our block registers the *terminatio* of an area sacred to Jove administered by one or more *tribuni plebis.*

The chronology of the inscription brings up another important point especially in light of the discovery spot. The paleography, directly inspired by that of Latin monuments, seems to provide evidence for a date within the second century B.C., if one looks at the parallels for the letter forms, especially for the *P* and the *R*, which are found in Latin inscriptions dated by the year or very nearly so.[9] The peculiar forms of these two letters as they appear in the *TBO* tend to "normalize" by the last years of the second century B.C., as attested by other inscriptions of virtually secure dates.[10] If one bears in mind the peripheral location of our text it is possible to concede a certain delay in the adoption of current inscriptional developments, but it is not possible to propose a date contemporary with the granting of municipal status to the indigenous community at *Bantia*—that is, at the earliest in the decade between 90 and 80 B.C. In other words, just from the paleographic evidence the distinct possibility emerges that the inscription may be placed at a date before the Social War. Such a possibility seems strengthened by the fact that the inscription is in Oscan and that the text refers to *tribuni plebis*, in all likelihood identical to the *tribuni plebis* of the *TBO* which are to be identified with the magistrates of the free Bantian community.

In summary, the inscription, written in epichoric language—to be considered a Lucanian dialectal variant of Oscan—and in the Latin alphabet, is most probably a boundary *cippus* datable to the end of the second or the beginning of the first century B.C.[11] It delineated sacred property of the greatest divinity in the local pantheon, which was administered by one or more *tribuni plebis.*

If we consider the nature of the text, it is possible that the missing portion may be negligible, unless we have lost the name of the magistrate (or magistrates), creators of the *terminatio* or something like:

Zoves; [*quidam*]
tr. pl. [*posuit vel sim*]

Apart from the unfortunate possibility that the name of the magistrate may be lost, the inscription, even though fragmentary, is fundamentally complete since we can establish all the terms of the juridical act enunciated by the inscription.

We must leave the chronology and significance of the new text as a *vexata quaestio.* Nonetheless, both the chronology and significance of the text are linked to the extraordinary juridical and administrative situation presented by the *TBO*, which was largely brought about by the Romanization and municipalization of ancient Italy. In turn the juridical and administrative aspects are related to the chronology and function of the political institutions attested to in the *TBO.* The bibliography for this subject is vast.[12] Nonetheless, by examining old and new data we may verify some of the basic elements regarding the Bantian statutes.

Some scholars attribute the *TBO* to the premunicipal phase; many others (including myself when many years ago a new fragment of the *Lex Osca* was published) to the period of the municipalization of the Lucanian community. The new document, with its paleographic, linguistic, and juridical data, seems to indicate that a date prior to the Social War is more probable.

Apart from the paleographic evidence, the political-administrative structure of the Bantian magistracy—*censores, praetores, praefecti, III viri, tribuni plebis, quaestores*—is certainly copied from Venusia.[13] In fact, such a complex hierarchy of magistrates does not reappear in municipal constitutions, but rather in the constitution of the Latin colonies prior to their transformation into *municipia*. This is also true for the *tribuni plebis*, now attested to as a functioning magistracy at *Bantia* by the new inscription as shown here. In another study I was able to demonstrate that the alleged municipal *tribuni plebis* are *tribuni plebis* of Rome,[14] where I concluded that the *programmata Pompeiana* for the election to *tr. pl.* of C. Tampius Sabinus and A. Fabius[15] are explicable in the light of special *comitia tribunicia* held in 12 B.C. among the *equites* by Augustus because of the scarcity of senatorial candidates, as noted by Dio Cassius and by Suetonius.[16] The other probable tribune of the municipal plebs, M. Vesiculanus V.f. of Teanum Sidicinum,[17] was one of those elected by this extraordinary *comitia:* in accord with the special provisions that Augustus offered, he later rejoined the equestrian ranks (the sources refer explicitly to this provision).

With the disappearance of the *tribuni plebis* from the horizon of the municipal magistracy, the Bantian statute seems more appropriate in the light of a "freely chosen" constitution of the *civitas libera* of *Bantia*. *Bantia* apparently suffered a strong economic, social, political, and cultural pressure from the nearby colony of Venusia in the second century B.C. That this is not a simple cultural pressure without social and economic consequences is shown by the recent discoveries of numerous *villae rusticae* of the second century B.C. within the Bantian territory. These *villae* attest to a profound economic integration between the two communities which were formally estranged and in origin organized on different socio-economic bases.[18] The juridical activity also provided a common link between the two colonies: it is not by chance that precisely at Venusia (and for all we know exceptionally at Venusia) the *tribuni plebis* appear to be active in the direction of an urban systemization (as the Q. Ovius Ov.f. of a famous Venusian inscription)[19] the same area in which the *tribuni plebis*—or the *tribunus plebis*—are operating in *Bantia* according to the new inscription.

Such activity in the case of *Bantia* seems to testify to a peculiar interest in the definition of the sacred property by the magistrates charged with the protection of the plebs. One could describe them as watchdogs of the traditional collective ownership which was evidently threatened by the growing expansion of private interests in the wake of development in the Roman or Roman-controlled territories. This growth is particularly evident from the presence of the *villae rusticae* in the area of *Bantia*. The new text of *Bantia* could well have been inscribed—but without insisting that the phenomena are contemporary—in the atmosphere which arose in Italy as a result of the Gracchan measures and in some manner continued by the board of III *viri a.d. a.i.*[20] We do not know if the drive towards Roman institutions may also have infused other peripheral Italian areas in the same way as *Bantia*. If this were the case, one could easily comprehend the limitation of the tribunician *intercessio* in the *TBO* without necessarily having to hearken back to Sulla.[21] This limitation of *intercessio* then may be treated as a local circumstance, a form of prevention of local "Gracchan" excesses introduced by social classes interested in the administration of land following the new trends appearing in the Roman territory. This same social stratum was the group most inclined towards a "Romanization" of the Lucanian community. Perhaps in this light, in situations where economic assimilation had played a part and in the alliances of "emerging" local groups within the Latin colony we can at least understand, if not explain, some of the motives of the unique defection of Venusia during the Social War.[22]

The *TBO* can probably be better understood in the climate of the decade prior to the *bellum sociale*, between 100 B.C., the date of the collapse of the subversive measures of Saturninus as implied in the *Lex Latina*,[23] and 90 B.C. when the allied revolt broke out. The *auguraculum* for which I have previously proposed an archaeological date between 80–60 B.C. can be easily anticipated by a decade, given the well-known impossibility of dating by decades black-glaze pottery found under the pavement of the *lapides augurales:* thus, the construction of the *templum augurale* would occur in the same historical atmosphere as the *TBO*. Note the more "modern" Latinization of the name of the chief divinity of the *auguraculum*, *Iovi* instead of *Zoves*, particularly in light of the present and certainly more ancient inscription.

The new inscription, with its linguistic, paleographic, and institutional-historical evidence (an official text in Oscan in a municipal Roman community would be inconceivable) justifies a chronology prior to the Social War, itself a process of spontaneous Romanization, already underway in the full second century B.C., in this small Lucanian community. Indeed, the *TBO* and *auguraculum* are the final acts of this Romanization, occurring before the outbreak of the Social War.[24] The microhistory of *Bantia* indicates a Romanization which assumes the form of an economic as well as an institutional homologation that, not by accident, reemerges in the "Roman" political apparatus of the Italic rebels with their *senatus* and their *imperatores*.

NOTES

I wish to thank particularly my friend and colleague A. Bottini, Soprintendente Archeologico Reggente for Basilicata for the graciousness with which he asked me to publish this first study of such an important inscription.

1. Already identified in *CIL* IX, 38, now the new excavations are verifying the size of the Lucanian and Roman city.
2. Information from Bottini.
3. Poccetti 1979: nr. 169 (see, however, the following note).
4. Vetter 1953: nr. 8 *iuveis* (Pompeii); Poccetti 1979: nr. 167 Διωϝηις (Rossano di Vaglio).
5. Porsia Gernia 1968–69: 334 ff.
6. See the indices for *ILLRP*, Vetter 1953 and Poccetti 1979.
7. But cfr. *ILLRP*, 486: "*Itus actusque est/ in hoce delubrum/ Feroniae ex hoce loco/ in via(m) p(oplicam)/ Campanam, qua proximum est/ p(edes) MCCX* [---]. On the left side: "*Fero[niae].*"
8. *ILLRP*, 478; cfr. also *CIL* X, 7931–32.
9. Cfr. for example, *ILLRP*, 124 (187 B.C.); 237 (146 B.C.); 467 (131 B.C.) with Degrassi, *Imagines, ad. titt.*
10. Cfr. *ILLRP*, 339 (108 B.C.); 342 (100 B.C.); 343 (99 B.C.) with Degrassi, *Imagines, ad. titt.*
11. Prof. Aldo Prosdocimi has brought this to my attention. L. Del Tutto Palma is now preparing a study on the linguistic interference between Oscan and Latin in the Bantine community.
12. The bibliography until 1963 on juridical aspects of the *Tabula Bantina* (Oscan and Latin) is found in the *Dizionario Epigrafico* IV, 715 f. sv. "lex". After the publication of the new so-called Adamesteanu fragment, Adamesteanu and Torelli 1969: 15 ff., Galsterer 1971: 191 ff.; Laffi 1973: 37 ff.
13. As many have noted, after Vetter 1953; Galsterer 1971: 191 ff.
14. Torelli 1984–85.
15. *ILLRP*, 1143; *CIL* IV, 16.
16. Dio Cassius LVI, 24.1; Suetonius *Div. Aug.* 40.1.
17. *CIL* X, 797 = *ILS*, 5004.

18. *ILLRP*, 690: *Q. Ovius Ov. f. tr. pl. viam stravit* (second century B.C.).
19. Bottini 1983–84 and *Società* 1981: 151 ff.
20. In addition to the classic studies by Brunt, see also the synthesis by Badian in *ANRW* I, 1, 688 and especially Gabba 1973: 193 ff. with complete bibliography.
21. This is the *communis opinio* on the limitation of the tribunician powers at Bantia (Galsterer 1971: 191 ff). After a careful examination of the evidence, these limits are not completely assumable into those put into force by Sulla. Only a part of these limits because of their simplicity can be considered independently in function of the defense of interest of the local ruling class represented by the Senate of Bantia.
22. Diodorus Siculus XXXVII, 2; Appian *B.C.* IV, 3; cfr. *supra*.
23. *Supra*, note 12.
24. *Supra*, note 12 and 14.

BIBLIOGRAPHY

Adamesteanu, D. and Torelli, M.
1969 "Il nuovo frammento della Tabula Bantina,"*AC* XXI: 1–17.

Badian, E.
1972 "Tiberius Gracchus and the beginning of the Roman Revolution," *ANRW* I, no. 1: 668–731.

Bottini, A.
1983–84 "Tombe di età romana a Venosa," *ASMG* XXIV-XXV: 215–31.

Degrassi, A.
1965 *Inscriptiones Latinae Liberae rei publicae Imagines.* Berlin.

Gabba, E.
1973 *Esercito e società nella tarda repubblica romana.* Firenze.

Galsterer, H.
1971 "Die lex Osca Tabulae Bantinae-Eine Bestandsarfnahme," *Chiron* I: 191–214.

Laffi, U.
1973 "Sull' organizzazione amministrativa dell'Italia dopo la guerra sociale." *Acta 6.* München.

Poccetti, P.

1979 *Nuovi Documenti Italici*. Pisa.

Porzia Gernia, M.L.

1968–69 "Contributo all'interpretazione del nuovo frammento della Tavola Bantina scoperto dall'Adamesteanu," *RendLinc* XXIV: 329–39.

Società

1981 *Società romana e produzione schiavistica*. 3 vols. Bari.

Torelli, M.

1968–69 "Un *templum augurale* d'Età Repubblicana a *Bantia*," *Rend Linc* XXIV: 293–315 (translated in this volume).

1980 "Aspetti Storico-Archeologici della Romanizzazione della Daunia," *Atti del Convegno di Studi Etruschi e Italici*, 325–36. Manfredonia (translated in this volume).

1984–85 "Tribuni plebis municipales" in *Sodalitas. Scritti in onore di Antonio Guarino*. Napoli.

Vetter, E.

1953 *Handbuch der italischen Dialekte*. Heidelberg.

7

HISTORICAL AND ARCHAEOLOGICAL ASPECTS OF THE ROMANIZATION OF DAUNIA

Drawing a comprehensive picture of the phenomenon of Romanization in the Daunian area of ancient Apulia helps to achieve a unified understanding of the Romanization process which has frequently been disarticulated by two diverse and separate fields of study. On the one hand, scholars of the indigenous world, for the most part archaeologists who pay careful attention to the development and structure of the local culture, have emphasized the destructuring nature of the Roman presence. On the other hand, scholars of the Roman world, usually historians, generally have emphasized the political and military procedures which were adapted from the formulae found at Rome, especially about the organization of the Roman commonwealth. In other words, the indigenous point of view and the Roman point of view are only occasionally tangential so that the two levels and types of documentation, archaeological and historical, are rarely studied together.

I believe it is possible to gather together the two types of evidence and methods in a preliminary manner and to consider the archaeological record for the Roman period more carefully.

Rome appeared on the Daunian horizon in 326 B.C.[1] From the pre-Apenninic foothills which flank the Daunian plain, the Samnitic peoples hovered threateningly around Arpi, the Daunian capital. The words of Livy (IX, 13) about the events of Arpi a few years after 326 B.C. explicitly illustrate the nature of the Daunian-Samnitic conflict: "... *Samnites, ea tempestate in montibus vicatim habitantes, campestria et maritima loca, contempto cultorum molliore, atque, ut evenit fere, locis simili genere, ipsi montani atque agrestes depopulabantur.*"

Enmity existed between the people of Samnium, *montani atque agrestes* but also living *vicatim*, and areas of Daunia, *campestria et maritima loca*, and, even though Daunia is not explicitly described, it is understood to be urban.

Against this background, the Romano-Apulian alliance of 326 B.C. took place, a *foedus* that Livy (VIII, 25) presents as the outcome of a *deditio in fidem*. It is not incidental that Velleius (I, 14) places the foundation of a colony at Luceria in 325 B.C. This information *a priori* should not be ignored but rather interpreted as the earlier occupation of the town by a Roman garrison otherwise known to have existed there in 319 B.C. (Livy IX, 26). The garrison of 319 B.C. is found in a city which in 321 B.C. was described as *socii boni ac fideles* (Livy IX, 2). The definite deduction of the colony in 315 (Diodorus XX, 72) or 314 (Livy IX, 26) constitutes an important event in the general picture of the Roman conquest. The significance of such an event may be understood by considering the political and economic situation of Luceria and concomitantly, the approach taken by Rome in the foundation of Latin colonies in those years.

The Samnitization process in the foothills, especially its chronology, is one of the more complex problems confronting historical-archaeological research of the period.[2] The boundary strip between Frentania, Irpinia, and Lucania, on the one side and Apulia on the other is characteristic of a frontier area. Larinum, a city whose onomastic is obviously Oscanizing and which minted coins with Greek and Oscan legends, is said to be a *polis Dauniōn* (Steph. Byz.). Teanum Apulum also minted coins with Oscan legends, but it was also the only city, together with Daunian Arpi, to issue silver coins. The case of Venusia is well known, thanks to the famous verse of Horace *Lucanus an Apulus anceps.* Ausculum Apulum and Vibinum are also very Oscanized centers. Luceria, at the beginning of the natural route across central Samnium, is also considered "very probably" a Samnitic city by Salmon, who thinks that the "boundary between Daunia and Samnium ran from Luceria to Venusia, turning west towards Aecae, Vibinum and Ausculum." This would place Teanum Apulum, Arpi, and Canusium outside of Samnium.

This uncertainty about the border leaves to Daunia only the two large centers of Arpi and Canusium with the ports of Sipontum and Salapia. Furthermore, it confirms the Oscanization process in the foothills, such as at Vibinum and Ausculum but also in the various peripheral areas of the plain such as Luceria. On the other hand, certain important elements in the tradition of the historical boundaries of Daunia, such as the cult of the hero-founder Diomedes,[3] exist from Canusium to Aecae, at Arpi, at Salapia, at Sipontum, at Venusia and Luceria, and all the way to Beneventum. This fact provides an outline of the "Daunian" sphere which is both precise and much larger than that which we find for the end of the fourth century B.C. The Osco-Lucanian presence in the area, which I see as rapport between classes rather than a mere traditional ethnic confrontation as presented in the ancient sources, is mixed with a large Daunian component. It is this large Daunian component that controlled both the major means of production and held a strong hegemony in the ideological sphere.[4] It was largely mixed with the Sabellic element, in a subordinate social position, which, in the course of the fourth century, was to emerge in the form of the protagonist of a class struggle. The interference of Rome thus appears directed towards eliminating this class conflict: the colonization first at Luceria and then Venusia must be different stages in this process.

The political and economic function of Luceria seems to be of a center crucial to the control of the vast Apulian plain, positioned as it is on a well defended height and at the crossroads of the great trans-Apenninic routes. The importance of the position and significance of the routes is underlined by recalling the direction of the march of the Roman army beaten at Caudium.

The Roman presence at Luceria consisted of a Latin colony of 2,500 colonists, normal for that time period. The long recognized military objective of Roman policy regarding the establishment of Latin colonies between the mid-fourth and mid-third centuries B.C., was to surround the Samnitic heart of the peninsula. The circumstances of the founding of Luceria as explained by Livy (IX, 26) appear controversial and confused because of their dramatic presentation, but are part of that encirclement of Samnium. The foundation of Luceria constitutes the most southeasterly and isolated point of the circle until the foundation of Venusia in 291 B.C., roughly a quarter century later.

The 2,500 colonists of Luceria must have disturbed profoundly the preexisting local agrarian structure as far as it can be known: they may also have altered the agricultural settlement pattern of the area. The centuriation traces found by Bradford and Jones[5] loosely confirm this level of disruption. One of the traces of centuriation, actually organized along *decumani* only, can be found east of Luceria and, following the reasoning of Toynbee and Frederiksen,[6] is part of the original division. I would place another very large trace of centuriation, in the area of Luceria, south of the previous line, but on a scale of twenty *actus*. Probably a third and smaller area can be located north-northwest of the city. Of the other land-divisions, one of sixteen *actus*, is east of Teanum Apulum, while two, both of twenty *actus*, are close to Ordona. There are traces of another division near Ausculum. This second group of agrarian divisions is not referable to the deduction of 314 B.C. The centuriation at Ausculum can probably be attributed to the colony of Firmum Apulum (about 5 km from Ausculum): this one was unknown until a few years ago and its existence was revealed by a republican inscription (*ILLRP*, 592) of either the Sullan or triumviral period. Those divisions at Ordona, a town incorporated into the Roman state as a *municipium* only after the Social War and remaining so throughout the empire, are rather more complex divisions, but they cannot be taken as part of the original *ager* of the *colonia Lucerina*. The centuriation near Teanum Apulum could instead be considered with the *ademptio* of the area in 317–6 B.C. which, according to the Liber Coloniarum, was distributed *lege Sempronia et Iulia*. Jones, who has dated the pottery from the area to about 120 B.C., seems to tie the centuriation to the Gracchan deductions which are attested to in the region by a Gracchan *cippus* found not far away at Celenza Val Fortore (*AE* 1973: 222).[7] These Latin colonies in the last years of the fourth century had an extremely strong cultural impact which can be fully assessed in both its form and scope. This, in turn, provides a useful indication of the origin of the colonists.

The Republican inscriptions from Luceria include a *lex de luco sacro* (*ILLRP*, 504), which Degrassi dated to a few years after the establishment of the colony.[8] The date is confirmed by comparing the amount of the fine levied in this *lex* with the amount in the analogous but slightly later *lex Spoletina* (*ILLRP*, 505–6). The document represents rather well the level of the Latinization which it was hoped would be or had already been easily achieved in the city either as it was being founded or within a few years of its foundation. The overview that emerges from an examination of the cultic activity is not very different. Cults are attested to at Luceria that are rarely found elsewhere, with the exception of Rome itself. The dedication to Fides (*AE* 1969–70: 159) of the late first century B.C. has parallels only in the well-known series of *cippi* from Pesaro (*ILLRP*, 14), in an archaic inscription from Lavinium (*EE* IX, 585), in an inscription of 10 B.C. from Capua (*ILS*, 3770), and in one from Auximum. Even more indicative is the dedication to Juno Populona (*AE* 1969–70: 154), an extremely ancient divinity, with a cult at Rome, Teanum (*CIL* X, 4789–91) and Aesernia (*CIL* IX, 2630). The inscription from Aesernia, like the unique widowhood of the goddess known from Seneca (*ap.* Aug. *de civ. Dei* VI, 10) and its association with the *ius Papirianum* noted by Macrobius (III, 11.6) illustrates the character of the archaic and marginal divine figure whom Seneca associated with Fulgura and Diva Rumina.

The presence of a rich votive deposit at Luceria is also revealing. The deposit was discovered by Bartoccini about two hundred meters from the church and monastery of S. Salvatore and was published by him in 1940.[9] The material includes heads and half-heads in the round, with or without the *velum*, statues of adults and babies in swaddling clothes, anatomical parts (torsos, legs, hands, feet, breasts, uteri, phalli) as well as human and animal statues. The heads-in-the-round which are not veiled are closely paralleled by material from Caere dated to the fourth-third century B.C. Even more important are the veiled female heads with braids on their temples, a type found only in the Latin area in the late fourth century at Ardea, Lavinium, Fregellae, and Luceria, where replicas seem to have been made from the same molds used in Latium. The infants in swaddling clothes are also important, as they are found in the Etruscan-Latin area, from Arezzo to Cales as well as in an episodic appearance in a deposit from the Italic temple at Paestum. The anatomical offerings include uterus models, which is striking since they are documented in the restricted area of southern Etruria and *Latium Adiectum*.[10]

By considering the Luceria deposit against the larger picture of the area of diffusion for this type of deposit, it is possible to be even more precise. In 1975, M. Fenelli[11] published a useful map of anatomical votive material. A.M. Comella[12] is now studying the problem in greater detail. From the distribution of Fenelli, one observation, made previously in the catalog of the exhibition *Roma medio-repubblicana*,[13] is readily apparent: the votive deposits containing anatomical ex-votos—busts, statues and statuettes (small bronzes and jewelry as well as ceramic offerings)—are typically products of the Etruscan-Latin and Campanian cultural *koiné* between the fourth-third centuries B.C.[14] The greatest concentration occurs between the territory of Vulci, the middle and lower Tevere valley, the Sacco, Liri, and Volturno valleys. Outside of these areas there are isolated but significant occurrences of this type of votive deposit: between southern Campania and eastern Lucania there are only two such deposits, one at Salerno and one at Paestum. Both were subject to Roman colonization: Paestum in 273 B.C. and Salerno in 194 B.C. In the Marsian and Sabine territory, deposits were found at Trebula Mutuesca, colonized in the early third century B.C., at Carsoli, a Latin colony in 302 B.C. and at Alba Fucens, a Latin colony in 303 B.C. Along the entire Adriatic side of the peninsula the examples of Hatria, a Latin colony of 289 B.C., and Luceria, a Latin colony of 314 B.C., are truly episodic.

It seems clear that the Luceria deposit does not merely represent an indication of a healthy cultural Latin type presence. This presence, in both the sense of religious ideology and in the more material sense as illustrated by the continuity of the traditions, manufacture, and perhaps use of the same molds for the production of these ex-votos, constitutes a primary documentation from which we can try to deduce the origin of the colonists. That origin is to be sought in the area of ancient Latium, as also seems likely from the date of the colony itself.

But the evidence provided by the Luceria deposit has not yet been exhausted. Unfortunately our information on the precise location of the deposit is minimal. Bartoccini notes that the votive material was found in an isolated area but also adds that according to tradition, repeated by several local sources, the nearby monastery of S. Salvatore was erected in 1301 on the remains of an earlier pagan temple. Whatever may be the actual place of the sanctuary to which the deposit belongs, the terracottas from the deposit, among which were also terracotta temple revetments, provide us with substantial details on the cult type. In addition to small statuettes of the goddess, the deposit also contained a splendid offering representing a helmeted bust of Athena. The bust is flat in back and lifesize. The image of Athena reminds us of the cult of Athena Ilias which Strabo (VI, 264) placed at Luceria. The cult mentioned by Strabo is almost certainly the same one that Ps. Aristotle (*de mir. ausc.*, 79) and Aelian (*nat. anim.* XI, 5) mention as both Daunian and as the repository for the votive gifts of Diomedes. It is accepted that the cult of Athena Ilias at Luceria should be distinguished from the cult at Salapia noted by Lycophron (vv. 1126–40), who claimed that young girls who sought refuge in the sanctuary could be granted the privilege of being freed from marriage. In reality, Lycophron placed the temple of Athena Ilias "on the hills beside Salapia," ναὸν δέ μοι τεύξουσι Δαυνίων ἄκροι/

Plate 7.1—Helmeted head of Athena fron the votive deposit at Luceria.

Σάλπης παρ' ὄχθαις. Furthermore, the literal translation of the phrases, "Daunian princes built for me a temple on the hills of Salapia," produces an obvious word play between ἄκροι and ὄχθαι. Lycophron continues to explain that these Daunian princes are those οἵ τε

Δάρδανον πόλιν/ναίουσι, λίμνης ἀγχιτέρμονες ποτῶν, "who live in the Dardanian city, near the waters of the swamp." Today Elpie/Salapia is recognized as a Daunian city, either of Rhodian or Chonian foundation and is not identified with "Dardania." The tradition of Lycophron has been rather curiously put in relation to the obscure *gens* of the Dardi mentioned by Pliny who records "*Diomedes ibi delevit gentes Monadorum Dardorumque et urbes duas quae in proverbii ludicrum vertere Apinam et Tricam*" or so it is understood—as by Berard,[15] the Δάρδανον πόλιν of the text as the "city (named) Dardanon." Neither interpretation is wholly satisfactory: the Homeric usage of the adjective Δάρδανος is of single termination (e.g. *Il.* II, 701 and XVI, 807) and warrants a translation as "Dardanian city."

The brusque insertion of a Trojan presence into the Daunian context by Lycophron can only be explained as an intentional allusion to Roman history—the poet's usual argument concerning the Trojan-Roman destiny in the Mediterranean. By describing the scene in a bird's-eye view (and thus near Salapia) Lycophron actually meant to indicate Luceria by his phrase *Dardanon polis.* Concomitantly, the splendid revetment fragment from the pediment found in the votive deposit at Luceria takes on a new significance. The nearly life-size sculpture represents the goddess Aphrodite in a *symplegma*, probably with Ares. The goddess is identified by her diadem and the gesture of *anakalypsis* as her left hand slips her dress off her shoulder, revealing her body. The iconographic type is that of the Venus of Frejus, in which some scholars recognize the cult image of Aphrodite *Nymphe*, Aphrodite the "bride" identified by both the gesture of *anakalypsis* and by the fruit offered in her right hand.[16]

The appearance of Aphrodite in her bridal dress on the pediments can be placed in rapport with the asylum offered to the *sponsae invitae* in the sanctuary, explicitly recorded by Lycophron (v. 1130 ff.). On the other hand, in the myth concerning the flight of Diomedes to the west, the goddess also played a precise role, complementary to that of Hera which is clearly stated in other verses of Lycophron concerning the metamorphosis of Diomedes' companions. Those verses point and counterpoint Troizen, the chief cult spot of Aphrodite Nymphe, and the epithet *Hoplosmia* of Hera Lacinia.[17] With this in mind, it should now be possible to find an explanation for the Athena Ilias sanctuary at Luceria and also for the dogs which were present there, according to Strabo. The dog, in fact, is the sacred animal of Aphrodite *en kepois*, the characteristic victim

Plate 7.2—Pedimental sculpture of the wedding of Aphrodite.

of the rituals dedicated to the goddess: the dog is also the animal that an ancient popular etymology would have as the eponym of Canusium.[18]

It is important to examine how the Latin colonization at Luceria may have appropriated this local cult, transferring to it all the values and religious trappings of the original tradition which are exemplified by the votive deposit of San Salvatore.

Even more relevant is that this Daunian cult is described as "Trojan." I believe that the colonists' strong interest in the sanctuary between the fourth and third centuries B.C. may be explained on the basis of their common Trojan origins, the same origin as that of the cult. The case of Luceria demonstrates well, as does the statuette of Aeneas and Anchises of Veii,[19] the fundamental ideological role of the Trojan legend in the Roman and Latin colonizations of the fourth century and what great refinement was used in the propaganda employed to conquer and colonize. The profundity and efficacy of the propagandistic works explain the interweaving of the Diomedes myth described by Dionysius of Halicarnassus (XII, 27) as well as in the famous episode in the *Aeneid* (Vergil XI, 234 ff.). The depth and effectiveness of the "Trojan" propaganda around Luceria and its sanctuary are visible in the definition that Lycophron gives to the city as Dardania, illustrating sufficiently that the cultural offensive launched by Rome based on the Trojan themes succeeded in touching worlds which were both cultured and protagonists in those years—the Greek world, and the Etruscan world (as the quotation of the François tomb seems to demonstrate).

Another central event in the Romanization of Daunia is the foundation of the Latin colony at Venusia in 291 B.C.,[20] a quarter of a century later. Our principal source of the historical circumstances of the deduction is a fragment of Dionysius of Halicarnassus (XVII-XVIII, 5) in which he digresses to state that the consul L. Postumius Megellus, conqueror of Samnitic Venusia, was denied a triumph which he then celebrated *sine auctoritate patrum:* he was also denied the right of choosing the colonists. The historical figure of Megellus is extremely interesting.[21] He was reelected consul for the third time for 291 B.C. despite his role of *interrex*. Megellus, who was active in Apulia, entered into a harsh conflict with his colleague Fabius Gurges who was occupied on the Pentrian front. Megellus wanted to take the place of Fabius Gurges in the siege of Cominium, and when this was not possible, committed the serious offense of using his soldiers for agricultural work on his own land. It is a long held view, amply discussed by F. Cassola,[22] that these episodes and their inclusion in the sources are the reflection of strong political and internal social conflicts at Rome. Three aspects of the event must be emphasized. First, the conflict which put Megellus against Gurges when both men were operating on contiguous battlefronts; second, the exclusion of Megellus from the number of *hegemones* who had the responsibility for the colonial deduction, and third, the name of the colony itself with the number of colonists assigned there, twenty thousand according to Dionysius.[23]

Venusia may also have first been established by Diomedes: "*Diomedes . . . Venusiam . . . in satisfactionem Veneris, quod eius ira sedes patrias invenire non poterat, condidit: quae Aphrodisia dicta est.*" (Servius *Aen.* XI, 246). Its placement in the upper Ofanto valley, between Daunia, Peucetia and Lucania is at a critical strategic point, the center of the peninsula between the two watersheds at the latitude of Irpinia.

The number of twenty thousand colonists has generally been considered unreliable. According to Salmon, the number should probably be six thousand colonists as at Alba Fucens, while Bernardi considers twenty thousand to be a copyist error and prefers to correct the number to two thousand. Beloch, although always critical of the ancient tradition, first thought twenty thousand to be accurate in light of the 228,000 hectares of the Venusian plain, but later concluded his argument by saying that such an immense territory would be distributed when the *ager* of Venusia was enlarged after the original colonial deduction.[24] The archaeological data of the territory now being collected by C. Andreau,[25] clearly illustrates the extent and type of settlement established in the area, and the argument of Beloch in favor of a restricted area for the Latin colony cannot be sustained by the archaeological evidence. From Gaudiano to Lavello on to Melfi and from the mountainous fringes to the vast Ofanto plain, no indigenous settlements can be dated to the periods after the beginning of the third century B.C. Additionally, A. Bottini says that in the habitations of Lavello the levels datable to this period reflect an abandonment of the site but that it is an abandonment without evidence of destruction.

In contrast, the epigraphic and archaeological evidence of Republican Venusia actually presents a very different picture than that seen at Luceria where the 46,411 hectares calculated by Beloch to be the extent of the colony is five times less than that of Venusia. No noteworthy epigraphic documents of the Republican period came out of the colony of 291 B.C. which are in any way comparable to the *Lex Lucerina*. This absence of important inscriptions, despite the number of inscriptions actually preserved, explains our very partial understanding of the civic cults. We are not able to associate any important inscriptions, urban or extra-urban archaeological remains or complexes with the civic cults of

Venusia, despite the similarity in the urban history of the two cities between the medieval and modern periods. The only votive deposit in the territory of Venusia, found at Monticchio,[26] has—understandably—a totally Samnitic and not Roman aspect as is illustrated by comparison with the deposit of Mefitis in the Valle d'Ansanto.[27]

Could the models of Latin colonization programmed by Rome in the cases of Luceria and Venusia be different? On one side, the picture of Luceria seems to be that of a deduction carried out on a medium-sized area, to which would correspond two or three traces of centuriation and a not very high number of colonists of prevalently Latin origin: the Latin origin was further emphasized by the use of a precise ideological framework, that of the "Trojan" origin. On the other side, Venusia was a colony deducted on to a very large area, up to now with no trace of centuriation known and perhaps with the inclusion of a large indigenous element, which is the only means of explaining the high number of colonists recorded in the sources.

Such a situation would seem to correspond to certain indications that tie the circumstances of the Venusian deduction to political and ideological events in Rome. We have seen the exclusion of Postumius Megellus from the rolls of the *hegemones* responsible for the selection of the colonists and his strong conflict with his colleague of 292 B.C. and proconsul of 291 B.C. Fabius Gurges. Gurges would have been supported by his father, Rullianus, in the war: Rullianus had already celebrated a triumph for his activity against the Samnites and the Apulians in 322 B.C. and was again active in Apulia in 297 B.C. Fabius Gurges himself may have dedicated the temple of Venus Obsequens in the Circus Maximus. According to Livy (X, 31) the dedication of the temple occurred in 295 B.C. and would have been effected *ex multaticio aere* exacted from *matronae ad populum stupri damnatas*. On this basis it is supposed that Gurges may have acted as *aedile*. Another tradition, recorded by Servius (*Aen*. I, 720) instead puts the dedication of the temple *post peractum bellum Sanniticum* in conjunction with the motivation *quod sibi fuerit obsecuta*. The second tradition is accepted by Schilling because of the epithet of the goddess, *Obsequens*, which he relates to the propitiation of the victory of Gurges.[28] Curiously, though, Schilling does not record another significant passage in the psuedo-Plutarchian *Parellela minora* (37 B). That passage, despite Jacoby's seemingly excessive doubts on its authenticity, states that "Fabius Fabricianus, relative of the great Fabius, following the sack of

Touxion, a Samnite metropolis, carried to Rome the Aphrodite Nikephoros worshipped by that people." The anecdote, taken from the obscure historian Dositheos, illustrates dubious moralizing sentiments with a kind of "retaliation" acted upon Fabius Fabricianus, who was killed by his wife and her lover. The event—whatever may be the actual location of *Touxion*, perhaps one of the many Samnitic cities[29] conquered in 292–91 B.C.—together with Cominium and Venusium—is to be put in conjunction, significantly, with the date offered by Servius in that it confirms a certain interest by the Fabii in the cult of Venus and at the same time for the "Samnitic" origin of the cult of Venus. The cult of Venus appears now in Rome for the first time after the archaic Fasti of Fortuna and Libitina and should be closely linked to the great popularity of the goddess within the Samnitic context, as both Wissowa and Latte have pointed out.[30]

These elements must be collocated with the incident concerning the "disgrace" of Postumius Megellus. It may be that there was direct interference by the Fabii, enemies of Megellus, in the colonization, which itself was a hostile act against Megellus. Additionally, the colonization was directed toward the recovery of the indigenous Daunian element with whom Rullianus must have had a close relationship as a result of his campaigns of 322 and 297 B.C. conducted in Apulia. I consider it very likely that among the anonymous Roman *hegemones* responsible—according to Dionysius—for the selection of colonists there may have been the Fabii, Gurges or Rullianus himself, who, relying on old ties with the dominant Apulian classes, may have reinforced those ties and resolved in a clear manner the Daunian-Samnitic class conflict. At the same time this would have assured the new colony an extension of territory and a number of colonists which Rome, still tied up on the two distant battlefronts of Etruria and Samnium and furthermore already depleted by the deductions for the other twelve colonies founded in those twenty years, would hardly have been able to find. That the beneficiaries of this new situation may have been the Daunian aristocracy would seem to be demonstrated by the prosperity of Canusium in the third century B.C. and by the diffusion of Canusian products into the territory of Venosa between the fourth and third centuries B.C.[31] Such a reconstruction seems not only to provide a reason for the singular anomaly in both the extent and number of colonists of Venusia but also helps to explain the even more unique name given to the colony which honors a goddess who appeared in Rome in those very years, perhaps as a direct consequence of the Apulian conquest.

The colony of Venusia represents an important event in the politics of colonization in Rome, neither more nor less an event than was the *prorogatio imperii* of Gurges in 291 B.C. These facts not only reveal the peninsular dimension of the political, economic, and military Roman presence but also foreshadow the future direction of the Roman presence in the provincial contexts. So, too, did the Fabii's choice of a *nikephoros* goddess who almost symbolized the Venus—*victrix*, *felix*, or *genetrix*—who watched over the fortunes of the great generals of the republic: Sulla, Pompey, Caesar.

NOTES

1. For these events and those of the successive conflict, see Beloch 1926: 392 ff.; De Sanctis 1956: 317 ff.; Toynbee 1965: 145 ff.; Salmon 1967: 214 ff. and 1969: 55 ff.
2. Salmon 1967: 26 ff.; La Regina 1980: 29 ff.
3. On the cult of Diomedes and its diffusion, Bérard 1962: 355 ff.; Pugliese Carratelli 1971: 53 ff.; Lepore 1979 and 1980: 317 ff.
4. Di Niro 1980: 53 ff.
5. Bradford 1950: 84 ff.; Jones's research has not yet been published but his conclusions are reported by Toynbee 1965: 563 ff. and Frederiksen 1971: 342 ff.; cfr. Salmon 1969: 168 and n. 25.
6. Toynbee 1965: II, 563 ff.; Frederiksen 1971: 342 ff.
7. Russi and Valvo 1977: 255 ff., where the *cippus* is attributed to the territory of the Ligures Corneliani.
8. Degrassi 1965: 504.
9. Bartoccini 1940: 185–214, 241–98.
10. Comella 1981.
11. Fenelli 1975: 206 ff.
12. *Supra*, note 10.
13. Torelli 1973: 138 ff.
14. On Fenelli's map, *supra* note 11: Paestum is nr. 70, Salernum nr. 56, Trebula Mutuesca nr. 50, Carseoli nr. 17, Alba Fucens nr. 47, Hatria nr. 10, Luceria nr. 64. The finds noted by Fenelli at Valva (nr. 21) and at Schiavi d'Abruzzi (nr. 76) are of a particular type probably because of Campanian influence, while the Apulian-Lucanian deposits at Accettura (nr. 1), Policoro (nr. 62), Gnathia (nr. 32), and Bastae (nr. 89) are not within the Etruscan-Italic

typology but rather fall into the area of Italiote influence or are in the Italic periphery of the colonial Greek sphere.

15. Bérard 1962: 66 ff. and n. 166 on 375.
16. See the remarks by La Rocca 1972–73: 419 ff.
17. Lycophron vv. 610–614; Bérard 1962: 358 ff.
18. On the cult of Aphrodite in an Italic context, Torelli 1977: 45 ff and 1980: 147 ff. The etymology of Canusium is found in Servius *Aen.* XI, 246.
19. Torelli 1973: 399 ff. and 1978: 226 ff.
20. For the ancient sources and modern bibliography see M.R. Torelli 1978: 50 ff.
21. *Supra* note 20: 43 ff.
22. Cassola 1962: 194 ff.
23. Salmon 1969: 62 and n. 80; Bernardi 1946: 277 ff.
24. Beloch 1880: 142 and 1903: 472 ff. For a synthesis on the territory and colony of Venosa (but not for a totally sound methodology), see *Fotografia* 1979: 87 ff. I thank Prof. D. Adamesteanu for bringing this to my attention.
25. This study is unpublished. See the short summary in *Ofanto* 1976: 30 ff.
26. Adamesteanu 1965: 135 ff.
27. Bottini and Rainini 1976: 359 ff.
28. Schilling 1955: 19 and 1958: 23.
29. Dionysius Halicarnasseus XVII-XVIII, 5.1: . . . ἄλλας πόλεις πλείστας . . .
30. Wissowa 1912: 290; Latte 1960: 183 f.; Lejeune 1964: 392 ff. For the connection between Venusia and Venus, cfr. Koch 1955: 23 ff.
31. I thank A. Bottini for this information.

BIBLIOGRAPHY

Adamesteanu, D.

1964 *Santuari di Magna Grecia: Atti Taranto* IV: 121–44.

Bartoccini, R.

1940 "Arte e religione nella stipe votiva di Lucera," *Japigia* XI: 185–214, 241–98.

Beloch, K.J.

1880 *Die Italische Bund unter Roms Hegemonie.* Leipzig.

1903 "Die Bevolkerung Italiens im Altertum," *Klio* III: 471–90.

1926 *Römische Geschichte bis zum Beginn der punischen Kriege.* Berlin-Leipzig.

Bérard, J.

1962 *Colonisation grècque de l'Italie méridionale et de la Sicile.* Torino.

Bernardi, A.

1946 "Dallo stato-città allo stato municipale in Roma Antica," *Paideia* I: 213–27.

Bottini, A. and Rainini, I.

1976 "Rocca San Felice: Il deposito del santuario di Mefite," *NSc:* 359–524.

Bradford, J.

1950 "The Apulia Expedition. An interim report," *Antiquity* XXIV: 84–95.

Cassola, F.

1962 *I gruppi politici romani nel III sec. a.C.* Trieste.

Comella, A.M.

1981 "Complessi votivi in Italia in epoca medio e tardo repubblicana," *MEFRA* XCIII: 717–803.

De Sanctis, G.

1956 *Storia dei Romani* II². Firenze.

Degrassi, A.

1965 *Inscriptiones Latinae Liberae rei Publicae: imagines.* Berlin.

Di Niro, A.

1980 *Sannio Pentri e Frentani dal VI al I sec. a.C.* (Cat. Mostra Isernia 1980). Roma.

Fenelli, M.

1975 "Contributo per lo studio del votivo anatomico: I votivi anatomici di Lavinio," *AC* XXVII: 206–52.

Fotografia

1979 *Fotografia aerea e storia urbanistica.* Roma.

Frederiksen, M.

1971 "The Contribution of Archaeology to the Agrarian Problem in the Gracchan Period," *DdA* IV-V: 330–57.

Koch, C.
1955 "Untersuchungen zur Geschichte der römischen Venus-Verehrung," *Hermes* LXXXVIII: 1–51.

La Regina, A.
1980 *Sannio Pentri e Frentani dal VI al I sec. a.C.* (Cat. Mostra Isernia). Roma.

La Rocca, E.
1972–73 "Una testa femminile nel museo nuovo dei Conservatori e l'Afrodite Louvre-Napoli," *AnnScAt* L-LI : 419–50.

Latte, K.
1960 *Römische Religiongeschichte.* München.

Lejeune, M.
1964 "Vénus romaine et Vénus osque" in *Hommage J. Bayet* (Coll. Latomus LXX), 383–400. Bruxelles.

Lepore, E.
1979 "Diomede" in *Atti Taranto* XIX: 113–32. Napoli.
1980 "L'Italia dal 'punto di vista' ionico. Tra Ecateo ed Erodoto." *Miscellanea di Studi classici in onore di E. Manni,* Vol. 4. Rome.

Ofanto
1976 *Civiltà antiche del medio Ofanto.* Napoli.

Pugliese Carratelli, G.
1971 "Lazio, Roma e Magna Grecia prima del secolo IV a.C.," *Atti Taranto* XI: 49–82. Napoli.

Russi, A. and Valvo, A.
1977 "Note storiche sul nuovo termine graccano di Celenza Valfortore," *MGR* V: 225–49.

Salmon, E.T.
1967 *Samnium and the Samnites.* Cambridge.
1969 *Roman Colonization under the Republic.* London.

Schilling, R.
1955 *La réligion romaine de Vénus.* Paris.
1958 "Les origines de la Venus romaine," *Latomus* XVII: 3–26.

Torelli, M.

1973 Review of "L. Vagnetti: Il deposito votivo di Campetti; M. Bonghi Jovino: Capua pre-romana: le terrecotte votive II," *DdA* VII: 396–406.

1973a "Le Stipi Votive," *Roma medio repubblicana Aspetti culturali di Roma e Lazio nei secoli IV e III A.C.:* 138–39. Rome.

1976 "I culti di Locri," *Locri Epizefirii, Atti Taranto* XVI: 147–184.

1977 "Greci e indigeni in Magna Grecia: ideologia religiosa e rapporti di classe," *StStor* XVIII: 45–61.

1978 *I Celti in Italia (Cat. Mostra Roma).* Roma.

Torelli, M.R.

1978 *Rerum Romanarum Fontes.* Pisa.

Toynbee, A.J.

1965 *Hannibal's Legacy.* Oxford.

Wissowa, G.

1912 *Religion und Kultus der Romer*[2]. Munich.

8

FUNERARY MONUMENTS WITH DORIC FRIEZES

"SPLENDIDI MONUMENTI TITULUS": Mommsen, in *CIL*, so describes the inscription from the sepulcher of *C.Nonius C.f.M.n.* five times *quattuorvir* from Isernia (*CIL* IX, 2642 = *ILS*, 895). The tomb was erected by his son, *M. Nonius Gallus*, who, according to the inscription, was *imperator* and *VII vir epulonum (Plate 8.1)*.

The tomb of *C. Nonius* is a characteristic and diffuse type of funerary monument which is composed of a "dado" (which usually carries the inscription) on a plinth. The lower part of the "dado" is decorated with a molding and there is a Doric frieze above the inscription. Above the "dado" and Doric frieze there was an epistyle, usually with dentils which was intended to carry either *pulvini* or acroteria or a superstructure imitating the facade of an *aedicula*. This type of funerary monument has been studied only as individual examples, or in regional groups, or with regard to specific details. There has been no general investigation of its typological origins, or of its diffusion and chronological development. I will attempt to present an overview of the type and to place its more significant architectural aspects within the historical-cultural context of the Roman world between the end of the Republic and the beginning of the Empire.

This class of funerary monument is very large. Within it, we can distinguish two distinct groups on the basis of origin and architectural form. The first group includes sepulchers of limited dimensions characterized by a pair of *pulvini* used as crowning elements above the epistyle. The second group consists of larger monuments with a superstructure in the form of a *naiskos:* in turn this may be crowned by a cusp or topped by

Plate 8.1—Isernia. Funerary movement of c. Nonius.

a cuspidated element. In this second type the dado is often compartmentalized by a row of Corinthian pilasters. Although the two groups evolve from two different types of structures they are still linked by architectural and decorative modules and models, that is, the altar and the base (that of a dedicatory offering, of a statue, or of a *naiskos*).

The first group, both structurally and typologically, repeats the altar form. An excellent example is the Isernian monument of *C. Nonius* of which only the central dado with the inscription and the frieze are preserved (the moldings of the base and crowning elements are lost). Given the modest dimensions (1.20 m high by 0.69 m wide, thickness unknown), one cannot imagine anything other than two *pulvini* at the apex: thus the basic form is that of a funerary altar. This monument gains particular importance because the inscription provides us with the useful *terminus post quem* of 29 B.C., if in that year *M. Nonius Gallus* was granted an imperatorial acclamation for his victory of the Treveri: this is not attested to elsewhere.[1] A funerary monument which was discovered beside the sepulcher of Ummidia Quadratilla many years after the excavation of the necropolis of Cassino also belongs in this category (Plate 8.2). It is also small (0.51 m high, 0.99 m by 0.88 m at the top, 0.63 m by 0.52 m at the bottom): the monolithic block which is preserved belonged to a funerary altar similar to that of *C. Nonius*. *Bucrania* or paterae are represented in the metopes: the motifs are alternated two by two, that is, two

Plate 8.2—Cassino. Epistyle of a funerary monument.

paterae and two *bucrania*. Additionally, the Ionic dentilated epistyle which is lost in the example from Isernia is preserved here.[2]

The Pompeian sepulcher of *M. Porcius*, which is interesting for the chronology of the group, also belongs to this same class. The funerary monument was on the Via dei Sepolcri outside of Porta Ercolano and is the third sepulcher on the left side of the street as one leaves the Porta Ercolano. It stands between the two funerary exedrae of *Mamia* and of *A. Veius.*[3] The sepulcher is simple. The cement core is hidden by blocks of peperino and is preserved to approximately half of the original height. Above a plinth used as a base, there is a lower molding and then the dado. Today, the elements of the superstructure which includes a Doric frieze and a pair of *pulvini* as crowning elements are leaning against the foot of the monument.[4] The inscribed cippus with the name of the owner is near the base of the plinth (*CIL* X, 997 = I², 1637=*ILLRP*, 650):

M. Porci M.f.
ex dec(urionum) decret(o);
in frontem ped(es) XXV,
in agrum ped(es)
XXV.

The measurements are in Roman feet, as was already noted by the eighteenth century excavators[5] and correspond to the measurements of the base of the monument (7.40 m by 7.40 m). It is not certain whether the statue of a man in a toga found in the course of excavation actually is the image of *M. Porcius* as was maintained by the excavators.[6] The tomb was built by decurional decree for one *M. Porcius M.f.* This name is known from Pompeian prosopography to be that of the very famous *duovir* who, in the earliest days of the colony, together with *Quinctius Valgus* built the odeion and amphitheater (*CIL* X, 852 = I², 1632 = *ILS*, 5267 = *ILLRP*, 645; *CIL* X, 844 = I², 1633 = *ILS*, 5636 = *ILLRP*, 646). His son of the same name with the title of *quattuorvir* (*CIL* X, 800 = I², 1631 = *ILS*, 6354 = *ILLRP*, 644) built the altar of the Temple of Apollo.[7] Provided that these two *M. Porcii* are not just one person, it is very difficult to establish which of the two may have actually been buried in the tomb outside of Porta Ercolano.[8] In any case the sepulcher cannot be later than the early Augustan age, after which the Pompeian family name of the *Porcii* ceases to exist.

The monument of *C. Maecius T., pu(pi) l.* in the Museo Civico at Rimini should be considered.[9] The metope frieze in two blocks placed on the dado which carries the inscription (*ILLRP*, 960) ought to belong to this monument notwithstanding the reasonable doubt of Aurigemma. The interest of this monument at Rimini, which is of modest proportions (the dado measures 1.22 m on the side), is that it belonged to a member of the freedman class and that its date cannot be later than the very earliest Augustan age—both on the basis of the epigraphic formula with "salve" and on the basis of the freedman's use of a *praenomen* different from that of his patron.[10]

In light of the chronological and general historical implications of this last monument, it is worthwhile to examine similar monuments at Benevento. There are three inscriptions and the remains of a Doric frieze. Two of the three inscriptions are preserved in the Museo di Benevento (Plates 8.3–8.4) but a careful search I made failed to trace the third inscription which Mommsen saw at "Vico Annunziata 11."[11] The first of the three monuments (Plate 8.3) is a large slab of local calcareous limestone (inv. nr. 1740: 1.32 m wide by 0.96 m high by 0.47 m thick): this large inscribed slab very likely covered a cement core. The inscription (*CIL* IX, 1624) reads as follows:

Plate 8.3—Funerary monument of a veteran of the VI legion and of some freedmen. (Museo di Benevento)

[---]o C.f. Ste(llatina) l(egionis) VI et
[---]o C.L. l(iberto) Pilomuso et
[---a]e C. l(ibertae) Edonioni et
[---]ae CN. l(ibertae) Saturniae
[---monument]um M. Semmius M.f. et P. Sextule[ius?---f.]
f(aciundum) c(uraverunt)
[quod pr]o sua parte facere no[luerunt].

The monument is also of considerable chronological interest. It belonged to one of the veterans of the VI legion who, along with veterans of the XXX legion, were sent by the triumvirs in 42 B.C. to the Latin colony of Beneventum which by that time had already become a *municipium*.

The other inscription, with two partial metopes and a triglyph, is also chronologically important (Plate 8.4). The block (inv. nr. 1741, 0.47 m wide, 0.75 m high, 0.28 m thick) carries the following text:

[---]Ste(llatina) Libon(i)
[---]II vir(o) i(ure) d(icundo)
[---tri]buno milit[um---]

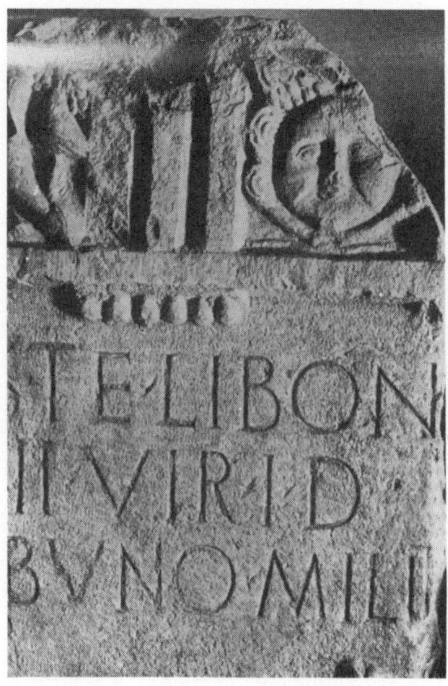

Plate 8.4—Funerary monument of a military tribune. (Museo di Benevento)

The inscription records that a certain Libo (both the *praenomen* and gentilician name are lost) was *duovir iure dicundo* of the colony and *tribunus militum;*[12] thus possibly an official of the legions of the re-establishment of Beneventum, if not a *tribunus militum a populo.* The date of the two Beneventum examples is not any later than the early Augustan period. The third inscription, which unfortunately I could not find, also ran beneath a triglyph-metope frieze as the *CIL* seems to imply by the notation *epistylium ornatum.* The text (*CIL* IX, 1604) refers to one *Avidienus T.f.*, centurion of one of the legions of the triumviral establishment and decurion of the colony. The date is identical to that of the preceding examples.

The last example of this first group is the so-called Doric monument, a sepulcher in peperino at the IV mile of the Via Appia, excavated, reconstructed and published by Canina.[13] The inscription is still *in situ*, albeit fragmentary and unclear (Plate 8.5). The *pulvino* in peperino on the sidewalk across the street also belongs to this monument. The presence

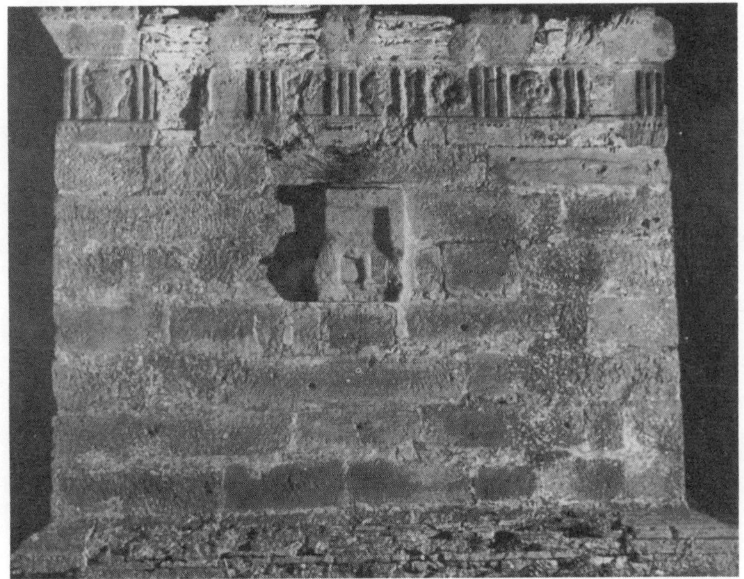

Plate 8.5—Doric funerary monument. Rome, Via Appia.

of this type of monument in Rome is interesting, the low relief of a possible gladiatorial combat inserted into the dado, although it is somewhat dubious that the relief really belongs there.[14]

The second group of monuments is less well represented. This second type, in the form of a *naiskos* in which the "dado" with a Doric frieze appears to serve as a support or base, has its distant origins in the typological tradition of the mausoleum. Evidence of this type of sepulcher is scarce because its considerable height is less well preserved. It is not by chance alone that we can securely cite only a single example, at Sarsina, and its state of preservation is due to exceptional circumstances. In Pompeii itself it is not possible to find any examples in such a condition to demonstrate beyond a doubt that the type existed in Campania as well. Monuments of this type would not have withstood an earthquake such as that of A.D. 62–63 even though excavation methods used in the past do not allow us to detect the existence of possible inherent structural collapse.

The mausoleum at Sarsina is the tomb of the *Aefionii*, and has recently been comprehensively published by the excavator.[15] This famous monument, partially reconstructed in the Sarsina museum, has three distinct parts. The large pedestal-like "dado" is a roughly cubic form with a

Doric frieze and an epistyle with *mensulae.* The central part takes the form of a Corinthian tetrastyle *aedicula* also of cubic appearance: this *aedicula* is topped with a spire. Four sphinxes are at the base of the spire which in turn is crowned by a Corinthian capital and a globular vase which resembles a cinerary urn. Unfortunately, in spite of the detailed publication by Aurigemma, many questions remain about the reconstruction, even if the general aspect is acceptable. In particular, most problematic to me is the placement of the meander frieze in the reconstruction, where it takes on the function of a support instead of its normal decorative use. Nonetheless, we are interested in the general appearance of the monument and it seems that the dado of the base probably supported a tetrastyle *aedicula.* We have therefore to attribute a similar function of support to all the other examples of funerary monuments characterized by a dado with the base partitioned by either Tuscan or Corinthian pilasters. Naturally, in almost every case we do not know what, in reality, may have been put on top of this base.

Another important mausoleum at Sarsina, that of *P. Verginius Paetus,*[16] also belongs to this group of monuments. Above a tall plinth, the dado is decorated with three Tuscan pilasters on each side which on the front side define the panels for the inscription and the reliefs. The text of the inscription, restored by Susini,[17] gives the name and the office of the person, *P. Verginius P.f. Pup(inia) Paetus, tri(bunus) mil(itum) a p[op(ulo)].* The reliefs bear the usual symbols of the rank and offices of *Verginius Paetus,* the *clipeus* and the *hasta,* symbols of his equestrian rank, the *fasces* and the *sella curulis,* symbols of his municipal offices (even if they are not mentioned in the preserved part of the inscription). Unfortunately nothing is known about the upper section of the monument as the tomb was very badly preserved. We can exclude from consideration, however, the proposed spire or pinnacle in stone or clay. An example from Rome itself, up to now unpublished,[18] illustrates the type sufficiently. This particular mausoleum was found more than fifty years ago and has been reconstructed in the Porta Maggiore piazza not far from the spot of its discovery (Plate 8.6 and Fig. 8.1a–8.1c).[19] The simple structure has a cement nucleus with a peperino revetment; the plinth, however, is in travertine. The facade (length at base 3.45 m) consists of two Corinthian engaged pilasters at the corners with the characteristic capital of fleshy acanthus leaves in the Hellenistic tradition.[20] These pilasters frame a travertine slab in the panel which bears an extremely damaged inscription.[21]

Plate 8.6—Right side of a funerary monument. Rome, Porta Maggiore.

On the sides, which are narrower than the facade (reconstructed lengths 2.70 m and 2.95 m) the panel is neither inscribed nor decorated. On the posterior facade, as on the short sides and the front, there are the usual engaged pilasters though we have to be uncertain about the moldings on the base which in any event are missing on the posterior side. A Doric frieze, in tufa with the usual bull's heads, rosettes and daisies in low relief as decoration, runs around the upper part. Above this frieze there was probably an epistyle, barely recognizable in an extremely corroded block at the top of the left side. As for the structure on top of this dado it

Fig. 8.1a

is only possible to put forward some hypotheses not unlike those suggested for the *P. Verginius Paetus* monument at Sarsina. The actual preserved height of this monument is about 3.70 meters.

To conclude the brief examination of this second type, it will be useful to consider an example from Modena with Tuscan pilasters which frame three panels (Plate 8.7). The panels are decorated with the *insignia* related to the juridical and social position of the proprietor, that is, the *umbo* and the *hasta*, symbols of the equestrian order and the *phalerae*, decorations received for military service as well as the cuirass of the Hel-

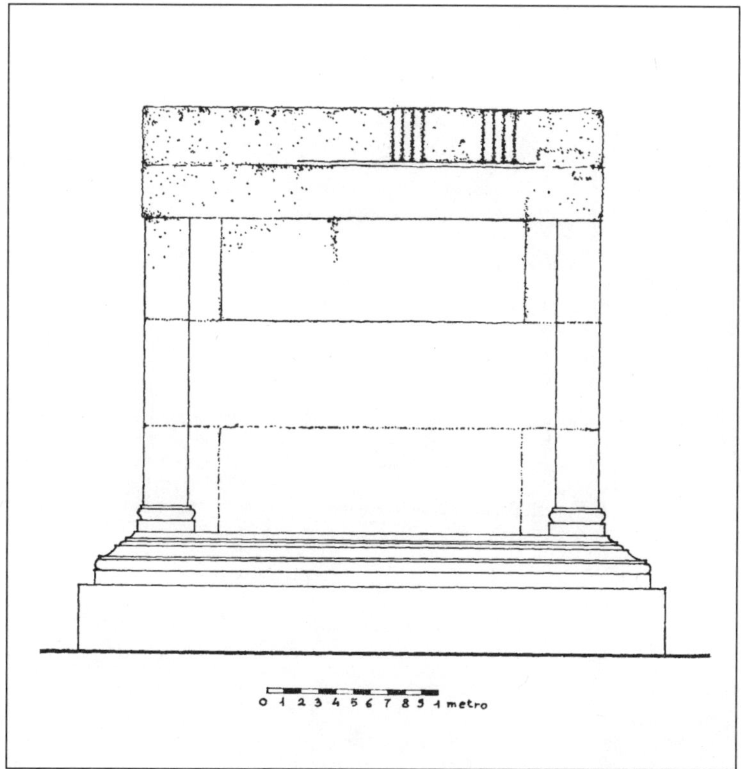

Fig. 8.1b

lenistic type. In the metopes there are the usual rosettes, flowers—eight petalled or swirled—and *bucrania*.

The decorative motifs of the metopes deserve some discussion. Even if it is premature to attempt a rough classification, it is still possible to outline a summary picture of the themes and significance of the motifs. The great majority of the metopes are decorated with motifs that are vegetal in origin and of Hellenistic flavor—often with a certain exuberance—as in the swirling flowers motif. Several symbols—such as wreathed bull's heads[22] and paterae—are also a favorite motif. Obviously such symbols enter into the cultic sphere and are common in the decorative repertoire

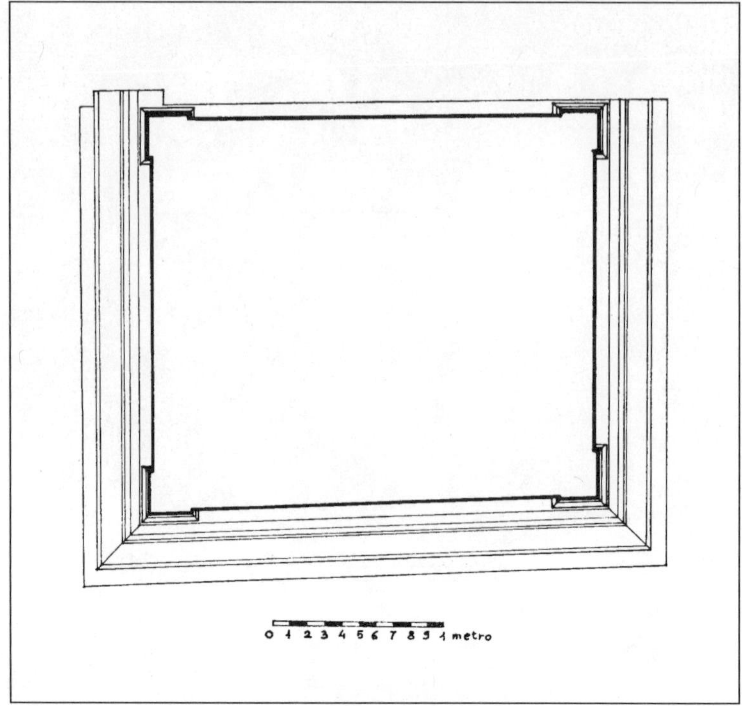

Fig. 8.1c

of contemporary religious monuments, such as altars and votive bases. Another series is mythic-religious in theme—centaurs, the she-wolf of Rome, and so forth. A final series is composed of subjects alluding to the life of the deceased or to daily life in general—arms, ships, various implements: these are found exclusively on central Italic monuments. It would be interesting to have a catalog of these motifs as they would shed much light on the question of so-called "popular art." The side of the Isernia monument of *C. Septumuleius Obola* is one of the best examples of this last decorative type (Plates 8.8–8.9).

The fundamental typological aspects of these sepulchral monuments are characterized by a Doric frieze. Of the two functionally distinct groups, the first group assumes wholly the appearance of an altar, the second group—often enriched with a series of Doric or Corinthian pilasters on the sides—acts as a base or a support intended to carry an *aedicula*-like structure (real or false is unimportant).

Plate 8.7—Funerary monument. (Museo di Modena)

The study of both the typology and the decoration of the prototypes of these funerary monuments finds excellent comparanda within late Hellenistic Italy. In minor centers, especially between the Republican and Augustan periods, there were workshops contemporaneously pro-

Plate 8.8—Right side of the funerary monument of C. Septumuleius Obola. (Museo di Isernia)

Plate 8.9—Funerary monument of C. Septumuleius Obola. (Museo di Isernia)

ducing altars, dedicatory bases, and sepulchral monuments, and not infrequently for the same clientele as was the case at Isernia.

Certainly the Hellenistic altars of both Capua and Pompeii attest to local production.[23] The use of "Doric" altars is doubtless older,[24] but it is only in the Hellenistic period that the practice of putting an Ionic cornice on top of a dado with triglyphs and metopes becomes widespread. This mixing of styles finds particular favor in the Italic areas.[25] Still, towards the middle of the first century B.C. this class of monument becomes less baroque in form: it suffices to cite the case of Pompeii, where the difference between the altar of the temple of Zeus Meilichios from the end of the second century B.C. and the altar of the temple of Apollo from about the mid-first century B.C. is clear. The taste for decorative solutions and effects moves progressively from the official to the private sphere. The Doric frieze is found first on minor decorative works such as on wellheads, and then on humble and modest objects, such as domestic fictile altars.[26]

The type of base or dedicatory support with a Doric frieze is amply illustrated throughout the Italic territory. An interesting dedicatory base from Alba Fucens (now in the Museo di Avezzano) should be considered (Plate 8.10). In this case we have a limestone rectangular block (ht. 0.80

Plate 8.10—Base of a honorary offering to Hercules. (Museo di Avezzno)

m, length 0.34 m, width 0.31 m) topped by a Doric frieze (the upper and lower cornices are missing) with sculptured metopes and the following inscription (*CIL* IX, 3907 = I², 1815 = *ILS*, 2489 = *ILLRP*, 146):

Herculei d(onum) d(ederunt)
milites Africa[ni]
Caecilianis;
mag(ister) curavit
C. Saltorius C.f.

The inscription celebrates a gift made by the African soldiers from Castra Caecilia[27] to Hercules, a highly venerated divinity in the Italic territories. The dedication seems reasonably old: the presence of these miltary men, who were probably organized as a group called together by a magister, could explain the military events at Alba Fucens during the Civil War.[28]

A similar monument in Capua on which the inscription is repeated on all four sides must have had an analogous function (*CIL* X 3790):

a. *Imp(eratore) Caesare (e) / T. Statil(io) co(n)s(ulibus), / bis ministri / faciun(dum) coe(raverunt):*
b. *L. Popillius Sp.f., / L. Popillius Hil(arius), / Q. Staed(ius) Prot(us?), Epicad(us) Pop(illi) L. s(ervus),*
c. *Musicus Popil(li) L. s(ervus), / Gluco Popil(li) L. s(ervus), / Felix Popil(li) L. s(ervus), / Glaucia Popil(li) L. s(ervus),*
d. *Sosus Pop(illi) L. s(ervus), / Eros Faber(i), / Eros Ingenui / Atticus Pop(illi) L. s(ervus).*

The monument, which I have not seen (nor do I even know if it still exists), must be the base of an offering dedicated by twelve *ministri* in the year 26 B.C.[29] as the consular date given in an abbreviated form indicates. A third monument with a definitely honorific character[30] is the dedication to *Sex. Appuleius Sex. f. imperator, consul, augur* and *patronus* of Aesernia (*CIL* IX, 2642 = *ILS*, 894). The small base (ht. 0.53 m, length 0.68 m, thickness 1.70 m) dedicated to *Sex. Appuleius, cos.* 29 B.C.[31] by the citizens of Isernia (Plate 8.11) was intended to support, probably, an equestrian statue of this man who was related by marriage to the house of Augustus. In the same Isernia museum there is also a similar base (Plates 8.8–8.9) with the inscription (*CIL* IX, 2668) of a local *quattuorvir C. Septumuleius C.f. Tro(mentina) Obola.*[32] The two monuments are very much alike and ought to come from the same workshop, perhaps even the same one which carved the Isernian monument of *C. Nonius.*

Another important predecessor of this type of structure is the podium of the "apsidal hall" at the Praeneste sanctuary which scholars date to the Sullan period (Plate 8.12).[33] Here too the powerful base with Corinthian columns has a characteristic Doric frieze and cornice decorated with dentils and ovuli. On the other hand, the same arrangement of a Doric frieze with an Ionic cornice occurs on other monuments in the sanctuary at Praeneste, for example, on the tholos and on the dedicatory base behind the eastern hemicycle on the "Hemicycle Terrace."[34] The initial mixing

Plate 8.11—Funerary monument of Sex. Appuleius, consul of 29 B.C. (Museo di Isernia)

of Doric and Ionic elements is definitely very old.[35] This is not the place to investigate the possible continuity between the late Hellenistic artistic traditions and the Italic *koiné* which is exemplified by the sarcophagus of Scipio Barbatus. The question of continuity can be put to many other aspects of the Italic Hellenistic representational sphere between the third and first centuries B.C. such as the figured capitals.[36] These architectural and structural concepts may derive directly from the great Hellenistic architectural motifs reflected in the Pompeiian Second Style wall-paintings. The time period of our argument, between the end of the Republican period and the beginning of the Empire, is shown by the architecture on the famous Boscoreale wall with the depiction of a philosopher and two members of the Macedonian royal family.

The presence and subsequent diffusion of the late Hellenistic motifs in first century B.C. Italy have been the subject of a number of studies which have demonstrated clearly that these figurative motifs were absorbed into the Italic artistic context. The Doric friezes with particularly rich metopal decoration illustrate this use of the late Hellenistic motifs. These friezes are widely represented in official art beginning with the Sullan age (without taking into account the precedents in the Italic *koiné*

Plate 8.12—Podium of the apsidal hall. Palestrina, Lower sanctuary.

of the third century B.C.) from the sanctuary of Praeneste onwards through the middle of the century, as seen in the propylon of Appius Claudius Pulcher at Eleusis,[37] and ending with the two monumental tombs at Gaeta, which belong to two famous aristocrats of the Caesarian senate, L. Munatius Plancus and L. Sempronius Atratinus.[38] On the "bourgeois" level the dated examples start from the triumviral age (the base at Alba Fucens, if one accepts the lower chronology) and carry on through the early Augustan period until the beginning of the first century A.D. In fact, most of the honorific and sepulchral monuments we have considered can be dated to that period, for example, the monuments at Modena and Benevento, both of which are connected with the establishment of colonies in the triumvirate and the early Augustan periods, as well as the monument from Sarsina of *P. Verginius Paetus, tribunus militum a populo* (an office known only in the early Augustan age)[39] and finally the Pompeiian monument of *M. Porcius* datable, at the latest to the last thirty years of the first century B.C. The diffusion of these motifs becomes more intense in the municipal area at precisely the moment in which the official milieu in Rome tended to abandon it and took up instead other themes of Hellenistic or classicizing origins. A comparison can be made between the mausoleum of L. Munatius Plancus at Gaeta, which is still tied to the decorative Hellenistic tradition—for example, in the plastically flat metopes—and the tomb of Caecilia Metella in Rome which is characterized by a frieze with bucrania and festoons of probable Rhodian derivation.[40]

Such a change occurs in perfect concomitance with the passage from the second to the third Pompeiian Style, which in turn coincides with the change in the use of the motifs from the official milieu of the capital to a more extended use in the municipal milieu. These funerary monuments represent a correspondence on a minor architectural level to the Pompeiian Second Style.[41]

In order to understand fully the taste which gave rise to this kind of architecture we must ask who commissioned these monuments. Before responding to that question, however, it is necessary to consider the areas of diffusion of these two types of sepulchers.[42] From the map (Fig. 8.2) one can see that in Italy two areas concern us. One area runs from the Po valley (including Aquileia and Istria) southwards, with the exclusion of most of Etruria (especially the coastal regions). The second area consists of the Apulian peninsula as far north as the Gargano-Lucera-Venosa-Ofanto line and of Calabria below the Vallo di Diano. These lacunae are extremely significant: these architectural formulae are absent in the zones of ancient cultures which had funerary and social traditions different from those of the rest of the peninsula. Above all, these lacunae were in the areas filled early on by large estates.[43] Instead, these monuments are concentrated in the areas where the military colonization of

Fig. 8.2—Distribution map of funerary monuments with Doric friezes. Shaded areas and cities marked with circles indicate the absence of the monuments.

the first century B.C. was more intense. Outside of Italy we find these same monuments in the area of Narbonne in great abundance (Plate 8.13), with a few examples in Gaul,[44] but with only one example at Barcelona (Plate 8.14). The frequent occurrence of this class of monument in the Narbonne area accords with the diffusion in the same area of many elements of Hellenistic culture. The monuments (and the paintings) of Glanum, the arches of Carpentras and of Orange, the characteristic and numerous friezes with arms in the Italic regions, the "Corinthian-Italic" capitals, and so forth, bear witness to this diffusion of Hellenistic ele-

Plate 8.13—Doric frieze. (Museo di Saintes)

ments.[45] The Spanish example falls into the same category, even if we might have expected there a greater representation. Previously the colonization of the first century B.C. was put forth as an explanation for this phenomenon but obviously colonization will not suffice to explain everything. If one takes into account the diffusion of the architectural type within the entire Roman world one would note that in the Roman colonies in the eastern portion of the empire—in Greece (Corinth, Philippopolis, Nikopolis) or in Asia (Antioch of Pisidia, etc.)—examples of this type of architecture are virtually absent. In our evaluation of such a phe-

Plate 8.14—Doric frieze. (Museo di Barcellona)

nomenon it is necessary to consider the cultural context in which the colonization occurred. The contribution of the "substratum" was a determining factor, either positive or negative. In other words, the areas and contexts in which such late Hellenistic figurative formulae are preserved for a longer time correspond, roughly, to the areas and contexts where, in the second century B.C. there is an expansion of "Italic" Hellenistic culture. The "Italic" culture, formed by a multiplicity of impulses, in which the emporium of Delos played an important role,[46] was widespread in the central parts of the Italian peninsula and where there were colonial deductions or where there was an enterprising merchant class, such as the Po and Rodano valleys.[47]

In the final analysis, the colonization of the first century B.C. was a phenomenon of return, of Italics substituting for Italics. The difference is that, before the mid-first century B.C., the culture and artistic production of the Italic centers were still able to compete with the culture and artistic production of Rome (as is demonstrated by the great "Sullan" sanctuaries of Latium or by the architecture of precolonial Pompeii) but in the second part of the century in these same Italic areas a perceptibly old fashioned culture took hold compared to the higher levels of culture in the capital.

Let us consider now the economic and social conditions of the proprietors of these tombs. In addition to providing chronological indications, the epigraphic material shows that those who built such monuments belonged to a class which, though inappropriately, we could define as "bourgeois." In the *municipia* and colonies such a "bourgeoisie" seems to be composed essentially of the local aristocracy, including the true groups of municipal nobility (decurions and magistrates) and those exponents of the mercantile aristocracy (for the most part freedmen) who were at that time in a rapid social ascent. At Rome, on the other hand, only freedmen, artisans, and merchants, for example the Vergilii Eurisaci, represented this "bourgeoisie." This, undoubtedly, is the *tota Italia* that swore fidelity to Augustus—officers and centurions of the army and the veterans from the colonies, the aristocrats of the *municipia*, the merchant class—and which constituted the core of the Octavian faction and was opportunely repaid in land and favors. These groups, already active in the age of Caesar, grouped spontaneously around the heir of *Divus Julius*, consigning power to him. The solidarity between the elite of the capital and these local clientele finds concrete expression in the analogies of orientation (although with a variety of formal levels) in the figurative arts existing at Rome and in the "Italic" *municipia* in the third quarter of the first century B.C. Once Augustus had consolidated his power and had undertaken his program of national restoration, the already latent distance between the center and periphery became more visible. Once the old solidarity was broken, the Italic periphery, by now worn out, at first tried to hold on to its obsolete cultural expressions. Later, the same Italic fringe attempted, without understanding, to adjust to the models of the capital city. The phenomenon grew with the logical, progressive absorption and the extinction of the municipal nobility in Italy. At Pompeii, even in Claudian times, a large part of the better names of the local aristocracy had vanished and the local *honores* became ever more the attributes of men of less illustrious extraction.[48] The tradition of the *Tullii*, of the *Veii*, of the *Mamii* passed into the hands of the rich but *ignobilis* Eumachia. The old tie between the ruling local class and the ruling central class was extinguished: thus the laughter of Petronius, the refined aristocrat of Rome, at the shoulder of Trimalchio, the pretentious neo-aristocrat from the province, became possible.

NOTES

1. The inscription is carved in an erased space: the stone may have been part of an older monument, though not much older. The victory over the Treveri in 29 B.C. is recorded by Dio Cassius LI, 20. To this military event all commentators are accustomed to attribute the acclamation which appears in the Isernian inscription. On this monument and on the others of Isernia, that of *C. Septimuleius Obola* and of *Sex. Appuleius*, cfr: Fuhrmann 1949: 45 ff.
2. In the Isernia Museum, however, together with numerous other fragments of Doric friezes, there are also preserved some epistyle fragments with dentils or *mensulae* which constitute the logical crowning element of those friezes.
3. The only synthetic study on this necropolis remains that of Mau 1908²: 425 ff.
4. See also the photograph of the monument in Mau 1908²: 429, fig. 253.
5. Fiorelli 1860: 235 (23 September 1769).
6. Fiorelli 1860: 239 (5 May 1770). It seems, however, far more likely that this statue, together with the other sculptures found with it, belongs to the sepulcher of *Mamia*, Fiorelli 1860: 239 (5 May 1770).

7. On the problem of these *quattuorviri* in relation to the *duoviri* of the colony, cf. Degrassi 1949: 281 ff. and Onorato 1951: 115 ff. (esp. 152 ff.).
8. Cf. Onorato 1957: 131 ff. who observes that neither *M. Porcius* nor *C. Quinctius Valgus* had descendents at Pompeii. Thus he is led to believe that the *M. Porcius* of the theater, the *M. Porcius* of the altar, and the *M. Porcius* of the funerary monument (built at public expense and thus belonging to a benefactor!) may be all the same person.
9. *NSc* 1940: 369–71 and figs. 6–7 and Degrassi 1965: nr. 321.
10. For the chronology of this monument, certainly one of the most ancient of the class, cfr. Degrassi 1941: 133 ff.
11. As in *CIL* IX, 1604.
12. The best datable testimony for this office is from Pompeii: *M. Holconius Rufus* is a *tribunus militum a populo* before 2 B.C. (cfr. *CIL* X, 837 and 890); *M. Tullius M.f.* is a *tribunus militum a populo* before 3 B.C. (cfr. *CIL* X, 820 and 824); *A. Clodius A.f. Flaccus* is *tribunus militum a populo* before 2 B.C. (cfr. *CIL* X, 890 and 1074). On the importance and the chronology of the office cfr. Mommsen 1871–88: 578 ff.
13. Canina 1853: 109 ff., tav. XXI.
14. The association between these monuments and reliefs with gladiatorial scenes is likely but not certain. Reliefs with representations of games are frequent in the area of diffusion of the monuments with Doric friezes and often have the same chronology, cfr. *Sabellica* : passim.
15. Aurigemma 1963: 23 ff.
16. Aurigemma 1963: 89 ff.
17. Susini 1955: 243.
18. Mentioned in *Bull. Comm.* 1925: 282; Lugli 1965: 151; Colini 1957: 3; Coarelli 1967: 66 note 4.
19. I thank Prof. G. Gatti for bringing this to my attention.
20. The same type of capital appears in many other funerary monuments of the same epoch; of different or uncertain typology see for example Tomb number 4 of the necropolis on Via Ercolanese, *NSc* 1943: 300 ff. which has a quadrangular plan with spires at the top.
21. This too is unpublished. The block measures 2.00 m. by 0.54 m. The letters are between 6 cm. and 5.5 cm. high. My reading is:

    [---]I[---]I[---]I[---]CIONI////// [---]TVRNISES-P-RVPILIVS-P-L-SABVRRIO-/////IMISQVE ARBITRA-P-RVPILI-P-L-SABVRRI-P-P-ET-HISTVMENNIAE-M-L-BASSAE.

22. On this motif, cf. note 45.

23. Capua, Koch 1907: 369 ff. and fig. 15; Pompeii, temple of Zeus Meilichios, Yavis 1949: 181 f.
24. Yavis 1949: 138.
25. Particularly inclined to these solutions are the Hellenistic milieus of Magna Graecia, as is widely acknowledged. See for e.g., the *arulae* and *epitymbia* of Centuripe; *NSc* 1947: 304 ff.; for Leontini, *NSc* 1954: 304 ff. and 339 f.; for Syracuse, *NSc* 1954: 218 ff.; for Akrai, Bernabò Brea 1956: 139 ff., tav. XXVII; for Taranto, Mansuelli 1963: 84 f., fig. 48. Magna Graecia is very early in this type of artistic expression, as is illustrated by the Doric *aedicula* of Megara Hyblaea dated to the end of the fourth-early third century B.C. in Vallet and Villard 1966: esp. 55.
26. On these minor objects of Hellenistic tradition, see the fundamental treatise by Pernice 1932: 12–37, figs. 7–23. The well head from the Casa del Citarista is particularly fine (Pernice 1932: 89, figs. 22, 27).
27. So Mommsen in *CIL* and Dessau in *ILS.*
28. In 44 B.C. the *legio Martia* was in existence (McKendrick 1954: 206–7). With this in mind we can consider the fragment from Pizzoli decorated with a triglyph and metope frieze and with the following inscription: *[---] et Sabino praef(ecto)I[---au]xiliariei Hispan[ei]* that the *Corpus* (*CIL* IX, 4503) says to be "*litteris pulchris et antiquioribus.*" Marmorale 1966: 185 thinks instead of the soldiers of Caecilius Metellus used against Jugurtha (thus *Caecilianis* = *Caeciliani*).
29. On the problem of Capuan *magistri* and of *ministri*, Frederiksen 1959: 80 ff., with bibl.
30. The monument is certainly honorific. In fact, the *Appuleii* seem to originate from *Luna* as the funerary inscription for the nephew of the consul of 29 B.C., son of the consul of A.D. 14, *Sex. Appuleius Sex. f.*, indicates in mentioning the tribe Galeria (tribe of *Luna*) and in fact found at Luni.
31. Thus I follow the opinion of Dessau in *ILS* cit., and of the authors of the *PIR*[2] A 961, 186 ff. against the thesis of Mommsen who identified our man with the namesake consul of A.D. 14. It would be difficult for the title of *imperator* to be taken up in this way by him given the tendency which was already evident in the first years of Augustus' reign to reserve the acclamation exclusively for the imperial family.
32. The character of the inscription, with the formula *ex testamento,* seems to be more funerary than honorific.
33. Fasolo and Gullini 1957: 42. This date is accepted on the basis of both the architectural and epigraphical evidence.
34. Fasolo and Gullini 1957: 148, tav. 21 (tholos), tav. 25, 3 (base).
35. *Supra*, note 23.

36. On the problem see most recently, *Sabellica:* passim. For the figured capitals in southern Italy, Neutsch 1965: 70 ff. On the figured capitals in general, cf. Mercklin 1962.
37. Giuliano 1965: 27 f. (with bibl.). To the examples already cited in the text one could add the external portico of the Basilica Aemilia, datable to the reworking of the building by Paullus Lepidus (Tobelmann 1923: 29, f. 35); the arch of Aosta and the La Turbie trophy (Formige 1949).
38. On the two tombs, see Giglioli 1921–22: 807 ff. and Crema 1959: 244 ff. Other examples (not numerous) of "bourgeois" funerary monuments exist in a circular form.
39. *Supra*, note 12.
40. Napp 1930.
41. On the close relationship between this architectural tradition and the Pompeian second style, Lugli 1900: 215 ff., and Beyen 1960: 385 ff.
42. I have based the discussion of the diffusion and location of the two types on what is published in the major archaeological journals (*NSc* in particular), in catalogs, and guides of Italian museums, in the *Corpus Inscriptionum Latinarum* and above all on my personal knowledge acquired over many years and innumberable trips for epigraphical research throughout central-southern Italy. Many colleagues—too numerous to list here—have contributed a great deal of information. G. Susini 1959: 324 ff. presented a careful study of the typology of Roman funerary monuments which, although limited to the Po valley, allowed a preliminary classification of the types. I hope to be able to finish a catalog of these friezes of which the present article could be considered a preliminary report. It is only with studies of this type that it will be possible, I believe, to organize the infinite and disordered heap of minor arts of varied inspiration, destination and use which go by the name of "popular" or "plebeian" art (cf. Bianchi Bandinelli 1967: 7 f.).
43. For the early diffusion of *latifundia* in Etruria it is sufficient to remember the famous analysis of Tiberius Gracchus (Appian, *Bell. Civ.* I,6). For Apulia, the epigraphic documentation is impressive already by the early imperial period with a very high percentage of slaves (*actores*, *pecuarii* etc.) in contrast to a scarcity of the local ruling classes. As Cicero (*ad. Att.* IX, 19.3) demonstrated, Bruttium, despite the Roman colony at Vibo, Croton, etc., was very little Romanized. For more than a century Sicily was in constant turmoil because of the slave revolts. On the entire problem, on which the agricultural works of Cato, Varro, Columella are very helpful and for the vast literature on the subject, see Frank 1933: 358 ff.
44. Esperandieu 1907–38: I, 158, r. 206; 160, nr. 211 (Arles); 319, nr. 480 (Nimes); 440, nr. 729; 447, nr. 744; 454 ff., nrr. 763–767; 456, nr. 769

(Narbonne); III, 40, nr. 1799 (Lyon); IV, 314, nr. 3328 (Langres); 426, nr. 3556 (Malain); IX, 148, nr. 7490; XIII, 20 nrr. 8143–44.

45. Most recently, Bianchi Bandinelli: 1965, 443 ff. and Picard 1963: 113. To Picard's examples, among which most remarkable is the strongly "Italic" flavor of the architecture of the temple of Valetudo (26 B.C.); I would like to add the altar found in the hall no. XXXV at Glanum (Rolland 1953: 7), closely resembling the Hellenistic ones from Delos (Yavis 1949: 149) which F. Zevi brought to my attention, in the characteristic appearance of wreathed bull's heads (not bucrania!), cfr. *ILLRP*, 961. The early Augustan altar from Anguillara is like these as well (Pallottino 1934: 146 ff., fig. 2; Hermann 1961: 84, nr. 10, fig. 5). This altar was dedicated by a freedman of Munatius Plancus but is unmistakably provincial in its style.

46. The importance of Delos in the formation of Roman and Italic artistic taste is a study which is still to be done. Studies exist, of course, on various aspects of figurative art but we do not have a synthesis which puts all the artistic perspectives in relation to the sociological, mercantile, and therefore "bourgeois" elements of the "Italics" (on which the old but still important work by Hatzfeld 1919 is still useful).

47. For this problem see Mansuelli 1963: 77 ff. and *supra*, note 45.

48. For example see the inscription of the *duoviri* of 26 (*CIL* X, 896), *M. Alleius Lucius Lebella and M. Stlaborius Veius Fronto.* Their polyonyms speak not only of the interweaving of the local and old aristocracy but also of how the ranks of that aristocracy had already become thinner under Tiberius. It is not improbable that the noble local tradition may have continued in the late Julio-Claudian period and that in the Flavian period it was continued by the freedmen of those same aristocratic families who carry on equally the family names and *praenomina* of their former *patrons.* On the economic and cultural decadence at Pompeii in the late Julio-Claudian period, see Zevi 1964: 16 ff., and his remarks on a "bourgeois" house in Regio IX.

BIBLIOGRAPHY

Aurigemma, S.

1940 "Iscrizioni inedite del Museo archeologico di Rimini," *NSc:* 362–74.

1963 "I monumenti della necropoli romana di Sarsina," *Bulletino del Centro Studi di Storia dell'architectura:* 23–45.

Bernabò-Brea, L.

1956 *Akrai.* Catania (Sicily).

Beyen, H.G.
1960 *Die Pompejanische Wanddekoration*. Den Haag.

Bianchi Bandinelli, R.
1965 "Naissance et dissociation de la koiné hellénistico-romaine," in *Le rayonnement des civilisations grècque et romaine sur les cultures périphériques: Actes du VII congrès d'Archéologie Classique*, 443–63. Paris.
1967 "Arte plebea," *DdA* I: 7–19.

Canina, L.
1853 *La prima parte della via Appia*. Roma.

Coarelli, F.
1967 "Un monumento funerario romano nell'abbazia di S. Guglielmo al Goleto," *DdA* I: 46–71.

Colini, A.M.
1957 "Resurrezione di un'antica statua," *Capitolium* XXII:14–16.

Crema, L.
1959 *Architettura Romana*. Torino.

Degrassi, A.
1941 "Il monumento Riminese di Q. Ovius Fregellanus," *Athenaeum* XIX: 133–40.
1949 "Quattuoviri in colonie romane e in municipi retti da duoviri," *MemAccLinc:* 281–345.
1965 *Imagines*. Berlin.

Esperandieu, E.
1907–38 *Recueil général des bas reliefs di la Gaule Romaine*. Paris.

Fasolo, F. and Gullini, G.
1957 *Il Santuario della Fortuna Primigenia*. Roma.

Fiorelli, G.
1860 *Pompeianarum Antiquitatum Historia I*. Napoli.

Formige, J.
1949 "Le trophée des Alpes," *Gallia Suppl. VI*.

Frank, T.

1933 *An Economic Survey of Ancient Rome I*. Baltimore.

Frederiksen, M.W.

1959 "Roman Capua: A Social and Economic Study," *PBSR* XXVII: 80–130.

Fuhrmann, H.

1949 *Zwei historische Reliefs vom Ausgang der Römischen Republik AA* II.

Giglioli, G.Q.

1921–22 *Architettura e Arti decorative I*. Roma.

Giuliano, A.

1965 *La cultura artistica delle province della Grecia in età romana*. Roma.

Hatzfeld, J.

1919 *Les Trafiquants Italiens dans l'Orient hellénistique*. Paris.

Hermann, W.

1961 *Römische Götteraltare*. Kallmunz.

Koch, H.

1907 "Hellenistiche Architekturstücke in Capua," *RömMitt* XXII: 361–428.

Libertini, G.

1947 "Centuripe-Scavi nella necropoli in contrada Casino," *NSc:* 259–311.

Lugli, G.

1946 "Le fortificazioni delle antiche città italiche," *MemAccLinc:* 294–307.

1965 *Studi minori di topografia antica*. Roma.

Maiuri, A.

1943 "Pompeii-Isolamento della Cinta murale fra Porta Vesuvio e Porta Ercolano," *NSc:* 275–314.

Mansuelli, G.

1963 "Les monuments commémoratifs romains de la vallée du Pô," *MonPiot* LIII: 10–93.

Marmorale, P.
1966 "Primus Caesarum," *Syntelia Arangio-Ruiz*, 1009–25. Napoli.

Mau, A.
1908 *Pompeiji in Leben und Kunst*². Leipzig.

McKendrick, P.
1954 "Cicero, Livy and Roman colonization," *Athenaeum* XII: 201–49.

Mercklin, E.V.
1962 *Antike Figural Kapitellen*. Berlin.

Mommsen, T.
1887–88 *Römisches Staatsrecht*³. 3 vols. Berlin.

Napp, A.E.
1930 *Bukranien und Guirlande*. Diss., Heidelberg.

Neutsch, B.
1965 "Tarentinische und Lukanische vorstufen zu den Kopfkapitellen am Italischen Forumstempel von Paestum," *RömMitt* LXXII: 70–80.

Onorato, O.
1951 "Pompeii Municipium e colonia romana," *RAAN* XXVI: 115–56.
1957 *Iscrizioni Pompeianae*. Firenze.

Pallottino, M.
1934 "Anguillara Sabazia. Aretta di peperino con dedica ad Ercole," *NSc:* 146–49.

Pernice, E.
1932 *Die Hellenistische Kunst in Pompeji V*. Berlin.

Picard, Ch.
1963 "Acrotères, antéfixes, chapiteaux hellénistiques à décor mêlé, humain et végétal. De Samothrace à la vallée du Pô et à Glanum," *RA:* 113–88.

*PIR*²
1897 *Prosopographia Imperii Romani*². Berlin.

Rizza, G.

1954 "Siracusa-Saggio di scavo a sud del Viale Paolo Orsi," *NSc:* 304–33.

1954a "Siracusa-Ara di Ierone," *NSc:* 333–83.

1954b "Siracusa," *NSc:* 218–304.

Rolland, H.

1953 "Fouilles de Glanum (1951–52)," *Gallia* IX: 3–17.

Sabellica

1966 *Sculture Municipali dell'Area Sabellica tra l'Età di Cesare e quella di Nerone. Studi Miscellanei X.* Roma.

Susini, G.

1955 "Documenti epigrafici di storia sarsinate," *RendLinc:* 235–86.

1959 "Nuove prospettive storiche: a proposito di alcune scoperte romane in Emilia," *Atti III Congr. Epig. Gr. Rom:* 321–46.

Tobelmann, F.

1923 *Römische Gebalke.* Heidelberg.

Vallet, G. and Villard, F.

1966 *Megara Hyblea 4, Le temple du IV siècle.* Paris.

Yavis, C.G.

1949 *Greek Altars.* St. Louis.

Zevi, F.

1964 "La Casa Regio IX.5, 18–21 a Pompeii e le sue pitture," *Studi Miscellanei V.* Roma.

NSc Concordance

1934 = Pallottino, M.
1940 = Aurigemma, S.
1943 = Maiuri, A.
1947 = Libertini, G.
1954 = Rizza, G.
1954a = Rizza, G.
1954b = Rizza, G.

9

PUBLIC BUILDING IN CENTRAL ITALY BETWEEN THE SOCIAL WAR AND THE AUGUSTAN AGE: IDEOLOGY AND SOCIAL CLASSES

THE AREA EXAMINED HERE includes the territories of the Augustan regions IV, V, VI, and VII which correspond approximately to the areas occupied by the Etruscans, Umbrians, Picenes, Sabines, and Samnites. Despite a minimal homogeneity in the levels of development,[1] the epigraphic and archaeological data allow us to confirm certain common tendencies in the socioeconomic sphere. Additionally, these tendencies appear to share a common origin.

The destructuring phenomenon of the Roman conquest of the third century B.C. had two aspects: first, *ademptio* of the territories belonging to a single community and, second, penetration of Roman economic and political forms including the circulation of Latino-Campanian coins and goods and the founding of Latin and Roman colonies. These aspects had a clear-cut effect on the structure of the local societies, reinforcing local oligarchies (or simply creating them where they were nonexistent) and marginalizing possible intermediate groups.

The ruling Italic classes appeared to be restricted aristocracies. For them, then, as for northern Etruria,[2] the Roman alliance had provided an efficacious instrument for the defense of established interests. The significance of the Roman conquest can be read negatively or positively: in allied communities elite groups became smaller (as is particularly clear in the documentation from necropoleis). On the other hand, the occupied territories were quickly transformed from what they had been previously. With regard to the latter, the situation in Samnium and in the Sabine region is very important. The presence of conspicuous contingents of Roman colonies in the Sabine land and in the territory of the

Vestini with organized immigration (and the contemporary absorption of old inhabitants by the concession of citizenship in 268 B.C.) is well attested to in the sudden and practically contemporary appearance of sanctuaries with Etruscan-Italic temple buildings. These sanctuaries functioned as centers of political and economic organization for large homogeneous parts of the territory which were notoriously nonurbanized. Formal temples like that of Villa S. Silvestro near Cascia[3] or those of Fontecchio or of Incerulae (Navelli) in the Vestini area[4] or Etruscan-Latin votive deposits like that of Trebula Mutuesca[5] are tangible proofs of this colonial presence in comparison with nearby areas belonging to *socii*, where nothing of the sort has been found in the archaeological documentation. In other cases, the foundation of a colony, such as Alba Fucens, Carseoli or Aesernia, even more clearly attests to the "importation" of an urban model in territories with previously *pagus-vicus* settlements. The pertinent archaeological evidence from the walls of the so-called Capitolium at Alba Fucens[6] and the imposing deposit at Carsoli[7] confirm the economic and ideological "Romanizing" impact in these areas.

Before grappling with the entire problem of euergetism in this area between the second and first centuries B.C. it is necessary to consider the local typology of monumental public buildings, sacred or profane, in these territories between the end of the third century and the middle of the second century B.C. The period before the Roman expansion, between the beginning of the fourth and the middle of the third century B.C. had been the arena of a formidable socioeconomic development in the entire peninsula. In the already urbanized areas, which coincides wholly with Etruria, this development was accompanied by intensive building, largely of cult buildings or walls in addition to a redevelopment of the urban and peri-urban road networks. In private buildings, while already known typological formulas for private habitations were consolidated, the principal activity was concentrated on a typological renewal for monumental tombs.[8] Differences in Latium, Etruria—especially southern Etruria—and Campania, an area of *koiné* which constitutes the well-known basis of the so-called "middle Italic" culture, are barely perceptible. In the less evolved areas, the fourth and third centuries coincide either with a definite urbanization (as in the Umbrian and Picenum region) or with the first monumentalization of central sanctuaries in the paganic territories of the Samnitic regions: even here no new building types are introduced, as the architectural forms are without exception derivatives of the Etruscan and Campanian areas.

The Roman conquest took place at a moment in which the social structures of central Italy were undergoing a profound evolution. The growth of civic bodies and the adjustment of already tested urban forms were accomplished without a substantial disturbance in the existing political framework. The skeleton of the sixth century B.C. *polis* was left largely intact in the new sociopolitical scheme. Architecture well illustrates the political aspect in the first phase of transformation. The evidence from fourth century B.C. Rome confirms a building trade all set to renovate that which already existed,[9] temples as well as public structures such as the *curia-comitium* complex or the city walls. It is helpful to consider what emerges from the collective building program in a Latin colony of the period. Cosa[10] was founded in 273 B.C., but in the first colonial phase and until the beginning of the second century B.C. the only public structures were the walls, the temples of the *arx* and the forensic square with the *curia*, *comitium*, *atria publica* and the small sacred area of Concordia. The building types found at Cosa are—on a smaller scale—those of the *urbs*. The only public buildings which are structurally distinguishable from sacred complexes (and this includes the *curia-comitium* complex) may be those which F. Brown[11] has rightly called *atria publica*. In this he follows in the footsteps of E. Welin,[12] using by analogy the complexes in the Roman forum. At Rome, these complexes served various functions. The *atrium regium*, the *atrium Vestae*, and the *atrium sutorium*, seat of the *tubilustria*, had sacred functions. Administrative functions were performed in the *atrium Libertatis*, linked to the activities of the censors or the *atria Licinia*, seat of public sales. The terminology *atrium/atria* and the discoveries at Cosa demonstrate that the architectural type of these buildings is absolutely identical to that of private habitations in which the *vestibulum* is framed by two or more *tabernae*. Many of these *atria*—such as the *atrium Titium* and the *atrium Maenium*, which were bought in 184 B.C. along with the adjoining four *tabernae* by Cato for the construction of the *Basilica Porcia*—must have been privately owned,[13] as the *atria Licinia* for public use. This fact, together with the strictly domestic aspect of the architectural type, demonstrates how, on both material and ideological levels, the domination of noble/ancestral buildings was still in vogue for the entire third century B.C. The architectural typology is in this sense revealing: the building trade of third century Rome is especially well documented in the second half of the century, as it simply retraced the developmental lines laid down in the preceding century, which in their time were not unlike the well-tested traditions of the late monarchic and the early Republican period.

The colonies, in particular the Latin ones with a high population density and large extensions of urban areas, adopted from close at hand the guidelines for the public buildings of the *urbs* without noticeable formal, material, or chronological gaps.

An actual break appears in the structures and architectural typologies of this historical block only in the first half of the second century B.C. Until that time, the building typology of Rome, its colonies, the urbanized areas of the *socii* and, in large measure, the nonurbanized central Italic zones,[14] is essentially the same. Indeed, the technical and formal solutions of architectural decoration for the entire third century—well illustrated for example by the terracotta temple revetments—are substantially homogeneous within the area.[15] With the beginning of the second century B.C. and through its first fifty years, the already implicit divergence between the center and the peripheral areas becomes greater, with evident guidance from Rome in the direction of the elaboration of new building types and, in the function of these new building types, new construction techniques.

Certain events are significant with respect to this occurrence: the erection of the *fornices Stertini* in 196 B.C., the construction of the *porticus Aemilia* and the emporium of 193 B.C., the birth of the first Hellenistic monumental systemization with porticoes bordering the city streets (like the porticoes between the *Porta Fontinalis* and the altar of Mars in 193 B.C.), the creation of the first basilica, the *Basilica Porcia* in 184 B.C. and lastly, the grandiose series of censorial buildings of 179 B.C. In little more than fifteen years, the face of Rome changed, assuming the appearance of a Hellenistic city.[16] Those buildings that had no facades were replaced by entirely new types, like the basilica which both took over the function and often the location of the old *atria*, or the *macellum* which took over the location and function of the old *forum piscarium* and of the *forum cuppedinis*.[17] If the basilica, whatever may be the ideological transference implied by the name, reveals a Hellenistic matrix in its architectonic form, then the *macellum* reveals, in its own etymology, the Punic origin of its type. The type may have been acquired through Sicilian channels, even if the influence of Carthaginian architectural forms could be rather direct as other "borrowings" demonstrate—for example, *pavimenta punica*, now found abundantly by the Germans at Carthage, or the *magalia*, the *aedificia quasi cohortes rotundas* as noted by Cato, and perhaps the *tholoi* of the *macella*—also the name of the suburbs of Sinuessa and Carthage.[18]

What of this sudden explosion of urban Hellenistic architecture in theses areas? Even if we do not have many extensively excavated cities such as Cosa and Alba Fucens from which to outline an organic picture of the construction activity in noncolonial cities, several observations can be made. There is no doubt that the reverberations of architectural Hellenization in the peripheral areas were immediate. A famous passage of Livy[19] describes the activity of the censors of 174 B.C.: walls, *tabernae* in the forum at Calatia and Auximum, at Pisaurum and Fundi, an aqueduct at Potentia in addition to minor works (due to a textual lacuna some are not comprehensible) at Auximum and Sinuessa. According to Livy, this initiative aroused local acclaim but also created a disagreement among the censors. The censorial activity was certainly without precedents: the activity of the lustral censors of ten years earlier,[20] who constructed buildings and roadworks in the territory of Antium and of Formia, as part of the normal censorial prerogative—at least from 312 B.C. onwards, the construction date of the via Appia—pertains to the communications network of the Roman territory or to territory controlled by the Romans. Instead, this action of 174 B.C. is novel (to the point of creating a conflict between the censors) and constitutes a glimpse of the new Italian political-economic situation in the years successive to the spread of the *luxuria Asiatica*. One must agree with Mommsen[21] about the juridical and administrative legality of the censorial action, which was aimed totally at the ager *Romanus* and *coloniae civium Romanorum*. The action of the two censors of 174 B.C., precisely because it was aimed at the *coloniae civium Romanorum*, was intended to offer a kind of compensation to *coloniae civium Romanorum* for the difficulties which they had suffered because the programmatic scarcity of land assignments granted to their colonists did not permit great accumulations of wealth. This, of course, is at complete variance with the situation of the Latin colonies, and thus necessitated public building initiatives of a certain importance in the *coloniae civium Romanorum*. Exactly in the same years, 191 B.C.,[22] there is documentation of difficulties in the *coloniae maritimae* in furnishing the normal military contingents and evidence that, still in the same time period, the new foundations of Roman colonies were given land assignments much greater than was traditional and included an elevated number of colonists as well.

The censorial benefactions of 174 B.C. provide the explanation for a series of unusual high-quality building programs in our area of interest. The examples of the temples such as that of Tortoreto in the area of the Roman colony of Castrum Novum[23] or that of Civitalba in the interior of Picenum,[24] with its splendid mid-second century B.C. architectural terracottas, are to be understood precisely as gifts of an urban character (for example, the temples ordered by the censor of 174 B.C. Q. Fulvius Flaccus at Pisaurum) to the colonies of Castrum Novum and to the *cives* of Sena Gallica or to the colonials of viritane deductions in the *ager Piceno-Gallicus*, where Civitalba is located. These last terracottas are artistically comparable to the terracottas of Luni, another Roman colony of 177 B.C., and provide evidence of other gifts made by the senatorial aristocracy of the period.[25] The most illustrative and significant testimony of this senatorial aristocratic interest in the peripheral Roman communities remains that of the *tituli Mummiani*, gifts *ex manubiis* (but made in his censorship, if we believe *Epit. Oxyrh.* LIII) to colonists of established cities (Parma, Italica) or to the colonists of viritane deductions (Sabini).

In the Latin colonies, the aforementioned example of Cosa provides useful evidence. While at Rome the *Basilica Porcia* was being built, followed in short order by two others—both larger—the *Fulvia et Aemilia* and the *Sempronia*, at Cosa the *atria*, characteristic of the preceding tradition, are built. It is necessary to wait until the middle of the second century B.C. for the construction of the Basilica at Cosa,[26] the oldest known outside of Rome up to now. This is also the first monumental public building of the city to be built in *opus incertum*, the extensive use of which—if not the discovery—is in strict rapport with the general building explosion in the Hellenistic culture at Rome and in the more advanced centers of Italy in Latium and Campania. A gap of more than twenty years separates the building of the triple arch at the forum of Cosa from its more ancient prototypes at Rome, the *fornices Stertinii* (193 B.C.) and the arch of Scipio Africanus on the slope of the Capitoline (190 B.C.).[27]

The separation between the center and the periphery becomes even more conspicuous within a decade. In the Latin colonies the emphasis is on cult buildings, rather than on the new Hellenistic typologies. The great Monterinaldo sanctuary[28] with its *porticus duplex* and temples decorated by lovely architectural terracottas of the late second century B.C. should be seen in the light of the building activity of the colony at Firmum. At Cosa itself the major energy is expended on the construction of the monumental "Capitolium" of about the mid-second century B.C.[29] while the few certain data from Alba Fucens lead us to regard in the same light the preeminent interest in public commissions oriented toward sacred buildings, in this case the urban temples on the surrounding hills.[30] The situation of the communities of *socii* is more complex. Here profound structural differences strongly influence the diverse orientation of the building activity: it is not possible to summarize this in a few lines.

In the Etruscan cities[31] the differences are especially great. In the northern region at Volterra and Arezzo there is great activity in the construction of sacred buildings as, for example, the urban temple (with the famous terracottas) on the acropolis at Volterra. At Arezzo, the immense extra-urban sanctuary with the theater-temple of S. Cornelio was the major undertaking. In these two cities, where there are no unequivocal data on the eventual process of superseding the old forms of dependency, this building activity is accompanied by a significant upsurge in artisan activity, from alabaster working to bronze and ceramic production. In the other two northern metropoleis, Chiusi and Perugia, the indications of the liberation process of the former *servi* are fairly clear. Chiusi presents a distinctly more backward picture than does Perugia, a city—as H. Rix pointed out—which is characterized by a greater social mobility. At Perugia, a massive wall circuit decorated by elegant doors in a Hellenistic vein provides evidence of a grandiose building program. Such manifestations appear to be absent at Chiusi.

If the decline of the coastal cities (Populonia, Vulci) corresponds to the growth of the Latin colonies like Cosa or the Roman settlements (colonies and *prefecturae*) like Saturnia with its ponderous polygonal wall or Heba to which the second century B.C. temple on the Talamonaccio hill probably belongs, Tarquinia has the appearance of a city without noteworthy building activity. Indeed, the separation into parts of the originally Tarquinian territory becomes even more evident as the independent communities of Tuscana, Ferentium, Blera, and Axia emerge.

The uniform scarcity of information—with the exception of Assisi which I will treat separately—prevents me from presenting detailed information about the Umbrian towns. The cities, especially numerous in this area as in neighboring *Picenum*, seem, however, poor in monumental testimony, with the occasional exception of temple buildings such as that of Monte Santo and of the Porta Catena at Todi.[32] *Picenum* has two particular situations worth emphasizing, that of Ausculum, with the great sanctuary on the Annunziata hill,[33] and that of the extra-urban sanctuary at Cupra,[34] both of which testify to the undertakings of the *Picentes socii* and of the *Picentes Romani*. For the territories of *Regio IV* the observations presented for Samnium-Pentri and the investigations of A. La Regina, J.-P. Morel, and F. Van Wonterghem[35] give detailed accounts of particular situations.

Thus, the great building renewal in Rome from the beginning of the second century onwards is only partially echoed in central Italy, with the exception of Campania and Latium. In the Roman colonies where direct Roman intervention is either known or postulated, energies are directed towards either a primary building program (roads, walls) or the completion of projects with a noteworthy ideological impact in a traditional sense, be they temple buildings or admittedly plundered statues given as *dona ex manubiis*. In particular, some temples, like those of Civitalba and of Talamone, seem to be associated with a commemorative intent and linked to the memory of celebrated Romano-Gallic battles of the third century B.C. Such sentiments were especially intense in the course of the second century B.C. in the climate of the conquest and colonization of the Transpadana and of the Transalpine Celtic areas.

The gifts of war booty made by L. Mummius to the Sabine centers of Trebula, Cures, and Nursia, on the one hand, and to the *cives Romani* of Parma and Italica, on the other, should be interpreted similarly.[36] The importance of Sabina, the probable home of the clients of the conqueror of Corinth, corresponds to the two establishments of Cisalpine and Spanish veterans, as is indicated by the likely *origo* of the colonists.

The public building activity in the Roman colonies, although emanating from the center, expresses itself in traditional forms that reveal clearly the persistence of a less developed viewpoint and social structure. Such a phenomenon of persistence, with the partial exception of Cosa, repeats itself in the Latin colonies, in the more developed communities of the *socii* at Arezzo and at Ausculum or in the traditional religious centers of the less urbanized centers, as at Cupra and Pietrabbondante. Epigraphic documentation for these developments is very scarce in general but practically nonexistent for all of Etruria and Picenum. It is barely perceivable in Umbria and the more northerly regions of Samnium. Only in southern Samnium, as it is in close contact with Campania, are the epigraphic data a little more substantial and indicate indisputably that the higher strata of society were responsible for these building activities. If by using the epigraphic data from the Etruscan necropoleis we might succeed in sketching a fairly clear picture of the local Etruscan aristocracy, the social structures of second century B.C. Umbria and Picenum are as vague and imprecise as ever. Where the local oligarchies are stronger and socially more robust, as at Volterra and Arezzo, the building activity appears more developed. This is evident in both a freedom of form and in traditional building types, for example, temples and walls in the public sphere and sepulchers in the private one. Where the Roman destruction was stronger, such as at Tarquinia, Falerii, or Vulci, the epigraphic documentation reveals clearly the progressive entry of alien elements into the local social structure, as is the case near the end of the mid-second century B.C. at Tarquinia. The alien elements in those cities in the late second century B.C. were composed of Latins and Romans, perhaps because of the Gracchan assignments.[37]

It is possible to formulate three general hypotheses from the data we have: First, the Roman colonies or at least the areas populated by *cives Romani*, beginning with the second quarter of the second century B.C., are characterized by frequent building donations by the senatorial aristocracy, under the censorial aegis or as gifts *ex manubiis* evidently motivated by their clients;[38] second, the Latin colonies show a certain retardation and a general indifference to the acquisition of new urban models. Generally, building construction follows a traditional form, primarily of temples and sanctuaries, and are consistently anonymous. Dedicatory inscriptions before the Social War are rare; third, in the *socii* communities, areas closer to the *urbs* (such as Etruria and southern Umbria), given the Roman socioeconomic pressure, show a halt in building construction. In the more developed and socially homogeneous areas (for example, Perugia, Arezzo, Volterra in Etruria, Ausculum in Picenum, Assisi and Gubbio in Umbria, the Pelignian and Pentrian areas of Samnium) there is evidence of a conspicuous construction of monumental buildings oriented entirely along the traditional lines of urban order and sacred buildings. Again, the epigraphic documentation is scarce with the partial exception of the Umbrian and Samnitic areas.[39]

In all these territories—Roman, Latin, or Italic—the gap between the center and the periphery is noteworthy. The new Hellenistic architectual types are slow to penetrate, largely because of the primarily socioeconomic rather than cultural nature of that gap. The building activity is concentrated above all on traditional forms, the aggregate expression of a mentality still firmly anchored to the old cultural *koiné* with the rare concession to Hellenistic models (as for example the diffusion—functional with a judicial use—of Hellenistic sun clocks) and in the private rather than the public sphere.

The new types of buildings are connected to the spread of *opus incertum:*[40] at Cosa in the second century B.C. the new building technique with a Latin-Campanian origin was universally used while elsewhere this technique is practically nonexistent until the end of the century and often not until even later, except for use in foundations and fill. There is still no map of the diffusion of the '*incertum*' beyond Latium and Campania. A map would well illustrate the profound dichotomy which existed in the heart of the peninsula between the "progressive" and "conservative" areas. The scanty epigraphic documentation of public works—which for non-Roman Etruria is totally absent—actually confirms the hypothesis formulated here. At variance with Rome, public buildings as instruments in the ideological and internal political struggle had a reduced importance. The great monumental undertakings of the peripheral areas—where they exist—seem rather concurrently to reaffirm the status of the local aristocracy in the face of the urban aristocracy and the hegemony exercised on the lower classes of the area.

If we compare this situation to what we know of the Latium-Campanian area, using the macroscopic examples of Praeneste and Capua or the archaeologically better known example of Pompeii and the more modest *municipia*, like small Alatri, with an extraordinary catalog of works in the new urban style completed at the expense of Betienus Varus,[41] an enormous economic and cultural chasm emerges with startling clarity between the richer more advanced area of Italy and the rest of the peninsula. Radically different levels of development exist instead in the rest of Italy, from the desolation of Magna Graecia to the densely populated Umbro-Picene countryside.

The years of the Social War and the new political reality expressed by the concession of Roman citizenship to the Italic populations initiate a different direction in local monumental buildings. This new direction, which had already been experimented with in Rome in the second century B.C., was destined to continue up to the early Julio-Claudian period. Temples, theaters, amphitheaters, baths, markets, basilicas, arches, aqueducts, and fountains in addition to streets and the urban infrastructure (*substructiones, porticus, pontes*) are now the most frequent projects. The politics of admissions into the Roman curia between Sulla and Caesar constitute an initial important line of division.[42] The local aristocrats of high standing were, to a large degree, admitted to the senate as were the "cream" of the old Samnitic districts, the Asini from the Marrucini, the Vettii Scatones from the Marsi, the Salridieni from the Vestini, and Poppaedii Silones, the Pentrian Papii Mutili. This was also true for certain families of Etruscan *principes* such as the Carrinates and the Caecinae from Volterra, the Perpernae, the Vibii Pansae, and the Volcacii of Perusia, the Saenii of Siena or from the Picene communities and from Ausculum, with the Ventidii and the Herennii and at Cupra with the Afranii and the Minucii. On the other hand, the Umbrian area as a whole seems to develop later than the areas around it. This primary admission carries the new senators and their families far from their roots. But it is not necessarily the case that the *laticlavus* carries with it the total abandonment of euergetic activity in the homeland. At the beginning of the first century B.C., the Caecinae built the theater at Volterra at their own expense. In the first years of the triumvirate, T. Labienus was the benefactor to his city of origin, Cingulum, an "oppidum" which he, according to Caesar (in 49 B.C.) *constituerat suaque pecunia exaedificaverat*. In 8 B.C. Asinium Gallus gave an adqueduct to his city, Teate. These euergetic donations are made concomitantly to enormous investments within the capital city. To point only to the Asinii, consider the library of Asinius Pollio in the *atrium Liberatis*. Private expenditures in the villa of *otium* and production, between the first half of the first century B.C. and the Julio-Claudian epoch spread beyond Latium and Campania and became diffuse throughout the entire central and northern peninsula.

On the local level, the emerging equestrians whole-heartedly carry the banner of the euergetic model, adopting various means according to the local circumstances. In Samnium, with the partial abandonment of the old "federal" sanctuaries such as Pietrabbondante, Schiavi, or Vastogirardi, there is an intense urbanization process. The case of Cluviae in the Carecine territory mentioned elsewhere with the vast building program of walls, theater and bath is inseparable from the social progression of the Helvidii Prisci from the local aristocracy to the Senate bench. No less important are a series of public works attested, archaeologically or epigraphically, to the period from the mid-second century B.C. to the beginning of the first century B.C. A few of them are those of Saepinum, associated with Naevius Pansa, ancestor of the consuls Neratii, that of Granius Cordus at Allifae, donor of the aqueduct and forefather of senators in the Tiberian age, that of Sex. Pedius Lusianus Hirrutus, builder of the amphitheater of the small *pagus* of Interpromium and the ancestor of Flavian senators, that of Octavius Segitta, father of a senator and donor of various public works in the Paelignan *pagus* of Superaequum, that of Octavius Laenas—also the grandfather of senators—with roadworks in Marsii Marruvium. All were *equites*, fathers or grandfathers of Tiberian senators: euergetism paid off and was contagious. The large and small examples of building activities carried out in *vici* and *pagi* are innumerable. Thus, in addition to demonstrating—as our much missed friend M.W. Frederiksen reminded us[43]—the great vitality in minor central Italic settlements between the late Republic and early Empire, public works are the sign of the tight interweaving of the collective psychology of the euergetic model and Hellenistic accomplishments.

In this phase and under this impulse which involves the width and breadth of ancient Italy, the habitat of paganic type in Samnium, Umbria, and Apenninic Picenum acquires an urban appearance as E. Gabba has so well illustrated.[44] This transformation often occurs by means of "global" beneficial activity by important people or families, such as Labienus at Cingoli, Quintius Valgus in the anonymous center near Frigento to the Helvidii Prisci at Cluviae.

Elsewhere, in the already urbanized centers such as the ancient Latin and Roman colonies, the fervor seems to fade. It is not that significant examples do not exist: the aforementioned theater at Volterra and the frenetic building activity in the colony of Castrum Novum near Caere and the work of L. Ateius Capito, grandfather of the celebrated jurist and consul of 5 B.C. and the extraordinary undertaking, slowly carried out within the century, of the sanctuary at Assisi confirms the diffusion of the model in these areas. One cannot deny that the process here underwent a noteworthy slowdown. The example of Alba Fucens, already a Latin colony, which had only in the late thirties of the first century a theater and amphitheater thanks to the munificence of the former *praefectus praetorio*, Q. Naevius Sutorius Macro, after many decades of building stasis, is truly revealing. One is not dealing only with urban models: that Tarquinia, for example, may be without a theater or amphitheater and should wait until the advanced first century A.D. to have a modern bath complex, confirms this belief. An explanation ought to be sought in the concatenation of two diverse and yet linked factors: on the one hand, the lesser socioeconomic vitality of many cities in the area and, on the other hand, the already accomplished integration of local elites into the Roman *Curia*, without a real replacement on the local level. Besides the "bourgeois" building activity we see the class of freedmen growing. The amphitheater of Lucus Feroniae is given by a *libertus*, M. Silius Epaphroditus, in the Claudian-Neronian epoch.[45] The road built by the *medicus*, P. Decimius P.l. Eros Merula, at Assisi or by the *Augustales* at Falerii[46] are eloquent examples of the emergence in this sector of the new reality of the Trimalchiones and of the crucial function of the euergetism in the dominant ideology, of which the "parvenu" freedmen, true heirs of the local aristocracy, are—in a debased form—the vocal interpreters.[47]

The profound architectural Hellenistic transformation in the second century B.C. is an exquisitely urban phenomenon. The colonies and settlements of the *cives Romani* were involved to some degree in this transformation, thanks to the censorial interventions and to the munificence of the members of the senatorial aristocracy, even if the projects are oriented toward more traditional forms, such as temples and war booty. The most various causes were involved here, from the inadequacy of local financing to the cultural and social traditionalism in the area, and to the needs of the urban aristocratic clients. The Latin colonies did not participate as much in the renovations, except for a few cases like Cosa, which because of precise economic reasons thanks to her maritime location, could maintain her position as an integral element of the more developed Latin-Campanian area. These settlements, especially those in the center of the peninsula, appeared little inclined to accept Roman technical and formal innovations until quite late and under the impulse of the direct insertion of the local ruling classes into the Roman political struggle, which was accelerated, if not initiated, by the consequences of the tragic episode at Fregellae. With the odd exception, such as Samnium, the building activity in the area of the *socii* is still more modest.

The true transformation occurs in the first century B.C., when the little or nonurbanized areas of central Italy see the arrogant entrance of the urban model, and when in the more properous areas of ancient urbanization the new building types appear. The phenomenon is composed of various aspects—ideological, social, economic. On the ideological plane, the significance of urbanization and of the new building typology for *urbanitas* is evident. It was central to the construction of the new political "consortium" which emerged from the Social War.[48] For the local aristocracy, for the intermediate classes who consequently stood forth in Roman politics, the picture of the city of origin is essentially that for any local ruling class in a society where the urban model is maintained as a discriminating point for belonging to the civil community. Where this is already in existence, the appreciation of a glorious and thus "civil" past assumes great ideological importance:[49] this gives rise to an insistence on the traditions of the *patria* in places with a long history and on famous documents with a great historical significance, which we see flower in the Etruscan cities, or on significant monuments, be they the "Ara della Regina" at Tarquinia or the sanctuary of Nortia at Spello.

The ideology and social structure are thus consolidated, becoming the cardinal point for the reproduction of the social structure itself. But such a process is not without a deep economic mechanism on which the basic techniques used for all these projects are especially revealing.

The most ancient phase of the appearance of the new building types in the early second century B.C., as noted, is characterized by the introduction of *opus incertum* on a large scale. *Opus incertum* is prevalently Latin-Campanian (which in fact delimits its diffusion) and is employed in building types between the last decades of the second and mid-first centuries B.C.

While this technique gradually spreads beyond the Latin-Campanian epicenter, the *urbs* begins to use the new reticulate technique which is tied to the process of "rationalization" of the most advanced slave mode of production.[50] As I have outlined elsewhere, this building technique was not as widely used as was the preceding *opus incertum* but was restricted in its greatest use to the area immediately around Rome and in the Phlegrean fields, in accord with the rise of speculative and deluxe buildings for primarily private rather than public use. Beyond this center, *opus reticulatum* was actually used for the great municipal building projects between the late first century B.C. and the mid-first century A.D.[51] But even this diffusion of technique reveals the socioeconomic situation: in the area of our analysis, the reticulate technique becomes less popular in favor of the older *opus incertum* and its variant with small square bricks. The farther one goes from the epicenter the more the typologically customary building projects are favored. It is not by accident that Vitruvius—an excellent example of the Italian "bourgeois" mental and cultural tradition—may speak of an "Italic common practice" and at the same time note as "ancient," but still more solid and secure, the *opus incertum.* The golden moment of our bourgeoisie can be placed at the juncture between the second and first centuries B.C. and Vitruvius was faithfully recording the prevailing sentiments regarding the more advanced production models between 40 and 30 B.C. It is not only attachment to a conservative mentality but also an awareness that these evolved production modes were essentially foreign to the economic interests of the municipal classes that he exemplifies.

NOTES

1. Torelli 1980: 75 ff. and *Società* 1981.
2. Torelli 1976: 97 ff.
3. Sensi 1977: 353 ff.
4. La Regina 1968: 387 ff. and 403 ff.
5. Santoro 1979: 215 ff. On the significance of this type of votive deposit and its relationship to the Romanization of the area, see Comella 1981: 717–803.
6. Mertens et al., 1969.
7. Cederna 1951: 169 ff. and Marinucci 1976.
8. Torelli 1981: 233 ff.
9. *Roma* 1973: *passim.*
10. Brown 1980.
11. *Supra* note 10: 33.
12. Welin 1953: 179 ff.
13. Livy XXXIX, 44.
14. For example, the monumental building,probably of the third century B.C. at Alfedena, in the heart of Samnium, which was published over eighty years ago by Mariani and has been justly brought to our attention again by La Regina 1976: 219 ff.
15. Strazzulla 1981: 187 ff.
16. Boethius and Ward Perkins 1970: 115 ff.; Coarelli 1976: 21 ff.
17. For the type, see Nabers 1969 and De Meyer 1962: 148 ff.

18. Cato *ap.* Servius *Aen.* 1, 421 (also a fragment of Sallust. *Hist.* and Cassius Hemina *passim magalia*). On Sinuessa, Livy XLI, 27; on Carthage, Plautus *Poen.* prol. 86 (cfr. Servius *Aen.* I, 368).
19. Livy XLI, 27; cfr. Gabba 1976: 316, n. 3.
20. The episode is certainly connected to that of 174 B.C. by Toynbee 1965: 233 and is in Livy XXXIX, 44.
21. Mommsen 1871–88: 429.
22. Livy XXXVI, 3.
23. Cianfarani 1970: figs. 107–10.
24. Verzar 1976: 122 ff.
25. On the Luni pediments, Coarelli 1970: 86 ff. At Luni the booty from Scarphaea was given by Acilius Glabrionus, *cos.* 191 B.C. (*ILLRP*, 321a).
26. Brown 1980: 56 ff.
27. *Supra* note 26: 56 ff.
28. Mercando 1976: 171 ff.
29. Brown 1980: 51 ff.
30. Mertens et al., 1969.
31. *Supra*, note 8 and Torelli 1981: 233 ff.
32. *Todi* 1981.
33. Pasquinucci 1975: 52 f., and Torelli 1977: 441.
34. Gaggiotti 1980: 283 ff.
35. Van Wonterghem 1976: 219 ff.
36. *ILLRP*, 327–31: a *titulus Mummianus* has been noted at Fabrateria Nova, probably coming from the ruins of Fregellae, see Castren 1978: 115 ff.). On the booty see Waurick 1975: 1 ff.
37. Torelli 1975: 187 ff.
38. A great deal of material is unfortunately unpublished. See for example the allusion to the generosity of an otherwise obscure *gens* Tongilia at Cosa in Brown 1980: 45, note 4. The epigraphic poverty *ante* 90 B.C. of colonies such as Aesernia, Alba Fucens, Narnia o Spoletium (contra Firmum Picenum *ILLRP*, 593–94 and Castrum Novum, also in Picenum, *ILLRP*, 566).
39. Materials presented in Vetter 1953 and Poccetti 1979 (see Poccetti 1979: 22 ff., for the publication of a sun dial from Mevania with an inscription in Umbrian).
40. Coarelli 1977: 1 ff.
41. Zevi 1976: 84 ff.
42. The entire problem, with respect to Etruria, Umbria, and Samnium, is treated by Torelli, Sensi, Gaggiotti in *Epigrafia* 1982: 43 and Frederiksen 1976: 341 ff.
43. Frederiksen 1976: 341 ff.

44. Gabba 1972: 73 ff., and 1976: 315 ff.
44. *ILS*, 6859.
45. *ILS*, 5369, 5373.
46. *Sabellica* and Bianchi Bandinelli 1967: 3 ff.
47. *Supra*, note 43.
48. Torelli 1975: 191 ff.
49. Torelli 1980: 139 ff.
50. *Supra*, note 16.

BIBLIOGRAPHY

Bianchi Bandinelli, R.

1967 "Arte plebea," *DdA* I: 3–19.

Boethius, A. and Ward Perkins, J.B.

1970 *Etruscan and Roman Architecture*. London.

Brown, F.

1980 *Cosa-The Making of a Roman Town*. Ann Arbor.

Cederna, A.

1951 "Carsoli. Scoperta di un deposito votivo del III secolo a.C.," *NSc:* 169–224.

Cianfarani, V.

1970 *Culture adriatiche d'Italia*. Roma.

Coarelli, F.

1970 "Polycles" in *St. Misc. XV Omaggio a Ranuccio Bianchi Bandinelli*, 77–89. Roma.

1976 "Architettura e arti figurative in Roma: 150–50 a.C.," in *Hellenismus in Mittelitalien* (ed. P. Zanker), 21–51. Göttingen.

1977 "Public building in Rome between the Second Punic War and Sulla," *PBSR* XLV: 1–23.

Comella, A.

1981 "Complessi votivi in Italia in epoca medio e tardo repubblicana," *MEFRA* XCII: 2, 717–803.

De Meyer, L.
1962 "L'étymologie de *Macellum* 'Marché'," *AC* XXXI: 148–52.

Epigrafia
1982 *Epigrafia e ordine senatorio: Tituli V.* Roma.

Frederiksen, M.W.
1976 "Changes in the Patterns of Settlement" in *Hellenismus in Mittelitalien* (ed. P. Zanker), 341–55. Göttingen.

Gabba, E.
1972 "Urbanizzazione e rinnovamenti urbanistici nell'Italia centromeridionale del I sec. a.C.," *SCO* XXI: 73–112.
1976 "Considerazioni politiche ad economiche sullo sviluppo urbano in Italia nei secoli II-I a.C.," in *Hellenismus in Mittelitalien* (ed. P. Zanker), 315–26. Göttingen.

Gaggiotti, M.
1980 *Umbria-Marche (Guida arch. Laterza).* Bari.

Hellenismus
1976 *Hellenismus in Mittelitalien* (ed. P. Zanker). Göttingen.

La Regina, A.
1968 "Ricerche sugli insediamenti Vestini," *MAL* XIII: 363–446.
1976 "Il Sannio" in *Hellenismus in Mittelitalien* (ed. P. Zanker), 219–54. Göttingen.

Marinucci, A.
1976 *Stipe votiva di Carsoli.* Roma.

Mercando, L.
1976 "L'ellenismo nel Piceno" in *Hellenismus in Mittelitalien* (ed. P. Zanker), 160–218. Göttingen.

Mertens, J. et al.
1969 "Alba Fucens I-II," *Etphilarchbelg.* Rome XII-XIII.

Mommsen, T.
1887–88 *Römisches Staatsrecht*[3]. 3 vols. Stuttgart.

Nabers, E.

1969 *Macella: a study in Roman Archaeology*. Diss., Princeton.

Pasquinucci, M.

1975 *Ausculum I*. Pisa.

Pietila Castren, L.

1978 "Some Aspects of the Life of Lucius Mummius Achaius," *Arctos* XII: 112–23.

Poccetti, P.

1979 *Nuovi documenti italici*. Pisa.

Roma

1973 *Roma medio-repubblicana: Aspetti culturali di Roma e del Lazio nei secoli IV e III a.C.* Roma.

Sabellica

1966 *Sculture Municipali dell'area sabellica tra l'età di Cesare e quella di Nerone. St. Misc X:* Roma.

Santoro, P.

1979 "La stipe di Monteleone Sabino," *Archeologìa Laziale* II: 215–16. Rome.

Sensi, L.

1977 *Manuali per il territorio-1 Val Nerina*. Roma.

Società

1981 *Società romana e produzione schiavistica*. Bari.

Strazzulla, M.J.

1981 "La produzione dal IV al I a.C." in *Società romana e produzione schiavistica*. Bari.

Todi

1981 *Todi-Verso un museo della città*. Todi.

Torelli, M.

1975 *Elogia Tarquiniensia*. Firenze.

1976 "La situazione in Etruria," in *Hellenismus in Mittelitalien* (ed. P. Zanker), 97–110. Göttingen. (Translated in this volume.)

1977 "Ausculum I," *Athenaeum* LV: 440–42.

1980 "Innovazioni nelle techniche edilizie romane tra il I sec, a.C. e il I sec. d.C.," in *Tecnologia, economia e società nel mondo romano*, 139–61. Como. (Translated in this volume.)

1980a *La cultura Italica*. Pisa.

1981 *Storia degli Etruschi*. Bari.

Toynbee, A.

1965 *Hannibal's Legacy*. Oxford.

Verzar, M.

1976 "Archäologische Zeugnisse aus Umbrien" in *Hellenismus in Mittelitalien* (ed. P. Zanker), 116–42. Göttingen.

Vetter, E.

1953 *Handbuch der italischen Dialekte*. Heidelberg.

Van Wonterghem, F.

1976 "Archäologische Zeugnisse spätrepublikanischer Zeit aus dem Gebiet der Peligner," in *Hellenismus in Mittelitalien* (ed. P. Zanker), 143–59. Göttingen.

Waurick, G.

1975 "Kunstraub der Römer. Untersuchungen zu seinen Anfängen anhand der Inschriften," *JRGZ* XXII: 1–46.

Welin, E.

1953 *Studien zur Topographie des Forum Romanum*. Lund.

Zevi, F.

1976 "Alatri" in *Hellenismus in Mittelitalien* (ed. P. Zanker), 84–96. Göttingen.

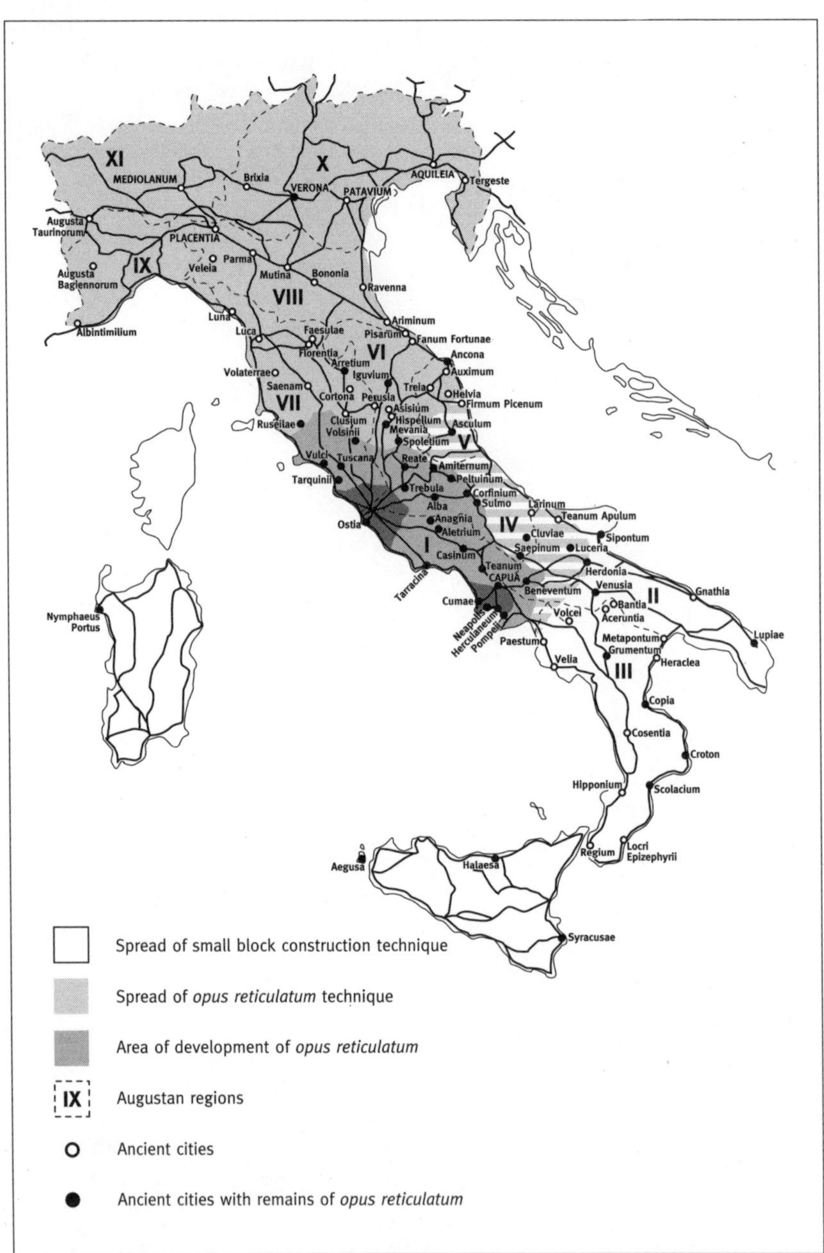
XI
X
MEDIOLANUM
Brixia
VERONA
PATAVIUM
AQUILEIA
Tergeste
Augusta Taurinorum
PLACENTIA
IX
Augusta Bagiennorum
Veleia
Parma
Mutina
Bononia
Ravenna
VIII
Luna
Albintimilium
Ariminum
Luca
Faesulae
Pisarum
Fanum Fortunae
Florentia
VI
Ancona
Arretium
Volaterrae
Iguvium
Auximum
Saenam
VII
Cortona
Perusia
Trela
Helvia
Firmum Picenum
Clusium
Asisium
Hispellum
Rusellae
Volsinii
Mevania
Asculum
Spoletium
V
Vulci
Tuscana
Reate
Tarquinii
Amiternum
Peltuinum
Trebula
Corfinium
Ostia
Alba
Sulmo
Larinum
Teanum Apulum
Anagnia
IV
Aletrium
Cluviae
Sipontum
I
Saepinum
Luceria
Casinum
Teanum
CAPUA
Herdonia
Tarracina
Beneventum
Venusia
II
Gnathia
Cumae
Bantia
Neapolis
Herculaneum
Pompeii
Volcei
Acerentia
Lupiae
Paestum
Metapontum
Grumentum
Velia
III
Heraclea
Copia
Cosentia
Croton
Hipponium
Scolacium
Regium
Locri Epizephyrii
Nymphaeus Portus
Aegusa
Halaesa
Syracusae
Spread of small block construction technique
Spread of *opus reticulatum* technique
Area of development of *opus reticulatum*
IX Augustan regions
Ancient cities
Ancient cities with remains of *opus reticulatum*

10

INNOVATIONS IN ROMAN CONSTRUCTION TECHNIQUES BETWEEN THE FIRST CENTURY B.C. AND THE FIRST CENTURY A.D.

Graeci e lapide duro aut silice aequato struunt veluti latericios parietes. cum ita fecerunt, isodomon vocant genus structurae; at cum inaequali crassitudine structa sunt coria, pseudoisodomon. tertium est emplecton; tantummodo frontibus politis reliqua fortuita conlocant. alternas coagmentationes fieri, ut commissuras antecedentium medii lapides obtineant, necessarium est, in medio quoque pariete si res patiatur; si minus, utique a lateribus. medios parietes farcire fractis caementis diatonicon vocant. reticulata structura, qua frequentissime Romae struunt, rimis opportuna est. structuram ad normam et libellam fieri, ad perpendiculum respondere oportet.

The Greeks build house-walls, as though they were using brick, of hard stone or silex dressed to a uniform thickness. When they follow this procedure the style of masonry is what they call "isodomon" or "masonry with equal courses." When the courses laid are of varying thickness the style is known as "pseudisodomon," a spurious variety of the former. A third style is the "emplecton" or "interwoven" in which only the faces are dressed, the rest of the material being laid at random. It is essential that joints should be made to alternate in such a way that the middle of a stone covers the vertical joint in the course last laid. This should be done even in the core of the wall if circumstances permit, and failing this, at least on the faces. When the core of the wall is packed with rubble, the style is "diatonicon," with single stones stretching from "face to face." Network masonry, which is very commonly used in buildings at Rome, is likely to crack. All ma-

> sonry should be laid to rule and level, and should be absolutely perpendicular when tested with a plummet.

This is how Pliny in chapters 171 and 172 of the thirty-sixth book of his *Natural History* presents his *summula* of building techniques, as it was customary to discuss the spread of the Greek techniques, the result of literary studies and an ages-old manual. Also customary are the rather summary notations on the Roman tradition, all tied to a practical remark on the various uses of concrete, its advantages and disadvantages. Thus, there is nothing new in Pliny's treatment. What does provide fresh interest is the comparison between the remarks of Pliny and the pages of Vitruvius (II, 8.5–67) where we find the same distinctions of *isodomon*, *pseudoisodomon*, *emplecton* and *diatonicon* with striking parallels (such as the mention of the use of *lateres* for the isodomic technique). Occasionally even the same word is found in the text of Pliny, to the extent that one wonders if Pliny derived some of his remarks from Vitruvius, as the *auctores* list of the thirty-sixth book of Pliny leads one to suppose.[1] This, then, is a comparative situation rich in possible interpretative developments.

Even more fascinating is the comparison between Pliny and Vitruvius regarding the Roman construction techniques. Vitruvius (II, 8.1) writes:

> *Structurarum genera haec sunt: reticulatum, quo nunc omnes utuntur, et antiquum, quod incertum dicitur. Ex his venustius est reticulatum, sed ad rimas faciendas ideo paratum, quod in omnes partes dissoluta habet cubilia et coagmenta. Incerta vero caementa alia super alia sedentia inter seque imbricata non speciosam sed firmiorem quam reticulata praestant structuram. Utraque autem ex minutissima sunt instruenda, uti materia ex calce et harena crebriter parietes satiati diutius contineantur.*

> These are the construction techniques: *reticulatum* which now everyone uses and then the older technique, the so-called *incertum*. Of the two, the *reticulatum* certainly looks better but is subject to fractures when the tufa and fill begin in every section to separate. Instead, the stones of the *incertum*, placed one on top of the other and linked together among themselves, create a structure which is not aesthetically pleasing but which is certainly more solid than the *reticulatum*. In any

event, both are executed in very small blocks, so that the walls, filled abundantly with cement (made of lime and of sand) may be more long lasting.

Vitruvius, writing at the beginning of the Augustan age, knew *opus incertum* as *antiquum* and attributed to the *opus reticulatum*—universally used by that time—greater visual appeal but lesser endurance. Pliny, writing in the Flavian period, ignored *incertum* and considered the *reticulatum* to be used with incredible frequency at Rome and, along with Vitruvius, maintained that the *reticulatum* was particularly subject to cracks. Nevertheless, Pliny, almost in response to Vitruvius' objections, suggests as a remedy the accurate use of the square, level, and plumb-bob instead of the liberal use of mortar.

Between these two judgements on the same technique, that of Pliny and that of Vitruvius, one can place the history of Roman construction technique in the period between the end of the Republic and the beginning of the first century of the empire. Thus the history of Roman building techniques is identified with the origin, the diffusion, and the end of the use of *opus reticulatum*. It is exactly this history and its connection to the economic history of the period that I would like to consider.

G. Lugli[2] dealt broadly with both the history and the more technical characteristics of *opus reticulatum* in his book *La tecnica edilizia romana con particolare riguardo a Roma e Lazio*. As the title of that work indicates and as all the reviewers and scholars who have used the book have had to acknowledge, Lugli's work begins from an entirely romano-centric and urban point of view. Thus, the relationship between the center and periphery of the empire is essentially not explored. A useful historical evaluation ought to largely leave aside Lugli's analysis and begin directly from the existing documentation.

It is necessary to reconstruct in an extremely detailed manner the area of diffusion of *reticulatum*, which Lugli[3] summarily traced out in order to define both the reasons for its development and the significance of its area of diffusion.

Starting from the Roman epicenter, *reticulatum*—from its initial appearance as *quasi-reticulatum*—was used for both public and private buildings. From the last decade of the second century B.C. the technique begins to be used, as F. Coarelli has recently established in a fundamental article.[4] After its "pioneering" use in the *lacus Iuturnae* in 116 B.C., structures such as the temple of the Magna Mater, temple B in the Largo Argentina, and the *Horrea Galbana*—all datable to the period between 110 and 100 B.C.—are all constructed in a rather developed *opus reticulatum*. The same developed *reticulatum* was used in contemporary urban habitations, a house on the Aventine and the well-known House of the Griffins on the Palatine. Although it was used in both private and public buildings, the new technique was slow to take over the scene completely. In the same buildings in which the first *reticulatum* occurs (temple of Magna Mater, temple B in Largo Argentina) *opus incertum* was still widely used in the foundations while in the great public undertakings of a few years later—such as the Tabularium of 78 B.C.—the more conservative technique was still amply employed. Specific public commitments of a precise origin may not be completely extraneous to the introduction of the new *reticulatum*. Most of the public buildings incorporating structural innovations are owed to the munificence of a few families: the *lacus Iuturnae* and the temple of the Magna Mater were built by the Metelli while temple B in Largo Argentina and—if, as I believe, Coarelli's identification is correct—the house of the Griffins are owed to the Lutatii Catuli.

But, in the years between the Social War and the Civil War, the technique quickly gained ground and seems to bridge that gap between technology used for support and technology used for aesthetics, the distance between *firmitas* and *venustas* of conservative Vitruvius which made the technique seem almost experimental at the initial moment of its use in Temple B in Largo Argentina. At Rome, in 87 B.C. walls were restored in *reticulatum*. At Ostia where there is much more abundant documentation even if the chronology is less certain, large expanses of the walls were built in *reticulatum* (ca. 70 B.C.) and in the same years, according to the new and convincing interpretation of F. Zevi,[5] the four small Republican temples were built which have the podium facades in *incertum* covered by tufa and, *venustum opus*, *reticulatum* on the other sides of the podium and in the cella. To these we can add two of the three temples[6] in the sacred area of Hercules and the small anonymous temple near the eastern gate of the *castrum*,[7] with their lovely revetments in *quasi-reticulatum*, dated to the same period, almost certainly before the building of the Sullan wall. More important, between 50 B.C. and the end of the Augustan period, at Ostia the use of *opus reticulatum* is widespread and not restricted to public buildings. It was used in the theater and the great storerooms for food storage (here I mean the *horrea* near the Roman port, those of Hortensius and those near the '*Semita dei Cippi*') but also in private houses, some of a certain level and size, others clearly of middle or lower levels, and in the tombs.[8]

In Rome, the years around the middle of the first century B.C. witness the uncontested triumph of *opus reticulatum*, which Augustus, his collaborators, and his generals used constantly in the Augustan building program, either in substructures or in revetments. From the theater of Pompey (55 B.C.) to those of Balbus (13 B.C.) and of Marcellus (13 B.C.), in the great Anio Vetus aqueduct, the acqua Marcia, and the acqua Alsietina (11–2 B.C.) as well as in Agrippa's constructions in the Campus Martius (25–12 B.C.), in the temple of Apollo on the Palatine (36–30 B.C.) and in the Mausoleum of Augustus (28 B.C.).[9] In fact, the buildings of the second half of the first century B.C. are characterized by the use of *reticulatum* revetments. The more monumental structures, such as the Temple of Mars Ultor (2 B.C.) obviously preserved the older techniques, isodomic masonry and mortar nucleus with block revetments: these buildings (if in reality they were holdovers) bear witness to the Vitruvian prejudice, in the use of *reticulatum* in constructions that were especially magnificent and of ideological importance. Nonetheless, it is important to note the use of *opus reticulatum* both in great public works, but also in more common popular architecture. The majority of *columbaria* in the Roman necropoleis, that of the Quinctii and of the Clodii, dated to after the mid-first century B.C. and up to those of the full imperial period, those of the Statilii, of the Arruntii and others, are all in *opus reticulatum*. Thus the appearance of *reticulatum* in these monuments proves that it was the typical construction technique used by speculators for the mass market.

Outside Rome and its harbor annex of Ostia, we lack certain fundamental elements on which to base an analysis. First, we have much less topographic knowledge about the area outside of Rome. For Ostia, an amply excavated city, and for Rome, there is elaborate literary and archaeological information about public and private monuments. Second, outside of Rome the consequent relative chronological certainty is also diminished. Few archaeological sites have been sufficiently explored and with sufficiently accurate stratigraphic observations. Furthermore, there are few cities with large enough excavated areas to allow comparisons, within and outside of the city, of the building techniques used or of the chronology of that use.

Nonetheless, certain useful elements do exist and we will discuss them as completely (and as cautiously) as possible. In the region south of Rome, which coincides broadly with ancient Latium Vetus and Latium Adiectum, *opus reticulatum* was generally used in the same way as it was in Rome. Undoubtedly, the number of public buildings in this technique is much less than at Rome. Great energy was expended by the local aristocracy in the late second century B.C. and in the first decades of the first century B.C. to give a Hellenistic appearance to the city and suburban sanctuaries. Certainly Praeneste, Tibur, Terracina, and Gabii enter into this category, but also elsewhere, in less macroscopic cases, the situation is identical. The almost pharaonic activity in extending and engrandizing Aletrium by Betilienus Varus, whose euergetism included all the streets inside the city, the entrance portico of the *arx*, the *macellum*, the *horologium*, the *campus* for the *ludi*, the facade of the basilica, fountains, and aqueducts: this must have left very little room for successive building initiatives.[10] My own research in three centers of Latium—Tibur, Cora, Anagnia (today better known thanks to the recent volumes of the *Forma Italiae* series)—only confirms this impression. At Tibur the principal public buildings, sacred or profane, of the city are virtually all in *opus incertum* or *quadratum:* the temple of Heracles, the buildings on the acropolis and of the forum,[11] the market,[12] and the city walls. The structures for roads with substructures within the city include six in *opus incertum* (and one in *opus quadratum*) as opposed to four in *opus reticulatum.*[13] Two of these pertain to the zone of expansion of the city to the southeast which took place after the second half of the first century B.C. On the other hand, the only public building securely non-republican in the forum area, the *Cesareum,*[14] datable to 19 B.C. on the basis of an inscription by a freedman of *M. Lartidius [quaestor pro] pr(aetore)*, father of *Sex. Lartidius* who is associated with *C. Asinius Gallus proconsul Asiae* in 5 B.C.,[15] is built in an excellent *reticulatum*. The amphitheater, the one great post-Republican building (dated at the latest to the middle years of the first century A.D.),[16] is also built in *opus reticulatum* and *mixtum*.

Instead, the panorama of luxury structures in *reticulatum* around Tivoli is exceedingly rich: five villas in *incertum* in contrast with at least ten in *reticulatum* (and *quasi-reticulatum*) and two with a phase in either *incertum* or *reticulatum*.[17] Thus, in addition to confirming the essentially *otium* character assumed by the territory of Tivoli in the late republic and the nature of the prevalent building activity in the early imperial period, the use of the new reticulate technique between the mid-first century B.C. and the mid-first century A.D. seems universal.

At Cora, the same situation exists. The walls and terracing, the temples and a public building (the only one known at the moment) are all in polygonal masonry and *opus incertum*.[18] Even simple walls are in *incertum* and only two are in *reticulatum*.[19] All of the four hundred villas found in the area are in polygonal masonry, *opus caementicium* with or without *incertum* revetments except for eight in *opus reticulatum*.[20]

At Anagnia, splendid ashlar masonry walls enclose the remains of an ancient city.[21] Among the ruins, there are five terracing walls and remains of two structures in *opus quadratum*, two in *opus incertum*. The only large public building known—perhaps the substructure of a sanctuary—is in *opus quadratum* and *incertum* with some later additions in *reticulatum*.[22] In the territory of Anagnia, there are fifty villas in concrete, polygonal masonry, and *incertum* with only four in *opus reticulatum*, but of those four, two have earlier phases in *incertum*.[23]

In Campania, *opus reticulatum* has long been acknowledged as a technique originating from an urban environment in contrast to *opus incertum*. Thus, the more vital centers, Puteoli first, then Cuma and Neapolis, may be where *opus reticulatum* was the most intensively and widely used. At Puteoli even the sepulchers are in *reticulatum*, not to mention some important public works such as the smaller Augustan amphitheater or, at Cuma, the so-called Capitolium, the colossal crypts of Agrippa and Cocceius, or at Neapolis the complex of public buildings beneath San Lorenzo and the so-called Tomb of Vergil.[24] A summary examination permits us to ascertain that around the epicenter of Puteoli, in the most important cities on the Gulf of Naples, *opus reticulatum*, introduced by Rome, has a use as extensive as that which the technique enjoyed in the capital and, by and large, in ancient Latium.

The diffusion of the reticulate technique is exemplified by the Vesuvian cities. At Herculaneum,[25] a city which developed greatly after the Social War in contrast to Pompeii, the principal public buildings are in *opus reticulatum*. The palaestra, the theater (dated to ca. 30 B.C.), the central and suburban baths, the great noble houses with a view of the sea, the houses of the Cervi, of Argus, of the mosaic Atrium and *Casa dell'Albergo* are all in *opus reticulatum*. Additionally, many constructions of a middle or lower level—the poorer or modest homes of the artisan or small businessman were also built in the same technique. There are also numerous houses and shops along the *insula orientalis* and the lesser decumanus which have walls completely or partially in reticulate.[26]

The picture of Pompeii is slightly different.[27] Proportionately, there are far fewer public buildings in *reticulatum*. Except for the minor public buildings, such as the bases in the forum or the added or restored walls, such as the *comitium*, the *odeon* stage, the facade of the Sullan Baths in the Forum or the restorations on the temples of Venus and Zeus Meilichios, only the Temple of Fortuna Augusta, the only public building securely dated to the Augustan age, has part of its walls in *opus reticulatum*. On the other hand, the majority of better quality houses, restored or enlarged between Augustus and Nero, are reticulate structures. Still, the use of the technique at Pompeii seems rather limited and superficial. There are very few tombs in reticulate at Pompeii and, as we shall see, the joint panorama of the city and necropoleis and of the building activity after the A.D. 62 earthquake offer useful points for general considerations.[28]

Let us move on to the Augustan regions of Italy, in order to complete and sharpen our information. Although we will certainly note isolated monuments, I am going to concentrate on those more fully explored sites which usually offer good comparisons and comparanda.

Bruttium and Lucania are two interesting cases. Roman Paestum, widely explored but inadequately published,[29] did not offer any examples of *opus reticulatum*. The basilica in the Forum[30] which has most recently been dated to the Augustan age, was built in a mixture of *incertum* and bricks. At Velia, *opus reticulatum* is virtually missing despite considerable building activity between the mid-first century B.C. and the mid-first century A.D. Copia-Thuri is another large city which has been extensively explored. Despite a number of remains dated to the early empire, only two buildings were constructed with *opus reticulatum:* an L-shaped portico[31] in the *Casa Bianca* area (possibly *horreum*) and a large public building which was later transformed into a theater. This last building was probably due to the generosity of L. Venuleius Brocchus, an important local man or, even more likely, to his father, as is demonstrated by two inscriptions by Brocchus which were found in this building and by the roof tiles stamped with the name of Cleandridas, the slave of L.

Venuleius. There are no reticulate constructions from the other large cities of the peninsula (among these is Locri, the object of huge excavations in both earlier and more recent times) nor from the area between Reggio Calabria and Vibo Valentia, nor in the other poleis of Magna Graecia. Nothing from Metaponto, virtually deserted from the time of the Roman conquest onwards, nothing from Herakleia which has also been amply excavated and whose territory has been studied in a *Forma Italiae* volume. Slightly different, but no less interesting, is the situation in the hinterland. We know nothing about Potentia. At Volcei (also treated in the *Forma Italiae* series) we know of the existence of just one monument in *reticulatum* but even that is really *opus mixtum*, a large villa in the area of San Nicola. In light of local epigraphic evidence, this villa is probably that of the Bruttii Praesentes.[32] The theater (perhaps that of a villa) at Gioiosa Ionica (despite what Lugli says) is not in reticulate but rather in *opus incertum*.[33]

Three centers provide a visible exception to the general overview of *Regio III*, Scolacium,[34] Grumentum, and Croton. At Scolacium the theater and the amphitheater were in *opus mixtum* and it seems that there was a mausoleum in *reticulatum*. At Croton, the remaking of the temenos wall to the Temple of Hera Lacinia was in *reticulatum*.[35] Doubtless in this last case we are dealing with a reworking of the wall which was tied to the Augustan religious restoration (as the sanctuary was prestigious in ancient Italy) and to the presence at Croton of a Roman colony. Grumentum, probably a Sullan colony,[36] had both its theater and wall in *quasi-reticulatum*. The wall is well-dated by inscriptions[37] to the years 57–51 B.C. The evidence from Grumentum, in fact, closely resembles that of Scolacium, a Gracchan colony of 122 B.C., reinforced by Nerva.[38] In both cases we have either a colonial foundation or a second colonial deduction. Grumentum became the pivotal point of Sullan control on the extreme southern part of the Italic revolt while the large public buildings of Scolacium—practically cathedrals in the desert of Roman Magna Graecia can be explained by the specific interest Nerva had in his only—for all we know—colonial undertaking in Italy.

There are other "cathedrals in the desert" in Apulia: the amphitheaters in reticulate at Lupiae, Luceria, Sipontum and the important complex of public buildings at Herdonia,[39] where in the late Augustan age the sixth phase of the wall, the baths, and the amphitheater are in *reticulatum* while the basilica, datable between 24 and 15 B.C., is in *quasi-reticulatum* and the *macellum* (possibly Trajanic) is in *opus mixtum*. Lupiae and Sipontum are certainly isolated episodes. Sipontum was a depopulated city until the Roman colonial deductions in 194 B.C.,[40] and the excavations of various urban areas there, unfortunately unpublished, have brought to light the exceptional quality of the construction of the amphitheater. Luceria is an Augustan colony and the amphitheater (also Augustan)[41] was a gift of the *eques M. Vecilius Campus*. Although the theater at Lupiae is built in *opus incertum*[42] it seems to be a unique case to judge from the other buildings excavated in the urban center. The extensive Belgian excavations at Herdonia have revealed a complex situation. Although the early imperial private buildings are not in *opus reticulatum*,[43] there was a substantial amount of financing available for public buildings. This availability of funds came about because the city was in the center of an extensive agricultural area and above all, on the road between Beneventum and Brundisium and thus essentially on the way to the east, as Strabo noted (VI, 3.7). The reason for the imposing construction of the *macellum* and perhaps the theater was the construction of the Appia Traiana. In comparison with this evidence from Herdonia, the vacuum in the area is noteworthy. Egnatia, amply excavated, has no monument in *reticulatum*.[44] Teanum Apulum, despite Lugli's indications,[45] has a city wall which possibly has an *incertum* revetment, while cities such as Bantia and Acheruntia[46] were completely without constructions in *reticulatum*. As already noted for Herdonia, the thoroughfare Brundisium-Venusia-Beneventum could be considered the only developed line in the region and the large cities along that road are the only ones with constructions in *opus reticulatum*—and only public buildings at that. Unfortunately, we know virtually nothing about Brundisium,[47] where there is no documentation of *opus reticulatum*. At Venusia with the so-called House of Horace and the amphitheater,[48] at Beneventum, with its primitive theater plan and the giant building in the Santi Quaranta area,[49] and at Aeclanum with its walls, there are greater ties with the more developed areas of Campania.[50]

In the *Regio IV* (*Sabini* and *Sannium*) we can delineate two areas, one with more direct contact with Latium and Campania where *opus reticulatum* was regularly used and the other where the episodic or exceptional use of the technique occurred. The first area takes in all of Sabina from Cures to Amiternum where the public buildings, and in part also the private ones, from the early imperial period are relatively consistently constructed in *opus reticulatum:* the houses from Trebula Mutuesca and Amiternum exemplify this situation.[51] To the southwest of this area, which runs from the Salaria as far as Ausculum,[52] there is the remainder of Samnium in which *reticulatum* was used only desultorally and occasionally. Only a few important cities (the capitals, let us say, of the old tribal areas) have a few buildings in *reticulatum* and certainly not all the cities have buildings in *opus reticulatum* and *mixtum*. The theater at Peltuinum and the two lesser remains—probably villas—at Civita di Bagno and Cepegatti are the total of the evidence that pertains to the teritory of the Vestini.[53] The small temple and theater of Chieti[54] are all the evidence for the Marrucinian territory, a few walls of unidentified buildings, together with a remaking of the sanctuary of Hercules Curinus at Sulmo and Corfinium[55] is what exists in the Pelignian territory while there is apparently nothing documented for the territory of the Frentani. Instead, the situation in the territory of the Carecini is exemplified by the city of Cluviae, brilliantly identified by La Regina, with its impressive remains at Piano La Roma:[56] here all the public buildings, walls, theater, baths are in *opus reticulatum*. This wholly exceptional case can only be explained by a specific act of public munificence. Luckily, in this case we know the personal politics and Cluvian origin of the famous conservative Elvidius Priscus[57] the only person to whom we can attribute such an exceptional and grandiose act. One can outline the same circumstances for the principal city of central Samnium, Saepinum.[58] Here the walls, in *opus quasi-reticulatum* and the buildings (in *reticulatum*) on the north side of the Forum, are the result of a direct action by the imperial house, as is shown by the well-known series of inscriptions on the city gates with the names of the dedicants, Tiberius and Drusus the elder in A.D. 4–7. The proof of the exceptional character of this munificence—and the construction technique linked to it—is found in the fact that the basilica, built in circa A.D. 1, and the theater, built between A.D. 10–15, presumably with local financing are not built in *reticulatum* but in small square blocks, a technique which remained in use locally until the late empire. The other well-documented example from Samnium, Alba Fucens, a Latin colony in the territory of the Marsi, does not conform to the observations made for Saepinum. Alba Fucens developed extraordinarily between the end of the second and the mid-first century B.C. as testified by a series of large buildings in polygonal masonry and *incertum*. The constructions in *opus reticulatum* with polygonal foundations include the theater, the amphitheater, and the exedra of the north terrace.[59] An inscription found in the amphitheater happily provides the name of the powerful benefactor, the praefect of the praetorium from A.D. 31–37, Q. Naevius Cordus Sutorius Macro.[60] These works, completed *ex testamento* after, perhaps, the death of Caligula, can find a good parallel with the mixed techniques used in another public undertaking in the area, the drains of Fucino, built contemporaneously to or slightly afterwards by Claudius in A.D. 41–52.[61]

In Etruria, too, *opus reticulatum* was widely used as far north as Tarquinia[62] where the Tullian baths, with the senator P. Tullius Varro as benefactor, were built using this technique. At Tuscana[63] the substructures of the Colle di San Pietro and the baths are in *reticulatum*. Farther north, the use of *reticulatum* is rarer. At Vulci it was used very little[64] but rather used more liberally as far as Volsinii and Rusellae. At Rusellae the substructures of the Forum, the amphitheater, the basilica, the baths (identified as a "villa")—in other words most of the public buildings are in *opus reticulatum*.[65] This impressive construction activity seems to be the product of the colonial deduction in the area, the chronology of which is tied by archaeological documentation to the Augustan age[66] rather than to the few and obscure literary and epigraphical sources. Volsinii, with its relative abundance of structures in *reticulatum*[67] is midway between the two situations at Rusellae and Vulci. Some of the large public works, for example, the baths, are in *reticulatum* while the private buildings remain tied to the more traditional *opus quadratum* and *opus incertum*, as is shown by the rich late Republican and Augustan *domus* at Poggio Moscini.[68] In effect, beyond Volsinii the occurrence of reticulate buildings is basically episodic. In the remainder of Etruria, only the amphitheater at Arretium[69] and a few remains in *opus mixtum* in the territory between Saena and Arretium, at Roma Vecchia,[70] probably the villa of a rich local *possessor*, are built in *reticulatum*. In archaeologically well-known cities such as Luna, Volaterrae, or Faesulae, revetments of small square blocks dominate as in the Volterra theater, dating from the beginning of the first century A.D. and in the theater and baths at Faesulae, also from the early imperial period.[71] The other less well-investigated cities—but still reasonably well-known—such as Florentia, Luca, Cortona, Perusia—also lack evidence for the use of *opus reticulatum*.[72]

The situation in Umbria and Picenum is scarcely different. The areas closer to the Valle Tiberina, such as Ocriculum or the great port building at the confluence of the Tevere and Paglia rivers,[73] are more within the sphere of Latium and follow the trend set there. Otherwise, the documentation for *opus reticulatum* and *mixtum* occurs only along the important lines of communication, the Flaminia and the Salaria, in a more sporadic fashion the farther one goes from the urban area. Still, at Mevania and at Spoletium, the technique is widely used. At Mevania, it is employed in the large building (possibly the substruction of a large temple) near the former Dominican convent, in another building near the Porta Foligno, and in some restorations of the city wall originally built in squared blocks.[74] At Spoletium, *reticulatum* was used in the theater and the public building complex beneath the Benedetti, Bandini, and Andreani houses.[75] Already at Carsulae,[76] even if the theater is in *reticulatum*, all the other buildings (all of the early empire) from the amphitheater to the small twin temples are made in small square blocks with or without supplementary brickwork. The same is true elsewhere: Asisium, Hispellum, Vettona, Nuceria, with the isolated exception of the theater at Iguvium and a little noted public building at Arna.[77]

The situation is no different in Picenum. A few isolated instances of *reticulatum*—the amphitheater and baths at Ancona,[78] or the walls of a sepulcher at Treia[79]—are to be compared to the splendid Augustan constructions in small square blocks at Fanum and with other structures of similar masonry or with stone and brick at important centers such as Auximum, Urbs Salvia, Firmum, Helvia Ricina.[80] Here, as in northern Etruria and Umbria, the same phenomenon as found in southern Latium is repeated, at least in part: a strongly developed area with a complete almost impenetrable resistence to the adoption of *reticulatum*. Thus, in these areas we find a material parallel for the words of the conservative Vitruvius, active in exactly this region, and the proof of a tenacious attachment to the traditional building techniques, to *opus quadratum*, and to structures made in small square blocks.

Northern Etruria, Umbria, and Picenum are strongly tied to a traditional culture, a way of building architecturally and structurally which is also peculiar to the other Augustan *regiones* of the north, to Veneto, to Emilia, to Liguria. Here there is virtually no use of *reticulatum*. With the singular exception of a very prestigious undertaking, the Verona theater,[81] all the cities in the region, from Aquileia to Tergeste to Ariminum, Brixia, Velleia, or Albintimilium—all very vital centers in the period of our interest—have a tangible and real explosion in public buildings and private projects in the traditional technique using small square blocks.[82] This mode of construction seems then to be singularly homogeneous along the Adriatic coast up to the very threshold of the area where *reticulatum* reigns. This common construction practice coincides with the most vital area of an Italic cultural *koiné* which was responsible for the transmission to the north—first to Cisalpina and then to the Narbonese area—of artisan practice and of artistic forms which constituted the skeleton of provincial Roman culture.[83]

We should turn back now to the main point of our argument, the question of the *opus reticulatum*. The map shows the distribution of this technique and of the contemporary use of small square blocks: this map permits us to synthesize that which we have analyzed. The epicenter of *opus reticulatum* was the urban area with its annex in the great emporium at Puteoli, where *reticulatum* was used at all levels, in both public and private buildings, created for luxury or for practical reasons. This epicenter dominated undisputedly what was done in public building in both urban and local spheres over a vast region—all of *Regio I* and the adjacent areas of the regions of Etruria as far as Rusellae, Volsinii, of Umbria along the Tiber River, of Sabine lands as far as Amiternum, of Apulia up to the Beneventum-Aeclanum line. Outside of this area, *opus reticulatum* was used episodically and in exceptional circumstances.

The line of diffusion of the construction technique follows the major road systems and the river systems which also constituted part of the communications network. *Reticulatum* was used not only for the large villas of *otium* in the imperial period from the Tuscan archipelagus to the Calabrian coast but also for the major villas of the inland areas which belonged to rich senatorial Italian families, for example, the houses of San Nicola near Volcei, or Roma Vecchia in northern Etruria, and are found in areas otherwise without examples of *reticulatum*. Luxury constructions, then, outside of the principal area of diffusion, occasionally prestigious buildings such as theaters, amphitheaters, baths (in the more prosperous cities) which were ordered by local patrons were also built in *reticulatum*. Those more prosperous cities with important buildings in *reticulatum* were often Roman colonies with an evident economic tie to the center.

The exceptional cases are almost always theaters and amphitheaters. This category includes Grumentum, Scolacium, and Copia in *Regio III*, Luceria, Lupiae, Sipontum, and Herdonia in *Regio II*, Saepinum, Alba,

Fucens, Cluviae, Sulmo, Teate, and Peltuinum in *Regio IV*, Ausculum, Treia, and Ancona in *Regio V*, Mevania and Spoletium in *Regio VI*, Arretium in *Regio VII*. Very often, at Cluviae as at Alba Fucens, at Saepinum as at Scolacium we know the names of the patrons, members of the imperial house (Saepinum), high-ranking officials (Alba Fucens) or large landowners of senatorial rank (Cluviae). The exceptional use of the technique and the high-level patronage emerge even more clearly when we leave the peninsula. Sicily had only three large buildings in *reticulatum:* the amphitheater at Syracuse, the unique quadrangular structure at Favignana and the remains of a building in the forum at Halaesa. The amphitheater at Syracuse pertains to the colony founded for Augustus' veterans;[84] the structure at Favignana, perhaps a guard tower or military *statio*,[85] could well be connected to Agrippa's reorganization of the imperial navy, for which there is extraordinary archaeological documentation at Misenum. The remains at Halaesa[86] are the most difficult to fit into the scheme and perhaps should be linked to the Augustan provisions made for *civitates liberae et immunes* for which there is some interesting numismatic evidence.[87] Sardinia offers only one example of *reticulatum*, the beautiful villa at Porto Conte, the Nymphaeus Portus in the northwest of the island,[88] certainly to be identified with an enormous imperial villa, specifically that of the concubine of Nero Acte.[89]

Still more singular are the extremely rare remains of *opus reticulatum* in the eastern provinces, of which there are two excellent examples. The first is that of Tulul Abu El Alayig[90] in Palestine near Jericho—a colossal villa over 150 meters long with niches and semicolumns and a central theatrical type cavea which can only be compared to the huge Italian imperial villas. A close parallel for this Palestinian villa is furnished by the Farnesina villa at Rome, also in *opus reticulatum*, which is attributed to Agrippa and actually reveals both the origin and destination of the grandiose complex which was a generous gift of Augustus or Agrippa to the ruling family of Judea. On a par with this building are the baths of Elaioussa, capital of Cilicia Aspera, which are built in an excellent *reticulatum*,[91] and ought to be considered a gift of Augustus to King Archelaos I of Cappadocia. Archelaos, in 20 B.C., changed to Sebaste the name of the city recently bestowed to him by the *princeps* of Rome.

These examples lead us to consider the organization of work which this technique presupposes and thus its economic significance. The very fact of finding *reticulatum* at a great distance from the center of the empire and thus from the center of the use of the technique, but also at closer range (in the areas of ancient Italy around the center of development), perfectly executed examples of *reticulatum* shows that the work was executed by organized squads of stone cutters, carpenters and masons who followed the entire undertaking from the quarry to the actual building of the wall. This then is the work of large *équipes.* The various components attended to their respective phases of construction, obviously following a division of labor and, by sea or by land, went from the center to the periphery, from Rome to the gulf of Naples to the Italian *municipia* and colonies for the large projects—theaters, amphitheaters, baths. Such buildings were *de rigueur* in the creation of the desired atmosphere of *urbanitas* around the various cities, and necessitated both the *venustas* of the reticulate technique and the expertise in planning works which were both exceptional and unknown in the preceding building tradition. It seems quite possible that the head of these large *equipes*, in addition to a *redemptor operis*, may have been an *architectus*, master builder, who would be necessary for the completion of works which were typologically and architectonically foreign to the normal building practice. We do not have an ordered study[92] of the epigraphic documentation on *architecti* or *redemptores operis* of the early imperial period but from a few examples we can extract some useful pointers. The close tie between these functions can be demonstrated by a number of literary and epigraphic sources, from the late imperial constitution[93] which make the architect and the contractor jointly responsible in the event of crimes against the construction workers/slaves. We know of the *architectones* who signed the lists at the quarry exits,[94] of the *architectus* and *faber navalis* from a Roman funerary epigraph,[95] of the *redemptor* and *pictor scaenarius* P. Cornelius P.l. Philomusus,[96] possibly the freedman of P. Cornelius, the architect from Ostia, and the *praefectus fabrum* of Lutazio Catulo and so forth. It is along this line then, linked as it is to the slave mode of production, that one can see, from the first half of the first century B.C. onwards, a progressive formal disengaging by the dominant classes from this lucrative but undignified enterprise.[97] Thus, one can also explain why the profession of *architectus*, after its late republican popularity among men of rank—C. Mucius, D. Cossutius, P. Cornelius, and L. Vitruvius—declines from the Augustan period onwards into *ars* executed by slaves and freedmen, often at the same rank as the *redemptores* themselves.

The technique of *opus reticulatum* as I have shown elsewhere and as F. Coarelli has so well demonstrated,[98] represents the "rationality" of an "example of pre-capitalistic development" in a production mode based on slaves. The availability of large numbers of slaves, in any case, cannot by itself explain the advance of the new technique over the old one, since convicted slaves and war prisoners had been working in quarries since Greek times. In fact, *reticulatum* demands a rather specialized type of manpower for the cutting of the *cubilia*, the building stone units of standardized size and format, and, so Pliny tells us, the actual wall construction needed the expertise of a good *faber*. The entire technique, and in particular the size of the *cubilia*, can be explained by a combination of motives which in any event can be justly attributed to the functioning of the slave production mode. The fundamental aspect is that provided by an embryonic tendency in the production to evolve towards a kind of "mechanization," in which there was a strict division of labor and cooperation-even though compulsory. The division of labor and cooperation together created the conditions conducive to the formation of servile *familiae* capable of producing foods and products in a rudimentary form of manufacturing. The example of the production of Arretine pottery, studied by G. Pucci,[99] provides sufficient clarification thanks to the quantity of data that we have on the subject. For the construction trade we can note the example of the servile *familia* of Crassus cited by Plutarch—the importance and authenticity of which has recently been questioned.[100]

Regarding the earlier use of *incertum*, the "rationalization" of the mode of production seems evident. For *opus incertum*, the quarrying of the construction material and the actual building of the desired structure (as was also true for the more ancient techniques, for example, *opus quadratum*) are two very separate elements of production and disparate in their respective need for forced labor. The quarry work could be entrusted to rather low level labor while the actual placement of the blocks required highly specialized labor, totally independent from the work done in the quarries. For *opus incertum* the mason was expected to understand the ordering of the larger and smaller blocks which had to be recut and laid in position in such a way as to create the minuscule mosaic (almost polygonal in appearance) of the wall surface. With the *reticulatum* instead, the mason only needed to place the *cubilia* which arrived ready to use from the quarry, thereby reducing the mason's necessary work time by eliminating the final finishing of the smaller and larger blocks once they were in place: this was now accomplished at the moment of the quarrying. Thus, the tendency toward standardization and "mechanization" of the production was reflected in the social condition of the workers which at the same time was lowered by the same tendency as was the rank of architect.

The embryonic nature of this process has well-known sources. I will only note one fact which is closely tied to this argument. It is only with capitalism that transportation distance and actual work time become central to economic choices and, in their abstract form, to theoretical dispute. In the Roman building trade, and in texts, we find evidence for the pressure of spatial and temporal factors exercised on the production process. Vitruvius (II, 8.7), speaking about *emplecton*, praises the Greek fashion and contrasts with the Greek the nasty results of the Roman way of doing things, which arise from the fact that *nostri*, our builders, are *celeritati studentes* "those who are in a hurry." And thus, in the quarry material from Anicianae near Lake Bolsena praised by Pliny (XXXVI, 168) or by Vitruvius (II, 3.4) instead of the ordering of time we have the ordering of space: "*quae si prope urbem essent, dignum esset, ut ex his officinis omnia perficerentur.*" But beyond these notations nothing else emerges from our sources, confirming once again the nature of the "limited development" of the ancient slave-labor economy.

Next to this tendency towards a partial mechanization of finished products in conjunction with the diffusion of the reticulate technique, there are also further political and ideological motives. In particular the necessities of *locatio* and *probatio*, in other words of accounts, critical for the great public undertakings and of the tenders given,[101] which from the second half of the second century B.C. assume gigantic proportions over a vast area. The "rationality" of the size of the *cubilia* could have enormously facilitated the accounts for the works. But the ideological motive also had its influence and importance. Vitruvius (but significantly not Pliny) considers the reticulate '*venustas*' an expression of the cultural hegemony of the urban model, derived from the ideology of *urbanitas* which the monuments in *reticulatum*—theaters, amphitheaters, baths—turned into a reality for the dominant classes of the capital as for those of the Italian provincial areas.

In this sense, the origin and development of *opus reticulatum* furnishes a tidy picture of the productive processes of the "classical" aspects of the slave mode of production. This is no less tidy than the picture of the decline of the same technique in which we find the reflection of large structural economic transformations but within the sphere of ideological transformation.

Opus reticulatum under Nero and the Flavians was replaced by *opus mixtum* where ever more obvious repetitions and joins in brickwork limited the *reticulatum* to very small surfaces of the walls. With Hadrian, the *opus mixtum* was replaced by *opus testaceum*, by brickwork. The limited development of this technique, largely urban and controlled by the dominant classes, is confirmed both archaeologically and epigraphically by the distribution of *lateres*. I will limit myself to several observations. The area of diffusion of *opus mixtum* and brickwork is noticeably more restricted than that of *opus reticulatum*. With few exceptions,[102] the reconstructions at Pompeii and Herculaneum after the earthquake of A.D. 62 imitate *opus mixtum* with brick courses and with revetments of *incertum* without any use of *reticulatum*. Only the big public enterprises of imperial benefaction in Latium and Campania[103] (in reality there are very few cases of nonimperial patronage) use the mixed technique perfectly, while in the north central part of Italy there are only a few timid appearances of *opus mixtum* but with the more usual revetments in small square blocks.[104]

The same diffusion of the urban brickwork (today well-known thanks to the work of the Finnish School)[105] reveals that the boundaries of the Italian market for the urban *figlinae* are narrower than previously thought, with only infrequent occurrences outside of Italy such as the exceptionally luxurious African constructions. The villa at Tagiura in Tripolitania has provided sixty-five stamped bricks representing six different workshops: all the workshops are Roman.[106] Additionally, the control of brick manufacture seems now to have been wholly imperial or senatorial: in the lists of the *domini* of *figlinae* of the second and third centuries initially compiled by T. Helen, of the 149 names, 79 are men of senatorial rank.[107]

The slow transformation of the construction tradition from *reticulatum* to *mixtum* and then to brick coincides with the slow decline of a mode of production: the shifting of interests towards the brick production cannot be separated from the prevalence of an agriculture in which—in place of specialized cultivation—grain becomes the dominant crop. The *lateres* are *opus doliare* as they often stamp the *figlinae*, products of factories engaged principally—or at least initially—in turning out *dolia* or large containers for grains.

But it is not my intention to foray into the other phase of Roman construction. The history of *opus reticulatum* is, as was said at the outset, contained between the two phrases of Vitruvius and Pliny. Vitruvius, the traditionalist who was living at the height of the new construction technique said, "*quo nunc omnes utuntur*" "that now everyone uses it": the second, sharp observer of his times and thus of the decline of the technique noted "*qua frequentissime Romae struunt*" "that the *reticulatum* was used very frequently at Rome" and was silent on its *venustas* touted instead by Vitruvius. And thus, as for agriculture, from specialised craft and culture one passes to a model of extensive exploitation of the soil,[108] in the same area where villas using slave labor dominated. In the same period (end of the first/beginning of the second century A.D.) from a stricter division of labor and higher level of cooperation suited to *opus reticulatum* one passed to a less complex technique with a reduced level of cooperation, suited to both the use of brick construction and to a different economic structure.[109] On this question, see the proceedings of the Seminario Internazionale di Studio held by the Istituto Gramsci (Pisa 4–6/1/1979) entitled *Forma di produzione schiavistica e tendenze della Società romana: I a.C.-II d.C. Un caso di sviluppo precapitalistico* (now published, see *Società* 1981).

APPENDIX: DATING OF SOME MONUMENTS FROM TIBUR ON THE BASIS OF EPIGRAPHIC TEXTS

The Caesareum of Tibur is dedicated *pro reditu Caesaris A[gusti]* by Diphilus, a freedman of Varena Q.f. and of M. Lartidius Sex. f. (*Inscr.It.* I, 1.74). This same Diphilus built the *mensa ponderaria* showing a reticulate wall between two projections built in *incertum* (Giuliani 1970: 62). He also dedicated two statues to his *patroni Varena Q.f. maio*r (I do not accept *maior* as a cognomen as others do) and to *[M. Lart]idius Sex. f. [q(uaestor) pro] pr(aetore)* (*Inscr.It.* I, 1.224–225). That this M. Lartidius may be the father and not the son of Sex. Lartidius leg. Asiae of 9 B.C. (as Syme maintains, 1956: 207 and on the basis of this, Petersen in *PIR* IV^2 L 115, L116 and Wiseman 1971: 62) may be demonstrated by more than one fact: one, the dedication to Varena uses still the formula with the dative in -ai; two, the archaic formula *s(enatus) c(onsulto)* on the dedicatory inscription to indicate the decurional decree cannot refer to the son (evidently already dead by the time of the dedication) of an Asian legate of 5 B.C. who thus lived between the late Augustan and the Tiberian ages. Nor does the fact that a fellow freedman of Diphilus may have died at Nola in A.D. 21. (*CIL* X, 1333) seem to contradict this chronology: we should remember the examples of imperial freedmen dated some fifty years after the death of the patron (Weaver 1972: 70 ff.). One other element should also be evaluated: *Inscr.It.* I, 140 was found together with the famous statue of the so-called "general of Tivoli" (we do not actually know how pertinent to one another they are) and is a dedication by one *[---]o/ [---]pro pr./ [---]trib.* The inscription is on 'giallo antico,' the same marble used for the M. Lartidius Sex. f. and Varena Q.f. dedications in the *mensa ponderaria:* this is a rather unusual stone for dedications at Tivoli. As Diphilus was *mag(ister) Herc(ulaneus)* it would not be surprising to find a dedication by him to his patron in the central sanctuary of this cult. Lastly, the *mensa ponderaria* was restored in the Flavian period (as the letters of the inscription would indicate) and that dedication was cut over the inscription of Diphilus: it is possible then that the restoration may have happened in a period rather distant from that of the original construction of Diphilus who seems to have been active between 30 and 10 B.C. rather than between A.D. 10 and A.D. 30. Whatever the *origo* of Lartidius, which Syme (*loc. cit.*) prefers to place at Pistoriae, it seems more consistent with the evidence that we have to situate him at Tibur.

The amphitheater is an example of another loose use of epigraphic sources. M. Tullius Blaesus, if he is identified with the curator in the dedication of L. Minicius Natalis (*Inscr.It.* I, 1.113) dated to about A.D. 150. (Thomasson 1960: 72) cannot be the donor of the amphitheater as all have deduced from inscription *Inscr.It.* I, 202 (*ILS*, 5630, cfr. Giuliani 1970: 739, note 174). As the text of *Inscr.It.* I, 202 shows, Blaesus is the author only of a modest embellishment or else of the *dedicatio* with the expense of 2.000 *sesterzi* and then (added in minute letters) of *operae n(umero) ducentae)*, that is, two hundred working days which simply cannot be sufficient—as anyone can see—for the construction of an amphitheater but only for a small operation of restoration, of embellishment and tidying up for the dedicatory celebrations.

NOTES

1. Lugli 1957: 363 ff.
2. Lugli 1957: 487 ff.
3. Lugli 1957: 493 ff.
4. Coarelli 1977: 1 ff.
5. Zevi 1973: 555 ff.
6. Zevi 1976a: 54 ff.
7. Unpublished, cfr. Lugli 1957: 495. I wonder if this might not be the temple of Tiberinus Pater, the cella of which was restored by P. Lucilius Gamala *filius* (*CIL* XIV, 376) in the early Augustan period.
8. *Ostia: passim.*
9. For all of these buildings see Coarelli 1974: passim.
10. Cfr. Zevi 1976: 84 ff. As to be expected the structures at Alatri are all in polygonal masonry or *opus incertum* (see Gasperini 1965).
11. Giuliani 1970: 56 ff., and note 3 (apsidal buildings beneath the cathedral). Rather than the basilica, it could also be a shrine of Hercules as dedications to Hercules Invictus and Hercules Saxanus were found both in the building itself and in the surrounding area (*CIL* XIV, 3548 and 3543).
12. Giuliani 1970: 218, nr. 114, although Boethius, against Giuliani, thinks it may be a "market" like that at Ferentinum.
13. Giuliani 1970: numbers 32 (*opus quadratum*); 59, 63, 75, 80, 114, 179 (*opus incertum*); 47, 50, 166, 170 (*opus reticulatum*).
14. Giuliani 1970: 62 ff., nr. 4.
15. See appendix.
16. See appendix.
17. Giuliani 1970: numbers 96, 107, 120, 131, 198 (*incertum*); 90, 92, 97, 106, 112, 117, 135, 207 (*reticulatum*); 209, 212 (*incertum* and *reticulatum*).
18. Vitucci Brandizzi 1968: numbers 1–28 (walls); 30, 35, 36, 38, 40, 41, 47, 48, 49, 51–54, 57, 61–63, 65, 68–70 (terracing); 44, 67 (temples); 32 (vaulted building).
19. Vitucci Brandizzi 1968: numbers 33, 45, 50, 56 (*incertum* walls); 42, 43 (walls in *reticulatum*).
20. Vitucci Brandizzi 1968: numbers 54, 72, 76, 111, 120, 173, 200 (*reticulatum* used in villas); for the villas with other construction techniques, see the index of Vitucci Brandizzi 's work.
21. Mazzolani 1969.
22. Mazzolani 1969: numbers 46, 48, 52, 63, 65 (terracing); 41, 42 (walls in *incertum*); 69 (vaulted building); 39, 54, 59, 67 (reticulate walls).
23. Mazzolani 1969: numbers 19, 93 (villas with reticulate construction); 104, 132 (villas in *opus incertum* with additions in *opus reticulatum).*

24. Lugli 1957: 513. For the public buildings of Naples, Napoli 1967: 412 ff. (also contains earlier bibliography).
25. Maiuri 1958: *passim*.
26. Lugli 1957: 513.
27. On this point see Maiuri 1942: *passim* and Lugli 1957: 504 and 512.
28. For example, see the large tomb at the crossroads of Via di Ercolano, La Rocca, and M. and A. De Vos 1976: 335, number 34.
29. Synthesis in *EAA* V, 829 ff. and in *EAA Supplement* 1970: 571 ff.
30. I thank A. Pontrandolfo and E. Greco for this information.
31. *Sibari* 1970: 555 ff. L. Venuleius Brocchus, local magistrate of Copia (possibly the son of the owner of the pottery factory?) should be put in relation to the Venuleius *III vir capitalis* (?) in 82 B.C.: for the latest article on this man, see Wiseman 1971: 272 number 475 (with preceding bibliography). P.G. Guzzo has very kindly provided me with the other information on Copia.
32. Bracco 1978: 62 ff., number 28. On Herakleia, Quilici 1967: *passim*.
33. Lugli 1957: 513 and arguments against in *EAA* III, 910 by Arias.
34. Arslan 1969–1970: numbers 20 (mausoleum), 30 (theater), 66 (amphitheater).
35. *NSc Suppl.* 1911: 61 f., and 83 ff.
36. Beloch 1927: 493 f.
37. *ILLRP*, 607–8.
38. *CIL* X, 103.
39. For the amphitheater of Sipontum, Serricchio 1978: 19, figs. 43–44. For the amphitheater of Lupiae, De Giorgi 1907: 131 ff. On the Herdonia buildings, *Ordona* 1972: 17 ff. (baths), 25 ff. (wall, second half of the first century A.D.), 33 ff. (basilica); *Ordona* 1975: 509 (*macellum*).
40. Cfr. the episode reported in Livy XXXIX, 23.3.
41. Bartoccini 1936: 1 ff. On the colony, Degrassi 1938: 129 ff.
42. *Bernardini 1959: 69 ff.; cfr. Bartoccini 1935: 103 ff.*
43. See for example the "suburban villa" in *Ordona* 1972: 10 ff.
44. *Egnazia:* 1965.
45. Lugli 1957: 505 and Russi 1976: 171 ff.
46. The excavations conducted by D. Manconi at Bantia (1972) had layers datable to the first century A.D.: I thank Dr. Manconi for this information.
47. Archaeological map of the city in Sciarra 1965: 77 ff. and an archaeological map for the territory in Quilici 1974.
48. Lugli 1957: 513.
49. Lugli 1957: 526 (The Santi Quaranta building); *NSc* 1924: 516 (theater).
50. Sgobbo 1937: 394 ff.

51. Trebula Mutuesca, Torelli 1963: 230 ff.; Amiternum, Lugli 1957: 505, 511 (theater).
52. Pasquinucci 1975: 33 (Corinthian temple), 46–47 (theatre); 104–5 (aqueduct and sewers).
53. La Regina 1968: 383 (Civita di Bagno); 396 ff. (Peltuinum); 421 (Cepegatti).
54. Cianfarani in *EAA* II, 550 ff.
55. La Regina 1966: 113, numbers 52–54 (Sulmo); Van Wonterghem 1976: I, 147 ff. (sanctuary of Hercules Curinus and Corfinium).
56. La Regina 1967: 87 ff. For the few remains in *reticulatum* at Terventum, see Matteini Chiari 1974: 559 ff.
57. Tacitus, *Hist.* IV, 5.1; cfr. Syme 1958: 559 ff.
58. *Sepino* 1979.
59. Mertens 1969: 76 ff. (theater); 86 ff. (amphitheater); 104 (exedra). There are a few ruins in *reticulatum* also at Antinium, Quilici 1966: 47.
60. De Visscher and Mertens 1957: 39 ff.
61. Lugli 1957: 526. A parallel is seen in the *specus* of the Anio Novus aqueduct between Capannelle and Rome in the same period, Lugli 1957: 523.
62. Pallottino 1937: 92 ff.
63. Quilici Gigli 1970: 154 (substructure); 163 (baths).
64. There are only bits of *reticulatum* known: Bartoccini 1960: 269.
65. Laviosa 1969: 577 ff. (with earlier bibliography). The "villa" is almost certainly an urban bath complex, Minto 1943: 554 ff.
66. As in Salmon 1969: 138 and Harris 1971: 310. The epigraphic evidence cited by Mazzolai 1959: 217 ff. is hardly indicative.
67. Buchicchio 1970: 19 ff. (archaeological map of the city) and in particular, 37 f. (baths).
68. Bolsena II 1971: 217 ff. (*nymphaeum* of 40–30 B.C. in *opus incertum*).
69. *NSc* 1950: 227 ff.
70. Tracchi 1978: 67 (number 29).
71. Lugli 1957: 639 ff.
72. See, for example, *Luni* 1973 and Sommella and Giuliani 1974: Luca; Maetzke 1941: Florentia; Neppi Modona 1977[2]: Cortona.
73. Pietrangeli 1943: 63 (theater); 66 (amphitheater); 67 ff. (baths of Iulius Iulianus); 78 (mausoleum). For the port on the Paglia between Umbria and Etruria, see *NSc* 1890: 72, 111, 144, 146, 181, 282 and *NSc* 1891: 23.
74. Pietrangeli 1939: 85 (substruction of the old Dominican convent); 90 (the building near Porta Foligno); 62 f. (rebuilding of the walls).
75. Pietrangeli 1939: 59 (theater); 64 (other buildings).
76. Ciotti 1976.
77. L. Sensi is preparing a monograph on Hispellum while L. Rose Bonci is studying Arna. I thank all of my other colleagues of the Institute of

Archaeology in Perugia for the information on the Umbrian centers that I have used here. For the buildings at Asisium and at Iguvium, Lugli 1957: 505 (Iguvium) and 511 (Asisium).

78. Moretti 1945: 61 ff. (amphitheater) and 70 (baths).
79. Bejor 1978: 63 (walls); 103 (mausoleum).
80. See also Gentili 1955 on Auximum; Napoletani 1907 on Firmum; Caraceni 1958 (Urbs Salvia); *NSc* 1971: 381 ff. and 402 ff. (Helvia Ricina).
81. Ricci 1895: 72 ff. (for the upper passageways with views including niches and semicolumns, also tav. 5).
82. Summary list in Lugli 1957: 642 f., where areas and chronological considerations are mixed without any historical perspective.
83. On this problem see Bianchi Bandinelli 1969: 58 ff. for a clear discussion.
84. On the amphitheater, Gentili 1948: number 3388.
85. Bisi 1967: 198, number 2842 (watchtower).
86. Cfr. *AA* 1954: 472 ff.
87. Grant 1969[2]: 195 ff. for the "foundation issue" coin with the head of Augustus and a Latin legend.
88. Maetzke 1959–61: 657 ff.
89. Meloni 1975: 154 ff. (with earlier bibliography).
90. On the problem (but with a different perspective) see Deichmann 1979: 473 ff.; on Jericho under Herod, cfr. Pritchard 1952–54 (but out in 1958).
91. Elaioussa, Keil and Wilhelm 1931: 222. For the confirmation of the use of *reticulatum* by another oriental *regulus* at Emesa, Butler 1904: 49.
92. Calabi Limentani in *EAA* I 572 ff., and 1960.
93. *Cod. Iust.* VIII.10.12.56.
94. *IGRR*, I, 529–30.
95. *CIL* VI, 338–33.
96. *CIL* VI, 9794.
97. See my remarks in Torelli 1980.
98. Coarelli 1976: 376 f., and 1977, n. 4.
99. Pucci 1973: 255 ff.
100. Plutarch *Crass.* 2.5. See, most recently, Frier 1981.
101. See De Ruggiero 1925. On the economic aspects in general of political buildings see Bodei Giglioni 1974.
102. On the central baths and on the honorary base in the Forum, Lugli 1957: 525.
103. Lugli 1957: 525–26. For example, the villas of Domitian at Circei (and the rebuilding of the Villa at Anzio); Trajan's villa at Centumcellae and at Arcinazzo; Hadrian's villa at Tivoli, and the entire area of Domitianic—Hadrianic imperial villas at Baia and Bacoli.
104. Lugli 1957: 654 ff.

105. *Lateres* 1977 and *Ordona* 1975; Steinby 1978: 1489 ff. under 'Zeigelstempel.'
106. Helen 1975: note 16.
107. Helen 1975: 257.
108. Carandini 1979: 91 ff.
109. On this question, see the proceedings of the Seminario Internazionale di Studio held by the Instituto Gramsci (Pisa 4–6/1/1979) entitled *Forma di produzione schiavistica e tendenze della Società romana: I a.C.-II d.C. Un caso di sviluppo precapitalistico* (now published, see *Società* 1981).

BIBLIOGRAPHY

Arslan, E.
1969–70 "Relazione preliminare sugli scavi effettuati nel 1966–69 a Roccelletta di Borgia (Scolacium)" 15–72 in *Centro Studi e Documentazione sull' Italia Romana Atti* 1969–70.

Bodei Giglioni, G.
1974 *Lavori pubblici e occupazione nell'antichità classica.* Bologna.

Bartoccini, R.
1935–36 "Il teatro romano di Lecce," *Dioniso* V: 103–9.
1936 "Anfiteatro e gladiatori in Lucera," *Japigia* VII: 11–53.
1960 "La tomba delle 'Olimpiadi' nella necroppoli etrusca di Tarquinia," *Atti VII Congresso Internazionale Archeologia Classica,* 177–90. Rome.

Bejor, L.
1978 *Treia.* Pisa.

Beloch, J.
1927 *Römische Geschichte.* Berlin-Leipzig.

Bernardini, M.
1959 *Lupiae.* Lecce.

Bianchi Bandinelli, R.
1969 *L'arte romana al centro del potere.* Milano.

Bisi, A.
1967 "Marettimo (Sicilia, Trapani), " *FA* XXII: 198.

Bolsena

1971 *Bolsena II, Les architectures (1962–67).* Roma.

Bracco, V.

1978 *Volcei (Forma Italiae III, 1).* Roma.

Buchicchio, F.T.

1970 "Note di topografia antica sulla Volsinii Romana," *RömMitt* LXXVII: 19–45.

Butler, H.C.

1904 *American Expedition to Syria.* New York.

Calabi Limentani, I.

1960 *Studi sulla società romana. Il lavoro artistico.* Milan.

Carpanelli, F.

1950 "Arezzo-L'anfiteatro romano," *NSc:* 227–40.

Caraceni, F.

1958 *I Salvii e Urbs Salvia.* Urbania.

Carandini, A.

1979 *Schiavi e padroni nell'Etruria romana.* Bari.

Ciotti, U.

1976 *San Gemini e Carsulae.* Roma.

Coarelli, F.

1974 *Guida Archeologica di Roma.* Verona.

1976 "Architettura e arti figurative in Roma: 150–50 a.C.," *Hellenismus in Mittelitalien* (ed. P. Zanker), 21–51. Göttingen.

1977 "Public Building in Rome between the Second Punic War and Sulla," *PBSR* XLV: 1–23.

De Giorgi, C.

1907 *Lecce sotterranea.* Lecce.

De Ruggiero, E.

1925 *Lo stato e le opere pubbliche in Roma antica.* Torino.

De Visscher, F. and Mertens, J.

1957 "L'Amphithéatre d'Alba Fucens et son Fondateur Q. Naevinus Macro, Préfet du Prétoire de Tibère," *RAL* XII: 39–49.

Degrassi, A.

1938 "Problemi cronologici delle colonie di Luceria, Aquileia, Teanum Sidicinum," *RFIC* CXVI: 129–43.

Deichmann, Fr. W.

1979 "Westliche Bautechnik im Römischen und Romaischen Osten," *RömMitt* LXXXVI: 473–527.

Egnazia

1965 *L'antica Egnazia*. Taranto.

Frier, B.

1980 *Landlord and Tenants in Imperial Rome*. Princeton.

Gasperini, L.

1965 *Aletrium*. Alatri.

Gentili, G.V.

1948 *Auximum*. Roma.

1955 *Auximum (Osimo). Regio V-Picenum*. Roma

Grant, M.

1969 *From Imperium to Auctoritas*[2]. Cambridge.

Giuliani, C.F.

1970 *Tibur I (Forma Italiae I,7)*. Roma.

Harris, W.V.

1971 *Rome in Etruria and Umbria*. Oxford.

Helen, T.

1975 "Organization of Roman Brick Production" in *Acta Inst. Rom. Fin.* IX.

Keil, J., and Wilhelm, A.

1931 *Monumenta Asiae Minoris Antiqua*. Manchester.

La Regina, A.

1956 "Cluviae e il territorio Carecino," *RAL* XXII: 87–109.

1966 "Sulmona," *Quaderni Istituto Topografia Antica Univ. Roma* II: 107–16.

1968 "Richerche sugli insediamenti vestini," *MemAccLinc* XIII: 363–444.

La Rocca, E., and De Vos, M. and De Vos, A.

1976 *Guida archeologica di Pompei*. Verona.

Lateres

1977 *Lateres Signati Ostienses Acta Inst. Rom. Fin. VII.*

Laviosa, C.

1969 "Rusellae: Relazione preliminare della Settima e della Ottava campagna di scavi," *StEtr* XXXVII: 579–609.

Lugli, G.

1957 *La tecnica edilizia romana*. Roma.

Luni

1973–77 *Scavi di Luni I-II*. Roma.

Maetzke, G.

1941 *Florentia*. Roma.

1959–61 "Scavi e Scoperte nelle Provincia di Sassari e Nuoro 1959–61," *StSardi:* 651–63.

Maiuri, A.

1942 *L'ultima fase edilizia di Pompeii*. Roma.

1958 *I nuovi scavi di Ercolano*. Roma.

Matteini Chiari, M.

1974 "Terventum," *Quaderni Istituto Topografia Antica Univ. Roma* VI: 143–82.

Mazzolai, A.

1959 "Epigrafi Latine inedite di Roselle e del suo territorio," *RömMitt* LXVI: 214–21.

Mazzolani, M.
1969 *Anagnia (Forma Italiae I,6)*. Roma.

Meloni, V.P.
1975 *La Sardegna romana*. Sassari.

Mercando, L.
1971 "Villa Potenza-rinvenimento di edificio romano con pavimento a mosaico," *NSc:* 381–401.
1971a "Villa Potenza-rinvenimento in proprietà AGIP," *NSc:* 402–17.

Mertens, J.
1969 *Alba Fucens I*. Roma-Bruxelles.

Minto, A.
1943 "Esplorazione scientifica di Roselle e del territorio Rosellano," *StEtr* XVII: 554–56.

Moretti, L.
1945 *Ancona*. Roma.

Napoletani, G.
1907 *Fermo nel Piceno*. Roma.

Napoli, M.
1967 *Storia di Napoli I*. Napoli.

Neppi Modona, A.
1977 *Cortona etrusca e romana*[2]. Firenze.

Neutsch, B.
1954 "Archäologische Grabungen und Funde in Sizilien von 1949–1954," *AA:* 466–706.

Ordona
1972 *Ordona V*. Bruxelles-Roma.
1975 "Ordona (Foggia)-Rapporto sommario sugli scavi belgi a Herdonia e nell'Ager Herdonianus 1971–73," *NSc:* 499–530.

Ostia
1953 *Scavi di Ostia I*. Roma.

Pallottino, M.
1937 "Tarquinia," *MonAntLinc* XXVI.

Pasquinucci, M.
1975 *Ausculum I*. Pisa.

Pietrangeli, C.
1939 *Spoletium*. Roma.
1943 *Ocriculum*. Roma.
1953 *Mevania*. Roma.

Pritchard, J.
1952–54 "The excavation of Herodian Jericho," *AASO* XXXII-III.

Pucci, G.
1973 "La produzione della ceramica aretina. Note sull'industria nella prima età imperiale romana," *DdA* VII: 255–93.

Quilici, L.
1966 "Antinio," *Quaderni Istituto Topografia Antica Univ. Roma* II: 35–48.
1967 *Siris-Heraclea (Forma Italiae III, I)*. Roma.
1974 *Repertorio dei beni culturali Archeologici della provincia di Brindisi (Quaderni dell'Amministrazione provinciale di Brindisi no. 11)*. Fasano.

Quilici Gigli, S.
1970 *Tuscana (Forma Italiae VII, 2)* Roma.

Ricci, S.
1895 *Il teatro romano di Verona*. Venezia.

Russi, A.
1976 *Teanum Apulum*. Roma.

Salmon, E.T.
1969 *Roman Colonization under the Republic*. London.

Sciarra, B.
1965 "Le statue di Brindisi," *RendAccNap:* 219–26
1965a "Nuove iscrizioni funerarie del Brindisino," *Epigraphica* XXVII.

Sepino
1979 *Sepino-Archeologia e continuità*. Campobasso.

Serricchio, C.
1978 *Note su Siponto antica*. Manfredonia.

Sgobbo, I.
1937 *Un Complesso di Edifici Sannitici e i Quartieri di Pompeii per la prima volta riconosciuti*. Napoli.

Sibari
1970 "Sibari-Scavi all Parco del Cavallo 1960–62, 1969–70 e agli Stombi 1969–70," *NSc Supplement*.

Società
1981 *Società Romana e Produzione Schiavistica*, 3 vols. Roma-Bari.

Sommella, P., and Giuliani, C.F.
1974 "La Pianta di Lucca Romana," *Quaderni Istituto Topografia Antica Univ.* Roma VII: 3–109.

Steinby, M.
1978 *Lateres signati Ostienses*. Roma.

Syme, R.
1958 *Tacitus*. Oxford.

Torelli, M.
1963 "Trebula Mutuesca-Iscrizioni corrette e inedite," *RAL* XVIII: 230–79.
1976 Discussion to F. Rakob, "Bautypen und Bautechnik," *Hellenismus in Mittelitalien* (ed. P. Zanker), 376–77. Göttingen.
1980 "Industria estrattiva, lavoro artiginale, interessi economici: qualche appunto," *MAAR* XXXVI: 313–24.

Tracchi, A.
1978 *Ricognizioni archeologiche in Etruria*. Roma.

Van Wonterghem, F.
1976 "Archäologische Zeugnisse spätrepublikanischer Zeit aus dem Gebiet der Peligner," *Hellenismus in Mittelitalien* (ed. P. Zanker), 143–59. Göttingen.

Vitucci Brandizzi, P.
1968 Cora (*Forma Italiae* I, 5). Roma.

Wiseman, T.P.

1971 *New Men in the Roman Senate.* Oxford.

Zevi, F.

1973 "P. Lucilio Gamala Senior e i Quattro Tempietti di Ostia," *MEFRA* LXXXV: 555–81.

1976 "Alatri," *Hellenismus in Mittelitalien* (ed. P. Zanker), 84–96. Göttingen.

1976a "Monumenti e aspetti culturali di Ostia repubblicana" *Hellenismus in Mittelitalien* (ed. P. Zanker), 52–83. Göttingen.

NSc Concordance

1890 = no author found
1891 = no author found
1911 = no author found
1924 = no author found
1950 = Carpanelli, F.
1970 = *Sibari*
1971 = Mercando, L.
1971a = Mercando, L.
1975 = *Ordona*

INDEX